# ABOUT THE AUTHORS

**Mike Rothmiller**
*New York Times* Bestselling Author
Mike Rothmiller has enjoyed a distinguished career in law enforcement working across US Federal and State agencies and with American and international intelligence services. He served for ten years with the Los Angeles Police Department [LAPD] including five years as a deep undercover detective with the Organized Crime Intelligence Division [OCID].

He was a member of the US Department of Justice Organized Crime Strike Force and provided secret Grand Jury testimony regarding the assassination of Senator Robert Kennedy. He conceived and directed global intelligence operations targeting multi-national crime groups, terrorism, and political corruption, from Chile to Washington and London to Israel. In his long career Mike Rothmiller has encountered all manner of mendacity and atrocity but he remains most shaken by his investigation into the death of Marilyn Monroe. He regards *Bombshell* as the rich and important culmination of a lifetime of inquiries which will achieve legal redress, posthumously in some cases, and correct the fabricated history about the death of Marilyn Monroe and those who used her.

Alongside his dedication to public service, Mike Rothmiller established a media career producing television documentaries and working as a correspondent and presenter for America's PBS, ESPN and other international television markets. He is a regular commentator on law enforcement and worldwide intelligence matters across America and throughout the world. He is a *New York Times* bestselling author of 23 non-fiction books.

DEDICATION
For my wife, Nancy, and the memory of Marilyn.

D0494575

**Douglas Thompson**
*Sunday Times* Bestselling Author
Douglas Thompson is the author of many non-fiction books covering an eclectic mix of subjects from major Hollywood biographies to revelatory bestsellers about remarkable people and events. Four of his books are at present being developed for global television, another for film in Hollywood by MGM. With Christine Keeler, he wrote her revealing memoir *The Truth At Last*. That instant bestseller was revised as *Secrets and Lies: The Trials of Christine Keeler* and the audio version recorded by actress Sophie Cookson who played Christine to critical acclaim in the successful BBC television series. His works, published in a dozen languages, include the television-based anthology *Hollywood People*, and a worldwide selling biography of Clint Eastwood. He collaborated with Michael Flatley on the *Sunday Times* bestseller *Lord of the Dance*. He divides his time between a medieval Suffolk village and California, where he was based as a Fleet Street correspondent and columnist for more than twenty years. www.dougiethompson.com.

DEDICATION
For Effie Perrine who began it all, and Robert Evans, Cary Grant, Lloyd Bridges, Mike Qualls, Richard Gulley, Alan 'Whitey' Snyder, Shelley Winters, Lauren Bacall, Yvonne De Carlo, Robert Mitchum, Bob Werden, John Huston, Judith Exner, Marian Collier Neuman, Angie and the many others who helped. And for Mike Rothmiller who placed the missing pieces and proved the power of the long arm of time.

# BOMBSHELL

## THE NIGHT BOBBY KENNEDY KILLED MARILYN MONROE

**MIKE ROTHMILLER
AND
DOUGLAS THOMPSON**

△L
**AD LIB**

First published in 2021 by Ad Lib Publishers Ltd
15 Church Road
London, SW13 9HE
www.adlibpublishers.com

Text © 2021 Mike Rothmiller and Douglas Thompson

Paperback ISBN 978-1-913543-62-4
eBook ISBN 978-1-913543-60-0

A CIP catalogue record for this book is available from the
British Library.

Printed in the UK
10 9 8 7 6 5 4

## AUTHOR'S NOTE

While *Bombshell* clearly demonstrates the illegal activities of the Los Angeles Police Department's [LAPD] Intelligence Division, it must be remembered the vast majority of those serving in law enforcement are dedicated, honest individuals performing a difficult job. During LAPD's decades of illegal intelligence operations, no cop outside of OCID, except the chief, knew the sinister depths of the operations.

Mike Rothmiller.

*'John hasn't called. Bobby called. He's coming to California. He wants to see me.'*

from Marilyn Monroe's diary, 1962, revealed for the first time in *Bombshell,* 2021.

# CONTENTS

# PREFACE: JOURNEY'S END

*'Breaking Up Is Hard To Do'*
— Neil Sedaka, number one, Billboard Top Hundred,
August 1962.

The beginning of the end of Marilyn Monroe's life began when a black Lincoln Continental appeared as a shimmer in the sun as it carefully turned out of Los Angeles International Airport onto Imperial Highway and pointed its deluxe chassis north toward Santa Monica and beyond.

In the grand theatre of gender what defined Marilyn Monroe as a woman was the way men looked at her. Yet, a sinister metamorphosis had overwhelmed important men in her life, that faction of the fabulous and famous, once devoted to and so transparently enthralled by her. By the time that highly polished Lincoln slowed gently, took a right at San Vicente Boulevard and turned east toward Los Angeles proper, the most fearful of Monroe's lovers was adamant about his intention to resolve the problem.

The conversation in the car had been muted but what he'd been told as he glanced out at the Pacific Ocean at the start of the tense drive convinced him entirely that the only solution left was for Marilyn Monroe to die. The driver suggested, again and again, that she might 'see sense' and be 'reasonable' but that brought not the smallest diminution of Marilyn Monroe's ability to trouble and disquiet one of the most powerful men in the world.

She knew more about illusions than any of them but this time she'd created not an intoxicating fantasy, but a nightmare.

'Men do not see me,' she'd complained, 'they just lay their eyes on me.'

That was before.

That Saturday, August 4, 1962, as the strong Santa Anas, the 'devil winds,' hazed the southern California coast, Hollywood's most marketable and dazzling star, the world's most popular sex symbol, was being viewed in an altogether different and deadly way by some feverishly determined individuals.

# PROLOGUE: RIP?

*'Truth is the daughter of Time.'*
— ancient proverb.

Even after life, Peter Lawford, actor, charmer, and longtime brother-in-law to the princes of the Kennedy Camelot, directly connects to Marilyn Monroe. He is the pointer to her crypt at Westwood Memorial Park on the westside of Los Angeles not too far from Brentwood where she died so many years ago. Natalie Wood is nearby on the Walk of Memory lane which skirts through the cemetery, but it is Lawford's memorial stone that leads the way to what, for millions, is an altar to Marilyn; the daily gatherings of fans and floral tributes testify to that. Her name, with the dates of her short life, 1926–1962, is marked out on the muted marble wall with fan wishes marked in cherry red lipstick and other delible notes faded by the heat, worn like her monument by the salty breeze blown in from the Pacific. Every visitor brings their own ideas and images along this particular memory lane, and Marilyn Monroe continues to accommodate each and every perception. In life it was her remarkable gift and curse: she could be anybody or anything you wanted her to be. Her ending came when she became trouble.

Truth, like all material, can be squeezed and bent, angled and cut into whatever shape is required, what conclusions need to be drawn, which lives, and careers, need to be saved and which are quite dispensable. Rarely has it been twisted so expertly as in the death of Marilyn Monroe.

This is a sensational book but what sets it apart from all others is that the source material is equally sensational. It calls on secret Los Angeles police intelligence files and first-hand and previously unheard testimony from the man who was present at the end of Marilyn Monroe's life. The man who watched her die.

It dismisses the bespoke *truth* offered for decades by Hollywood and Washington and tabloid clairvoyants to explain the confected 'impenetrable mystery' about the death of Marilyn Monroe, and her associations and involvement with President John Kennedy and his brother Robert Kennedy, Attorney General of the United States.

Marilyn Monroe died at her Spanish Colonial home Cursum Perficio, 'Journey's End,' which sits at the end of a deceptively quiet driveway (*cul-de-sac* is too grand a word) in Brentwood, West Los Angeles off San Vicente Boulevard, a ten-minute drive west to Santa Monica and the Pacific Ocean. Since then, there have been tens of thousands of theories and a library of books [700] exploring them, as well as scores more films than Marilyn Monroe ever made, searching for an answer to whom or what killed the most renowned sex symbol of the 20th Century. The conclusions stretch from anodyne to the ridiculous.

This book asserts that Robert Kennedy and Peter Lawford were with Marilyn when she died. Their involvement in her death becomes rigorously clear as the pages turn and the story of Marilyn Monroe and her sexual encounters with President Kennedy, and her affair with Robert Kennedy, unfolds with chilling clarity. For the first time, we hear her 'talk' of them in her diary, of making love to President Kennedy and falling in love with his brother.

Mike Rothmiller was an eleven-year-old baseball fan living in South Gate, a then condensed suburb to the south-east of Los Angeles, when Marilyn Monroe's death, then aged only 36, was made public on August 5, 1962. Young Mike Rothmiller couldn't miss the event, it was all over the news, giant newspaper headlines, especially the Hearst-owned *Herald-Examiner* which his father had delivered to his doorstep. Still, he was far more interested in his little league baseball team than the sudden demise of Marilyn Monroe. He could never have imagined, and never have believed, that years later, he would be the person to have uncovered the answers to the greatest questions surrounding her death.

Or known that such knowledge would, perhaps, cost him his life.

# PART ONE

## Black Sunset

*'On August 9, 1969, I was sitting in the shallow end of my sister-in-law's swimming pool in Beverly Hills when she received a telephone call from a friend who had just heard about the murders at Sharon Tate Polanski's house on Cielo Drive. I remember all of the day's misinformation very clearly, and I also remember this, and wish I did not: I remember that no one was surprised.'*
— **Joan Didion,** *The White Album*, **1979.**

# I: Summertime

*'I never said it was always wrong to enter fairyland;*
*I only said it was always dangerous.'*
— G. K. Chesterton, *The Innocence of Father Brown,* 1911.

The variety of the traumas in Marilyn Monroe's life ran like an afternoon television soap opera, but still the death of the most talked about and lusted after woman in the world managed to shock and surprise. Why would Marilyn Monroe kill herself? Suicide was the initial and, shortly thereafter, official verdict from the doctors and the police, and enthusiastically endorsed by the politicians. In 1962, these were the people you trusted, believed and paid deference to. The Eisenhower era was not long gone, and respect was all, the moral guidelines as neat and sharp as a military crew-cut.

So, like many, Mike Rothmiller, in his growing years, thought Marilyn Monroe, either intentionally or accidentally, took an overdose of sedatives and succumbed. However it happened, esteemed authority insisted she had died by her own hand.

He was 21 years old when he joined the Los Angeles Police Department [LAPD] in 1972, and Marilyn's death was seen in his work circles as an early bookend of the decade just ended. More raw was the final bookend, the 1969 murders committed by the Charles Manson Family, which harshly concluded the 1960s for California, violating forever the summer of love. People stopped wearing flowers in their hair.

As a young officer, Rothmiller was keen, able and had paid his own way through college. He felt an obligation to serve and

17

was drawn to the police, like many before him, by the television series *Dragnet*. The LAPD-endorsed, police procedural show was focused on honesty and integrity. It was the good guys versus the bad guys, with scarce room for ambiguity. Yet, the killings inspired by Manson had wiped out illusions as well as lives and brought unease to a now fearful and increasingly paranoid California. People were asking questions about how such an atrocity could happen, about the police and about the rumours of the past. There was a heightened awareness that nothing was ever black and white. Mike Rothmiller heard scary tales of misdeeds, abuses of position and privilege, and rumours of a cover-up involving the death of Marilyn Monroe. It was coffee shop conversation around Parker Center, the police department's downtown headquarters named after the former chief, the contentious 'founder' of the modern LAPD, William Parker. Soon, in 1975, it would be the centre of a reluctant, media-driven internal police investigation which would, once again, conclude that Marilyn Monroe had killed herself. In time, Mike Rothmiller would come to learn that the official conclusion was absurd.

When that particular fuss over Marilyn Monroe had faded away, and the 1978 headlines were worrying instead about the 'Hillside Strangler' discarding dead women around the Los Angeles freeway system, the man who had led, organised and controlled the 1975 inquiry into Monroe's death, Daryl Gates, was now Chief of Police. He signed off on Mike Rothmiller's promotion and assignment to work as an undercover detective for Gates' old command, The Organized Crime Intelligence Division [OCID]. As a 'rookie' spy and the youngest detective in the division, Rothmiller was designated desk/office duty for his first weeks in the intelligence unit. The atmosphere was like working at Moscow's 'House of Government'. The 'office' was a windowless, three-storey grey brick building squirrelled away on the fringes of downtown, an architectural embarrassment, like the Greyhound Bus Station across the street. But Rothmiller soon found the work fascinating.

He recalls the otherworldly, *Twilight Zone* atmosphere of his first days in late 1978 as a detective within OCID. The intent was to help newcomers like him familiarise themselves with how the office operated. His first assignment in his new role was to compile an inventory of the office supplies and make sure the four lieutenants and Captain Stuart Finck who ran the division had plenty of paper and pencils. The lieutenant who was his immediate superior was not a street cop but a paperwork pusher, a pseudo-manager. He wanted to know how much lead was left in used pencils. Rothmiller thought he was being hazed, but he wasn't: he was simply being made to mark time. He resolved always to *look* busy.

It wasn't difficult. Only half a dozen steps away from his desk was a wall holding what, at first glance, appeared to be a set of giant locked bookshelves, but up close they were overloaded floor to ceiling rolls containing thousands upon thousands of secret dossiers. Nearby was a series of chest-high filing cabinets holding the keys to the dossiers. Even if he felt a little like Aladdin, he didn't need an *Open Sesame!* to access the contents. Inside these filing cabinets were names on index cards with a code system linking to the corresponding files stored on the shelves. There were thousands of cards dating back nearly five decades. Rothmiller had time and worked out the filing codes and how they related to the location of each set of files. Many were cross-referenced. A subject could have been dead for years, but their file kept growing and remained 'active' – granted immortality within the OCID if any associate remained alive. As the local industry, Hollywood and all its players were overwhelmingly represented.

Secured within the cabinets each 5 x 7 inch index card contained a photo of the person, their personal information and numbered single sentences [covering the front and back of the card] describing the listed intelligence reports. The numbers before each sentence told the detective where to find that report within OCID's intelligence treasures. In some cases, a person had accumulated dozens of cards since their dossier was extensive and collated over decades. Rothmiller learned that there was a secret internal OCID filing code. An asterisk marked on an index card indicated there was another, highly confidential file relating to the individual.

A detective's intelligence report received a minimum of two reviews and approvals. Depending on the sensitivity of the information, the report would be placed in the secret OCID files or the super-secret Confidential Files [*Cfs*]. The secret records were housed in the OCID office lieutenant's room. The *Cfs* were stored adjacent to the office lieutenant in a lockable room called 'the vault' or 'the safe'. The most highly guarded documents were held by the OCID captain and the Chief of Police in their private safes. The Chief of Police also maintained a secret file on all media reporters and news executives in southern California. It is understood the secret media file was still being used in 2021.

The vault was only a couple of yards away from the wall of intelligence reports. Marilyn Monroe, the Kennedys and many others were linked by forty or fifty index cards with each card corresponding to thirty or more bulging intelligence files. *Cfs* didn't exist officially as a safeguard for subpoena purposes. There were also 'ghost' files. These comprised such sensitive material – actionable against the LAPD for how the information was compiled as well as their provocative content – that they were held in public storage units rented by OCID detectives and paid for in cash from the aptly named Secret Service Fund. There was another group of highly classified intelligence reports called 'white papers'. They were not written on LAPD letterhead or traceable to the LAPD. They were not considered official LAPD documents and were not available for scrutiny outside of OCID. Indeed, so sensitive was the material, normally of a political nature, that it was held in the Chief of Police's private safe. If a 'white paper' somehow found its way to the media, anyone outside of OCID or, in the worst case, into a legal proceeding, the LAPD representative testifying under oath would state that the document was an obvious forgery since all LAPD forms are marked with identifying nomenclature. In most instances, once the Chief of Police had read a 'white paper', it was supposedly destroyed. As an OCID detective, Mike Rothmiller understood this hide-the-document ritual and periodically was required to engage in this practice.

Mike Rothmiller's initial assignment was a bureaucratic ritual, but when he had finished sharpening pencils, he began reading the classified files. This cache of secrets he now had unencumbered access to, changed his perception of so much of what he, and the rest of the world, had been led to believe. Along with salacious details of political and Hollywood scandals, was the evidence of the cover-up surrounding Marilyn Monroe's death. The civic leaders had deemed it a suicide or, possibly, an accidental overdose. That was the official story, and a lifesaver for the LAPD who grasped for it like a falling trapeze artist. Despite the shaky evidentiary scaffolding, it was on what all consequent verdicts were built. Yet, Mike Rothmiller now believed that Marilyn Monroe's death was in no way self-inflicted. The evidence he uncovered in the OCID files convinced him she had died by the hands of another.

He became absolutely certain as he worked his way through the information, from one cross-reference to another, from one secured area of the OCID third floor offices to the inner sanctum containing the Holy Grail, the extraordinary floor to ceiling top secret files, a world of money shots. What struck him was there was no dust, no sense of damp displacement: this material was still in use. He was impressed by the clever way the document folders were linked by coded cards which could be 'lost' or switched, sending files into an abyss of deniability [if sought by a pesky court order, LAPD simply replied they had no such file] while still remaining intrinsically secure and available to those with the code and keys to unlock this fortune of information. These were secrets which were deployed by several LAPD Chiefs as efficiently as J. Edgar Hoover used the FBI's intelligence files against America's political giants.

OCID's massive storehouse was located in the secure and windowless Fort Davis. The reinforced building was designed to withstand a violent attack and named after the stocky former LAPD Chief [1969–1978] Ed Davis, who had warned terrorists he'd 'hang 'em at the airport'. Inside was a wealth of public documents, newspaper and magazine articles, information provided by criminal and non-criminal informants, and gleaned from other law enforcement and intelligence agencies. There were OCID detectives' personal reports detailing the results of covert surveillances, wiretaps, black bag jobs [Watergate style break-ins] and confidential witness testimony. The secret dossiers contained every tidbit of rumour, innuendo, fact and supposition each and every OCID cop had come across. In these files, Rothmiller got his first glimpse of the truth about the events before, during, and after Marilyn Monroe's death. He also found what so many had sought and just as many had dismissed as fantasy: placed, rather haphazardly, amid all the paperwork in the *Cfs* files was a document marked with the words 'Monroe's Diary'. Rothmiller eagerly sought out Marilyn Monroe's diary from which he was able to copy extracts, make notes about names and circumstances he recognised. As he read it, he knew instantly why it had been so desperately sought after and declared officially 'lost.'

Rothmiller began studying the files expecting to escape the office work boredom by reading the innermost secrets of the Mafia, a real-life version of Mario Puzo's *The Godfather*. He did learn intimate details of America's Five Families and their cosy relationships with many of the nation's leading politicians. He reviewed wiretap transcripts – some legal, most not – and thousands of informant debriefings presenting a potpourri of sensitive, salacious and actionable material, much of it backed up with hard evidence.

Several letters written by Mafia Godfathers were in files which were packed with graphic crime scene photographs demonstrating the competence of Mafia hitmen and women. Of course, the OCID Mafia dossiers were justified in terms of public safety and crime prevention – if not all the methods used to compile them – and they revealed a world known to a select few. What Rothmiller didn't expect to find were the huge number of confidential dossiers maintained on individuals who were *not* involved or even suspected of any type of criminal activity. He quickly realised the potential power and leverage the files supplied uncovering dossiers on politicians; television and movie stars as diverse as Robert Redford, Rock Hudson, Burt Lancaster, CBS newswoman Connie Chung and entertainer Michael Jackson; and sporting figures like Muhammad Ali whose name he came across early on as he had started, in the natural order of things, with 'A'. The first politician he found was Joseph Alioto, the Mayor of San Francisco, who'd been in office throughout the Black Panther marches and the hunt for the perpetrators of the 'Zodiac' murders, and the 'Zebra' racial killings. Alioto had also run in a Democratic primary for California Governor. Well, if the San Francisco mayor was on the books of LAPD what about Tom Bradley, the Mayor of Los Angeles? There he was in the 'B' index, a bulging file on the former LAPD police-lieutenant-turned-politician and longtime nemesis of Chief Daryl Gates.

The files were the ultimate scandal sheets: gripping, intriguing and loaded with impropriety, shaming the efforts of the supermarket tabloids, and they were supported by illegal electronic surveillance, photographic and audio ['bugged'] evidence, testimony from paid informants, from illicit break-ins, and political intelligence supplied from investigations by OCID's Quiet Team. That team's only job was to gather criminal or potentially embarrassing intelligence on politicians of all stripes, from the President of the United States down. The very existence of the Quiet Team was known only to the Chief of Police, who they reported to, their captain and other OCID detectives.

It didn't take Rothmiller too long to get to 'K' and the intelligence index card for President John F. Kennedy. This card was cross-indexed with Robert F. Kennedy, Ted Kennedy, Peter Lawford, Marilyn Monroe and many others, including a list of Mafia leaders throughout America. There were bundles of them, some annotated, some with pencil marks, some with parts redacted – scribbled rather than blacked out – and a few with dates listed. The records consisted of thousands of pages ranging from newspaper articles to private letters; CIA secret information and wiretap transcripts to covertly taken photographs – including one of President Kennedy and Marilyn Monroe in a warm, private embrace.

Many of the files had been duplicated, sometimes triplicated, and held in different cabinet drawers or driven off the premises to decoy storage units. During his assignment within OCID, Mike Rothmiller learned from several senior detectives that recorded conversations from the illegal wiretaps and buggings of Marilyn Monroe and Peter Lawford's homes were still in existence. They were held by a trusted OCID detective who, against the LAPD code, stored them at home on the orders of Chief Daryl Gates. Most detectives kept copies of 'very interesting' files at home. Rothmiller never listened to the tapes but read some of the transcripts of the conversations and believes the recordings still exist. He was not alone when he read the transcripts and was not able to take notes. The secret dossiers on the three Kennedy brothers contained paperwork covering every conceivable aspect of their public and personal lives, the assassinations of JFK and RFK, and the role of Senator Ted Kennedy in the death of Mary Jo Kopechne at Chappaquiddick.

There were scores of classified intelligence reports garnered from the FBI, CIA and other US government agencies, and some from foreign intelligence services delving into the Kennedy brothers' sexual trysts, their father Joe Kennedy's Mafia ties, and references to personal contacts with characters the FBI labelled as 'Communist or foreign spies'.

With John F. Kennedy there was an excessive amount of information regarding his long affair with Judith Campbell

Exner who was also sleeping with Mafia chief Sam Giancana and mafioso Johnny Rosselli. Giancana and Rosselli had plotted with the CIA to assassinate Cuban President Fidel Castro in 1962, when tensions between East and West, Kennedy and Khrushchev, Cuba and the USA, were strung to the limit and, for once, could truly be described as nuclear. Exner was herself potentially politically explosive. The files indicated that when the then junior Senator from Massachusetts [1953–1960] had ambitions of running for President, he had supposedly 'ended his affair' with Judith Exner [Exner told Douglas Thompson in 1976 that the affair continued during JFK's Presidential campaign]. The OCID documents make it clear J. Edgar Hoover had told Robert Kennedy that JFK was recorded on a wiretap speaking 'fondly' with Exner while she was at the Chicago home of the Sicilian-born Sam Giancana. That single piece of intelligence guaranteed Hoover would remain the director of the FBI throughout any Kennedy Administration [Hoover died in office on May 2, 1972].Yet, when it came to arranging his secret sexual trysts with Exner and others, JFK behaved like a pubescent schoolboy: he wasn't temperate. He might have suspected that the FBI, CIA, his sworn enemy, the Teamsters Union boss, Jimmy Hoffa, Giancana or a foreign intelligence service would be recording every call to any of his lovers' phones.The FBI was recording *all* of Judith Exner's telephone calls. And OCID were 'tapping' into that and much more. There were accurate reports of Peter Lawford sleeping with Christine Keeler, the teenager at the centre of the Profumo scandal which brought down the UK Government of Harold Macmillan in 1963. Lawford was also the link between the English good-time girl and Scotland Yard informant Mariella Novotny – hostess of London's infamous 'Man in the Mask' party – and President Kennedy's 'traveling girls' during his election campaign. British actress Shirley Anne Field revealed that Lawford tried to entice her into the arms of the President. And there were the details, the minutiae, of Lawford's longtime connection with Marilyn Monroe.

J. Edgar Hoover knew the high currency of obtaining the most intimate and damaging details of an aspiring President. As did LAPD Chief William Parker and his protégé Daryl Gates, his one-time chauffeur, and bodyguard, whom he would later appoint captain and leader of OCID. Although geography often concentrated their focus on the kings and queens of Hollywood, their eyes and ears were always open to potential scandals in Washington D.C.

The relationship between President Kennedy, Attorney General Robert Kennedy and Marilyn Monroe met all the criteria for LAPD spying. It was espionage to combat enemies but also to help friends. Ultimately, the only cops who mattered knew almost every secret and kept them in the OCID files, which was where Mike Rothmiller discovered the exactitude of the complex circumstances and cause of the death of Marilyn Monroe. Before, and most efficiently *from* August 9, 1950, when he was appointed Chief of the Los Angeles Police Department, William Parker maintained a close-to-the-chest working relationship with the Kennedy family. As important, his LAPD intelligence captain, James Hamilton, was an intimate friend of the Kennedys and regularly ran secret LAPD intelligence operations on their behalf. The tall, rugged Hamilton particularly bonded with Bobby Kennedy who, like Chief Parker, was a victim to bouts of depression that sometimes resulted in violence – 'Black Bobby' was a sometime nickname JFK gave his younger brother. Parker, also a Roman Catholic, if a Calvinistic one, was a man who fought to control his thirst for whisky [double shots of Bourbon de Luxe, 'Parker specials'] and B&Bs [brandies and Benedictine], was sympathetic to the perils of mood swings.

Captain James Hamilton very much saw himself as the Kennedys' 'protector', especially of Bobby with whom he established a strong friendship. OCID knew every time the Kennedys were in southern California as Captain Hamilton would serve as their bodyguard and chauffeur. Hamilton was also their concierge and would quietly assist both John and

Robert Kennedy during private visits to California by arranging accommodations under a banal alias or his own name. He personally handled their various requests with the cooperation of Chief Parker.

One OCID report details a sex party held at Frank Sinatra's secluded and recreational home in the San Fernando Valley, at the top of Winnetka Boulevard in Encino where it dead-ends at the Santa Monica Mountains. As well as a stable of active young women, there was unlimited alcohol and limited drugs [no one wanted overdosing starlets]. The report listed party guests including Sinatra, Dean Martin, Sammy Davis Jr., Peter Lawford and John Kennedy. Interesting guests, but a Hollywood sex party will surprise few.

More intriguing was that Captain James Hamilton and another OCID detective provided security at the party. 'Party girls' were checked for 'wires' which might be used to record indiscretions. If the media had shown interest, or a curious neighbour had turned up, the moonlighting policemen would crush that interest. Then, before the days of chattering news helicopters and picture snatching mobile phones, the cops had the power to remove anyone from an area. And they would. Forcibly. Potential intrusion and publicity were always prevented.

Chief 'Whisky Bill' Parker's fantasy was the thought of being appointed FBI director if JFK was elected President. Yet, he knew J. Edgar Hoover was the past master of political extortion and was in heated competition with him when it came to accumulating illicit information on the Kennedys and their associates. Still, on the Kennedys in Hollywood, the LAPD always had the big edge on the Feds. Especially through Captain Hamilton, the head 'spook' of the intelligence division who shared a key and the security combination on their secret files only with Chief Parker. The men trusted each other with their careers which amounted to their lives. Hamilton was the well-paid consultant and adviser on the big screen version of *Dragnet* [September 1954] and was portrayed in the movie by the solid, tobacco-voiced Richard

Boone. It was impeccable public relations. Hamilton became the fixer, the enabler of the LAPD. In December 1954, he dedicated his time to 'educating' the writer Ian Fleming, the then largely unknown – especially in America – creator of James Bond, in the ways of the Mob, the Mafia, drugs and the perils of Las Vegas. This material later found its way into 007 adventures.

If you were a friend, Parker and Hamilton, and therefore the total power of the Los Angeles police had your back, your total well-being, protected. They were the long arm of the law; there was nothing they couldn't or wouldn't do.

Mike Rothmiller's friend's grandfather was a founding member of 'The Original Gangster Squad' which later morphed into the OCID. When his friend's grandfather retired, he was replaced by his son, also an LAPD officer. Detective Con Keeler was also an intelligence cop at the time. He confirmed to *Los Angeles Times* reporter Paul Lieberman, how Chief Parker used OCID for 'other chores.' And on one of those occasions it was used to preserve the reputation of President John F. Kennedy. Con Keeler recalled a delicate moment when it was Marilyn Monroe's Hollywood screen goddess rival Kim Novak who was JFK's desired target.

'Parker was always fearful that something might happen in LA and embarrass the city, though this attitude was rare in the era before the Kennedy assassination. So, Kennedy himself comes to town, and they assign a car to watch him. I was like a supervisor then, and the guys are reporting to me.

'So, he [President Kennedy] goes to the hotel where he checks into a bungalow, and then they see him crawl out of a window and get a cab. A cab – the President of the United States...

'Oh, my...

'So they call me.

'"What should we do?"

'"Follow him."

'So they do... to Kim Novak's house.

'I call the Secret Service which is supposed to be protecting him: "Do you know where your man is?"

"'He's asleep.'"

"'You better check where…'"

Another item went into the OCID file on actress Kim Novak, Sinatra's co-star in *The Man With the Golden Arm* [1955] and *Pal Joey* [1957].Whenever a Kennedy was in town, whatever a Kennedy did, whomever a Kennedy saw, the OCID and the chief knew about it – and filed it for a rainy day.

As such, it was a monsoon moment when Mike Rothmiller got a detailed look into the intricate reports surrounding the events before, during and after Marilyn Monroe's untimely, unnatural and now, to him, uncertain death, her murder.

Mike Rothmiller has since twice testified under oath, in relation to other sensitive matters: that the LAPD's top-secret dossiers existed and had grown and been used with abandon for nearly 40 years before he joined OCID, the one-time 'Gangster Squad' of Con Keeler.

He wanted to know the full truth and, as he graduated as one of the most respected, and noticeably successful, members of LAPD intelligence, he gathered more testimony and evidence from colleagues and through his own, shrewdly discreet inquiries. He had to be careful, for it was the hierarchy of the LAPD who ferociously protected the legend of Marilyn Monroe's final hours; some were involved in the deception at the beginning and the disingenuous inquiries which followed. His was a painstaking inquiry. Eventually, he had most of the answers and his conviction, but needed, desperately wanted, first-person confirmation, an eyewitness to what had happened the night Marilyn Monroe died. But what chance?

In the movies, the lifeblood of the city he lived in and patrolled, there was always that cliffhanger moment and that magical witness would emerge. But that was, indeed, much too Hollywood to dream about. Yet sometimes the magic works. It was not a mistake, an error of judgment or foolishness by the conspirators which allowed Mike Rothmiller to confirm how Bobby Kennedy had a hand in Marilyn's unnatural death. It was, as it so often is, chance which intervened, and on the detective's day off.

Weeks had become months and then years, and he pursued his career with OCID while conceiving and directing international intelligence operations, but Mike Rothmiller could not shake off his nagging certainty that Marilyn Monroe had been murdered. What he called his 'investigator's instincts' wouldn't allow him to. But how? The circles around the conundrum he confronted were too tight, too cleverly drawn for an easy solution and too many people were dead. When not overtaken by immediate duties, his thoughts would swirl around and around seeking a tiny break which would lead him to the heart of the matter.

As it was, a visit to Hugh Hefner's Playboy Mansion was something of a busman's holiday. It was his job to gather intelligence on the lives of celebrities, entertainment executives, sports figures, politicians, professional and college coaches, the wealthy, Mafia figures and any person of interest to – in this case with much irony – his boss, LAPD Chief Daryl Gates. He acknowledges, in fairness to Gates, that he wasn't the first LAPD Chief to employ the self-aggrandising benefits of intelligence gathering on friend and foe. The inside track on anyone perceived as wielding power or influence was a decades-old tradition when Gates became chief. As the former commander of OCID, he possessed first-hand knowledge of the virtually unlimited supply of scandalous information contained within the ever-expanding dossiers maintained in the division's tightly secured walls. He and the hand-selected detectives of OCID, including Mike Rothmiller – particularly the team of detectives whose *only* responsibility was targeting politicians – understood that an arm could easily be twisted, and a foe converted to an ally with the simple mention of a career-ending embarrassing incident or the revealing of covertly taken photographs. Daryl Gates and other LAPD Chiefs enjoyed, in the days when it mattered, hearing the steamy tidbits of who was gay and who was straight in Hollywood. And most of all, Gates relished his intelligence briefings when they included photographic evidence of a movie star's private activities or their *extremely personal* encounters with men, women, children, animals or any combination thereof. In the purest sense, he was a voyeur commanding a secret army of City-paid peeping toms who were accountable only to him.

Many of those incorrigible characters, at one time or another, were seduced by the bountiful temptations of the world of the Playboy Mansion – a mock Gothic-Tudor marvel bizarrely enhanced by aged dark wood carved so it appeared to be from trees which grew perfectly straight to the sky. Gates always wanted an update on the peccadilloes of the prominent citizens of Los Angeles and powerful visitors to the city. The now disgraced entertainer, Bill Cosby, was a regular, and the late Hugh Hefner's Mansion was a place to gain some of that.

When Rothmiller drove off Sunset Boulevard and up Charing Cross Road to the mansion, it was his day off. That Saturday morning in the spring of 1982, he didn't divulge to his passengers the secrets of the Holmby Hills neighbourhood although he knew them, most discreetly disguised behind the overgrown purple-flowering bougainvillea and cloaked by the power of extravagant wealth and influence. He was content to leave that dignified façade undisturbed.

He was taking his wife, Nancy, and two of their friends on a tour of the Playboy Mansion. He wanted to impress them and for them to enjoy themselves with a look at the grounds, portions of the main house, the pool and grotto, guest house, game house, koi ponds and Hefner's private aviary and zoo. A security director led them around and pointed out a Matisse painting with a cigarette hole burned through it by the Beatles' John Lennon. He said the security team wanted to 'kick Lennon's ass' and eject him from the property, but Hefner wisely advised otherwise. 'It's worth more *Lennonised*.'

As his friends examined the Beatle-burned artwork, he heard a television playing steps away in what seemed like a cloakroom. He looked inside the tiny den and saw a boozy Peter Lawford.

He was half-asleep, his matted hair spiking up at the sides, and sitting on a small sofa while staring at a tiny, flickering television.

Rothmiller did a double take for this was a frailty of the man he knew from the movies and television. He felt sad to see how far this man had deteriorated, from being the star of films like the original *Ocean's Eleven*, *The Longest Day*, and the eponymous *The Thin Man* of the popular 1950s television series. But this haunted-looking man *was* Peter Lawford. And sitting right in front of him. Only in the days before, Rothmiller had once more been reviewing significant portions of OCID's dossiers on Lawford, Marilyn Monroe, JFK, and Robert Kennedy. Rothmiller had so many things to ask Peter Lawford… but how?

He had serious questions regarding the activities surrounding Monroe's death, questions which tugged at his sense of justice. Questions, he believed, Lawford could answer to complete his intelligence investigation. His investigation had involved speaking with witnesses and informants, police officers who responded to Marilyn Monroe's home the night she died and those working intelligence at the time. Whirling around his mind was the evidence, both hard and circumstantial, that had convinced him that her death was a homicide. And that Robert Kennedy, Peter Lawford and at least two members of LAPD intelligence were present and intimately involved in her death and the ensuing cover-up, for cover-up there most certainly was; he had read the evidence.

Now, by that happenstance which bedevils conspirators, an encounter only five miles from where Marilyn Monroe died, presented Rothmiller with the possibility to interview the last known living person to see Marilyn and, as he knew from the OCID files, Robert Kennedy, that fatal evening. The thought of officially interviewing Peter Lawford taunted Mike Rothmiller. What were the chances? Was this chance cruelly teasing him?

Lawford seemed bedazzled, out of it, but seizing the opportunity the detective slipped his business card into Lawford's shirt pocket truly never *expecting* a result but *hoping*, *hoping* very much, that the man who had kept so many secrets would remember he had the card, find it and call him. And somehow supply the missing piece of the puzzle of Marilyn Monroe's death, a puzzle he was aware now genuinely obsessed him as it had so many others for such a long time.

Rothmiller already knew unequivocally that Robert Kennedy had been in Los Angeles on the day Marilyn Monroe died, a fact that had been denied and obstructively hidden for many years by the LAPD. Yes, he knew there had been a cover-up led by the LAPD. But of *exactly* what and how? He wanted more.

## II: Death by Conspiracy

*'Hollywood is a place where they'll pay you a thousand dollars for a kiss and fifty cents for your soul.'*
— Marilyn Monroe, 1958.

Instructively, as a metaphor for the turbulence of fame, on the last day of her life, Marilyn Monroe spent time with her Hollywood publicist, Patricia Newcomb, and with her psychiatrist, Dr. Ralph Greenson, at her home Cursum Perficio.

As ever, her housekeeper, the manipulative Mrs. Eunice Murray, was there, always busy and listening at 12305, Fifth Helena Drive, the home she had found for her employer and the first the nomadic star had ever owned by herself. Marilyn was talking of boosting her career and getting herself mentally prepared for it. She was also attempting to deal with her love-infatuation with Robert Kennedy, and her feelings of being abused by his brother, the President of the United States.

It's impossible to establish how medicinally exacerbated her frustrations and anger over the Kennedys had been in the prior weeks and months. That Saturday, she was livid. Wiretaps and testimony show she was threatening to go public with her sexual relationships with the President *and* Attorney General of the United States. Earlier, her anxieties appeared to have eased, as evidenced by her diary, where she wrote: 'Bobby called. He wants to see me.' Such serenity was brief.

The visit didn't go so well. Peter Lawford picked up his brother-in-law from Los Angeles International Airport at noon on Saturday, August 4, 1962, in his Lincoln Continental and drove first to his beach house where their conversation was heard on electronic 'bugs'. From there, the two men drove to Brentwood and visited Marilyn's home, which was also wired for sound by Rothmiller's informant, a former LAPD cop turned private investigator Fred Otash. They arrived around 2 p.m. [In a statement, held in the OCID files and read by Mike Rothmiller, Robert Kennedy confirmed the afternoon visit and acknowledged he had seen Marilyn several times that year].

From tapes and testimony, Marilyn and Robert Kennedy ignored the Spanish themed buffet [$49.07] brought from her local, Briggs Deli ['Wines, Spirits, Unusual Foods'], around the corner at 13038 San Vicente Boulevard, and indulged in a Mexican stand-off rather than a late lunch. It became more animated when Marilyn yelled that she was going to tell the world about the true nature of her affairs with the Kennedy brothers. With 1962 sensibilities and politics, and with national security an issue, it was the potential guillotine for the present and any future Kennedy administration. She said she was going to hold a press conference that Monday.

One report had Kennedy demanding to be given what was assumed was Marilyn's diary. Another said that the row between them became so heated Marilyn grabbed a kitchen knife and went for Kennedy but Peter Lawford intervened, and it ended in a shame-faced scuffle. With that, the lunch guests left, Lawford having called in Marilyn's psychiatrist, Dr. Ralph Greenson, who turned up around 3 p.m. Patricia Newcomb, who had slept over at Marilyn's on Friday night, left and Dr. Greenson took over. In the subsequent days, months and years, neither he nor Eunice Murray made public mention of the presence of Robert Kennedy that afternoon.

The OCID copy of her much-sought *missing* diary emphasises Marilyn Monroe's feelings and frustrations about the Kennedys. Marilyn sought solace, telephoning José Bolaños, the Mexican writer who had been invited as her escort to the 1962 Golden Globe Awards at the Beverly Hilton Hotel [Marilyn won the Henrietta Award for *World Film Favourite*] the previous February, and she talked openly to him that evening: 'I'm going to tell the world about them. They used me. I'm not a whore.'

The wiretaps heard it all. She was going to go public with her Kennedy affairs. A concerned José Bolaños warned her against it, especially revealing 'national security' details she knew from JFK's remarks about Cuba and Castro. Marilyn talked to lots of people on the phone that day and into the evening including Peter Lawford, although the official telephone company records of these calls swiftly vanished. In her diary on August 3, 1962, she noted: 'Peter said Robert will come tomorrow. I don't know if he will.'

It didn't seem a concern for Marilyn: even in her chemically disorientated mind, she appeared to those listening in to have determined to take more control of her professional and personal life and to do her 'dirty washing in public', no matter what happened, and no matter who did or did not turn up.

Marilyn Monroe, not long after she was voted the world's favourite star, was treated as a commodity, an unwanted commodity. As it was, her dead body was shifted around like a mannequin in a movie, positioned this way and that. There is one 'death' photograph of Marilyn holding a telephone. In another photograph, she is still naked but in a different position and there's no telephone. Much had gone on after the event and all of it to cover-up what did happen, that trick of shaping events to however you want them to appear. These photographs didn't reveal the truth, something vividly confirmed by Peter Lawford when he later confessed the facts to Mike Rothmiller.

Lawford was a tense man but could be good company [Douglas Thompson met and talked with him several times in the 1970s and visited him in rehab at the Betty Ford Clinic in Palm Springs, California, in 1984] with his stories of his glorious early days in Hollywood when all was happy and hopeful, of the Rat Pack period when the fun was controlled by the whim of Sinatra, nothing that couldn't be eased by a fifth of bourbon and a Las Vegas chorus. He was a wary person with that lost look of an insomniac. Disquietingly, after the death of Marilyn Monroe, he became a better actor, one who knew his lines impeccably and played the role of his life for almost the rest of his life. In so many ways, during that August weekend of 1962, Peter Lawford's displaced life, which had been disassembling for so long, was also destroyed.

This became all too apparent to Mike Rothmiller almost two decades later. A week after his encounter at the Playboy Mansion, Rothmiller got a message from the OCID's downtown office that 'a Mr. Lawford had telephoned.' He went to a gas station near downtown to return the call from a public telephone. [In those pre-cell/mobile phone days, detectives carried a large bag of coins for making sensitive calls out of the office and would never use OCID's telephone credit card since it left a trail as to the number called].

Lawford answered almost immediately. He seemed free of the influence of booze or drugs, yet Rothmiller had to revive his memory of the details of their meeting at the Playboy Mansion. Lawford, whom Rothmiller found paranoid – understandably, he thought – quizzed him several times about who he was 'with.' Rothmiller slowly spelled it out that he was a detective with the *Organized Crime Intelligence Division of the Los Angeles Police Department*. Still, Lawford repeatedly asked if Rothmiller was with the CIA. Rothmiller explained to Lawford that *he* was not under investigation: 'I'm LAPD, not the CIA and I merely want your opinion regarding a few issues from many years ago.'

Peter Lawford cautiously accepted the low-key approach. Rothmiller was curious about why he was so keen to know if he was with the CIA but lost that thought when they arranged to meet the next day, a Saturday, at a park off Sunset Boulevard, a rare walking area in car–dominated Los Angeles near the Playboy Mansion. It was a remarkable conversation which began a sequence of events and conversations that imprinted on Mike Rothmiller's brain. Now revealing this conversation for the very first time, quietly, slowly and with ease, Rothmiller presents the circumstances and details of something he has held to himself, for his, and his family's well–being, for nearly four decades. There is no grandstanding about what he has to say: it is a report of a conversation which turned into a police interrogation and overtakes everything we thought we knew about the mysterious death of Marilyn Monroe. The language is often that of a police statement, echoing the dogmatic fluency Rothmiller was trained in.

Lawford was 30 years old in 1954 when he married Patricia Kennedy, the sixth of Joe and Rose Kennedy's nine children; his bride was twelve days younger than him. It was that cachet-by-marriage which allowed him to introduce his brother-in-law to Marilyn Monroe. JFK was a Marilyn enthusiast from their first meeting, but Lawford had no sense then of the collateral damage which would result from the future President's sexual recklessness. As Mike Rothmiller prepared to talk with Peter Lawford, the detective was certain from his investigations and the secret files that there was a conspiracy to eliminate Marilyn Monroe, and it came from the highest levels of government. So, it wasn't just Lawford who was nervous that day, both men were deeply concerned about the consequences of what discovering the truth might create. Rothmiller sensed fear and shame in Lawford, saw pain and puzzlement in his eyes and the haunted look of a bad conscience. The whites of his eyes were yellowish from a bad diet. Rothmiller, cautious at what personal danger he was inviting, was, at first, careful in his approach during his extraordinary encounter with Peter Lawford in 1982:

'I arrived early and began scanning the area for Lawford or others who may have learned of this secret meeting. In intelligence work, you cannot accept anything at face value; including those who may be an ally, or worse, an adversary. I waited and waited. It was more than an hour after the agreed meeting time before I concluded he was a no-show. While I was preparing to leave, I spotted him cautiously walking into the park. He was slightly hunched over and slowly ambling. He'd stop, look around, and then proceed. I quickly approached, introduced myself, and we moved to a nearby park bench. It was clear he didn't remember me and was extremely nervous and guarded.

'Several more times, I reassured him that I wasn't with the CIA and asked him why he thought I was. His response was fascinating. Angrily and suspiciously, he said: "Because you guys have been watching me for years." Was this fact or the tangled thoughts of a troubled man? Or did he spot OCID detectives surveilling him and concluded they were the CIA? It was a question I could not answer.

'After several tense moments of small talk, he asked what I wanted. I said some questions had arisen regarding the death of Marilyn, and I wanted to hear his side. He immediately retorted that the cops spoke with him years ago and he told them what he knew. I asked him to indulge me and explain what happened the night Marilyn died.

'It was apparent he found my question irritating, yet he rattled off an abbreviated, choppy edition of his long-ago scripted speech. When he finished, I said: "That's not what happened." His body language telegraphed a volatile mixture of anger and fear that I questioned his response.

'"What do you mean?"

'I then proceeded to explain some of the details I already knew, including the work Fred Otash performed for him before and immediately after Marilyn's death, Marilyn and John F. Kennedy's prior rendezvous at his house and some of his and Robert Kennedy's activities on the day she died.

'He stared at me in silence, and I knew I had touched a raw nerve. Then I added the finishing touch: "Did you know that your home and Marilyn's was bugged, and the telephones wiretapped by LAPD intelligence and others?"

'He was stunned.

'LAPD intelligence documents indicated that he had long suspected his home and Marilyn's were bugged and their telephones tapped by some agency; he didn't know who, but always suspected it was the CIA. I provided the confirmation of what he had long suspected and feared. People were listening.

'Indignantly he retorted: "I told them what I know, and I have nothing more to say." He slowly stood and glared at me.

'It was apparent my soft interview approach had failed, requiring me to elevate the meeting from an interview to an adversarial interrogation. Unfortunately, he forced me to take an unpleasant step. I had no idea if my tactic would work or if he'd tell me to go fuck myself and walk away. I quickly stood and faced him. In a stern voice, I said: "We both know the story you gave is bullshit."

'He hesitated, staring at me. I leaned into him and in a low voice said: "Here's the deal. I've heard the tapes from your house and Marilyn's. I have a list of the telephone calls made from your house and Marilyn's. I know what happened that night, and I'm not going to stand here and listen to your bullshit."

'I paused: "You have a choice. Answer my questions, and this will be the end of it. If not, others may learn we met and will have serious concerns about what you told me."

'There was dead silence. I didn't relish pressing such a frail, haggard and pitiful soul. However, I knew Marilyn's death was a homicide, and I wanted more proof. The items I rattled off were part of a proven interrogation technique. The interrogator states facts the subject knows to be true, interlaced with others they believe or fear to be true. The more they think you know, the more likely they'll talk.

'However, I was truthful when informing him what might happen if he didn't answer my questions. LAPD fiercely guarded its dirty secrets, and Marilyn's death was one of their biggest. Without question, LAPD had the power, knowledge, and ability to silence anyone they deemed a threat. I did not doubt for a moment that a paranoid man like Chief Daryl Gates would take the ultimate step to silence any, and all, he viewed as a significant threat to his power base. I worried that if I wrote a detailed intelligence report regarding our meeting, others would leak the information and that would undoubtedly ensure Lawford's untimely silence and perhaps mine.

'Peter Lawford paused and stared at me before sitting back down on the bench. He slowly dropped his head and cradled it in his hands while resting his elbows on his thighs. My questions and statements were designed to impress upon him that I knew details that only an intelligence agent would know. More importantly, I possessed devastating information he never knew existed until today. His reaction was indicative of a person who had been carrying a heavy burden of guilt for many years. Hopefully, I had found him at the stage in his life and in a state of mind that would allow him to unburden himself.

'Without looking up, in a hushed voice, he asked: "What do you want?"

'"Just a few answers."

'For several moments I allowed him to ponder the situation in silence. I could only imagine the pain of those dark days racing back from the deep recesses of his mind where they had remained hidden for so many years. Without question, this was difficult for Lawford; I believe in his way, he felt responsible for Marilyn Monroe's death.

'I still had no idea how he would respond. Would he walk away? Tell me what truly happened? Or stick to his and the LAPD's long-standing scripted story? My wait was as tense as his.

'I asked him to look at me and said something along the lines of: "You're not in trouble, and we're not coming after you. Marilyn, the President and Bobby are dead. So are many others. I know Marilyn's death was not your fault. You were in the wrong place at the wrong time. It was a long time ago."

'The ensuing silence was deafening for us both. I felt the anxiety of the moment and adrenaline pulsing through my body, not knowing if I had pressed too hard or not hard enough. The painful introspection he was experiencing was plainly visible by his trembling hands. At that moment, the knot I felt in my belly told me that I had blown it and he was going to say he didn't remember anything.

'Slowly he looked up, and in a low nearly inaudible voice, he asked again, "What do you want to know?"

'Having prepared myself for him to say, "I don't remember" and walk away, his response momentarily stunned me. I slowly lowered myself to the bench and turned to him. I took a moment to compose myself and started the questioning.

'And he told me what really happened the night he watched Marilyn die.'

# III: Captain Fixit

*'[LAPD Detective Harry] Bosch had an idea what was coming. The fixer was here now. The investigation was about to go through the spin cycle where decisions and public pronouncements would be made based on what best served the department, not the truth.'*
— *Angels Flight* by Michael Connelly, 1999.

On the morning of Sunday, August 5, 1962, at 9 a.m. exactly, Robert Kennedy, the Attorney General of the United States, his wife Ethel and four of their children, attended Roman Catholic mass at St. Mary Parish, Gilroy, California.

At the same moment, Captain James Hamilton was conferring at LAPD HQ with Chief Parker, to construct and establish a cover-up of the great sin of murder.

Homicide investigators say you have to catch a killer within the first 48 hours or you are swamped in ongoing and sometimes futile inquiries. It works the other way if you want to 'lose' a killer. Captain Hamilton was clever at cementing disinformation into the foundations of his fabricated timeline of events. His manipulation of the autopsy, the doctors, the police and the fake news began in the minutes following Marilyn Monroe's death.

That morning, as the Robert Kennedy family prayed 310 miles away at the ornate St. Mary's in Gilroy, Captain Hamilton was about to make a simple story so complex, the truth so disassembled, the evidence and the crime scene so compromised that it would confuse the narrative for decades and invite crystal-gazing conjecture for just as long. He scripted Peter Lawford's cover-up story, the one he would repeat all but word for word until he spoke truthfully to Mike Rothmiller. It was Captain Hamilton who orchestrated the catalogue of malicious misunderstandings which would make the world believe Marilyn Monroe's death was self-inflicted. But, from the start, there was a wrinkle in his narrative, one that would rip to become a tear and eventually leave a gaping hole in the truth as presented by LAPD: the whereabouts of Robert Kennedy when Marilyn Monroe died. He was with his family for the scheduled Sunday service at the historic Gilroy church which is an hour's drive from downtown San Francisco. He had *not* been in Los Angeles the day Marilyn Monroe died. How could he be in two places at once?

Publicly, that alibi stood up for many years. The prolific biographer Donald Spoto [*Marilyn Monroe: The Biography,* Chatto & Windus] in 1993 determinedly dismissed any suggestion that Robert Kennedy had been anywhere near Los Angeles on the last day of Marilyn Monroe's life. Yet, a year earlier LAPD

Chief Daryl Gates in his biography [*Chief: My Life in the LAPD,* Bantam, 1992] had confessed: 'The truth is, we knew Robert Kennedy was in town on August 4. We always knew when he was here.' It had always been that way with the Kennedys, before and most certainly after the Democratic National Convention [July 11 to July 15] in Los Angeles in 1960 when JFK won the Presidential nomination. Chief Bill Parker's intelligence squads had their own suites at the Biltmore Hotel to monitor and help his campaign. When several hundred supporters of Adlai Stevenson [the Democratic nominee in 1952 and 1956] tried to make their views heard at the LA Sports Arena where the convention was being staged, the chief's men swiftly broke up their efforts. Still, Chief Parker was dismayed about what they were protecting. He was tentative about the Kennedy connection to Frank Sinatra ['totally tied to the Mafia'] and upset by what he saw as immoral behaviour by Peter Lawford, but he was loyal to the Kennedys, as were his inner circle. Several others knew the truth about Bobby Kennedy's whereabouts when Marilyn died, most obviously Peter Lawford. He had witnessed Marilyn, within moments, become comatose and, within minutes, lifeless. Peter Lawford had stared at Marilyn, lying motionless, and knew she wasn't simply 'out of it'. There was a void where she should have been, where she'd always been. He'd known she was dead.

In the aftermath of watching Marilyn Monroe die, Peter Lawford's mind was, understandably, a tumble of fears and his spinning brain suddenly seized up; he stopped thinking: he had, in real time, lost the plot. He had to drive Bobby Kennedy to the airport but found himself confused as to what direction to go.

Which was why at 12.10 a.m. on August 5, 1962, he was steering his Lincoln Continental the wrong way by going east on Olympic Boulevard at 70mph, twice the speed limit. He was stopped at Olympic and Robertson by Beverly Hills policeman, Lynn Franklin. In his report of the incident [*The Beverly Hills Murder File,* 1st Books Library, 2002] Detective Franklin's patrol car's flashing red light gets Peter Lawford to pull over. The cop then recognises Lawford and the Beverly Hills Police 'celebrity rules' kick in: 'Pete, what the hell do you think you're doing?'

Lawford was thinking enough to pull rank: 'I'm trying to get the Attorney General to the airport.'

At that point, Franklin, who died of natural causes in 2005, wrote that he turned on his flashlight and shone it on the back seat and directly into the face of Robert Kennedy.

'He didn't look happy,' commented Franklin.

Lawford said he was going to the Beverly Hilton Hotel to collect the Attorney General's luggage. [Robert Kennedy was not officially registered there that night, nor was anyone named James Hamilton.] Franklin said there was a third man in the car who he would later say he recognised as Dr. Ralph Greenson, Marilyn Monroe's psychiatrist. The 'why' of Greenson's presence in the car is something that has never been explained in the complex conspiracy. [OCID detectives later told Mike Rothmiller they believe Dr. Greenson was picked up after Lawford and Bobby Kennedy left Marilyn's home that night.]

Franklin told Lawford: 'Well you're heading in the wrong direction. It's [the hotel] behind you.' He also reported he heard Robert Kennedy shout urgently from the back seat, 'I told you, stupid!'

'That was all he [Robert Kennedy] said during the encounter.'

With a warning to 'be careful, drive slowly' the Beverly Hills policeman allowed Lawford and his passengers to be on their way and Lawford swept his car around on the always busy Olympic Boulevard and headed west toward the Beverly Hilton and Los Angeles International Airport and anywhere else he might be directed to drive to.

Mike Rothmiller did not need Lynn Franklin's evidence to know that Robert Kennedy had been in town that day as it was all a matter of OCID record. What did intrigue him was that in the years after that incident, Detective Franklin survived two attempts on his life.

In his 2002 book Franklin ponders:

'The significant thing that might be related to the hit attack on me was that I was the only witness that I know of, certainly the only one wearing a badge, who could testify that the Attorney General of the United States, Robert Kennedy, had been in Los Angeles in the middle of the night, going in the wrong direction at high speed, trying to get out of town as fast as he could... Sam Yorty, who was then the mayor of Los Angeles, told me that his police chief, William Parker, had assured him that Kennedy was in Los Angeles that night but Yorty didn't know what evidence Parker had, and Parker has long since died of a heart attack.'

Mike Rothmiller also eventually found himself with information no one else knew. After their 1982 interview, he was aware that both he and Peter Lawford could be in danger. Today [in 2021] Mike Rothmiller cannot be certain if there was a very real attempt to kill him because of what he learned about the death of Marilyn Monroe and the cover-up to protect the Kennedy family. He had been involved in many risky undercover operations involving the Mafia and Mexican cartels and death threats were part of the job... *yet*.

Only weeks following his intense interrogation of Lawford, on a muggy night in August 1982, he was near home, driving his unmarked police car, when a gunman on a motorbike roared up alongside him and sprayed a magazine of bullets at him. The burst from the machine pistol shattered the peace of the Orange County street and Mike Rothmiller's life. He'd sensed the 'hit' seconds before it happened, braking and veering over a dirt embankment. Even in the thundering chaos, he heard the bullets being pumped toward him, saw the flash of the weapon like a jumping light. He was thrown or he rolled out of the car and landed hard on the ground, winded. He tried to reach his police radio, but the only communication he got was a voice asking: 'Are you alright? Are you OK?' Instinctively, Rothmiller reached for the .38 revolver. It was as out of reach to him as his radio. Happily, the voice belonged to a fireman who lived nearby and heard the shots and the sound of the car crashing. The cops were on their way, there were sirens in the distance, and so was Rothmiller's would-be assassin. The full-face helmeted, black leather-clad gunman vanished as quickly as he had appeared. He'd left his target bleeding from the side of his chest, with excruciating pain in his back and no feeling in his legs. Rothmiller vaguely recalls the sirens and a helicopter clattering above him and voices – lots of voices –but what they were saying he couldn't quite comprehend.

What his dulled brain suddenly realised was that his wife Nancy might also be in danger – the gunman had probably followed him from his house. The cops took off for his home as the paramedics began treating him on the spot.

Rothmiller could no longer feel the right side of his body as the paramedics worked him into a neck brace and, with an IV dangling from his arm, stretchered him into an ambulance and off to Fountain Valley Regional Trauma Center. He heard a paramedic say he'd been shot and, more ominously, another medic urging the ambulance driver to speed up: 'Faster, we're losing this guy.'

The emergency trauma team turned that around; it wasn't a gunshot, but a wound in his side sustained in the crash that was causing the bleeding. It was a critical time. There was no internal bleeding, but his spinal column had been damaged and severely bruised. When he came to, his wife was there. She was safe, but he still didn't feel that way especially after a visit from his OCID lieutenant. His LAPD colleagues and investigators from the Huntington Beach Police Department found several bullets lodged in his car. They were from a .22 semi-automatic pistol, a weapon with a recoil-reducing barrel – perfect for high-performance assassins. At the time, it was the preferred tool for assassins in South America.

Just as disturbing were the instructions from his OCID chiefs: don't tell the local cops too much and don't divulge the cases he was working on or discuss possible motives. He followed his orders, but the investigators were desperate to discover a motive.

'They were asking him the same questions over and over, and he was clearly in shock. He was shaking. I knew I couldn't make them stop. I started to pass out. A nurse gave me smelling salts,' remembers Nancy Rothmiller, who was put under police guard. Her husband was registered in intensive care under a false name, and full security procedures were set up to protect them.

Nobody, outside those who masterminded it, knows who was behind the 'hit' on Mike Rothmiller. That night he had been returning from a clandestine meeting in California's Mojave desert; it was only days after his real identity was revealed to operatives in the secret CIA operation supplying weapons to the Nicaragua Contras. He had been undercover many times on just as tricky and dangerous assignments and had never been attacked.

He was heavily drugged, and in that deep, semi-conscious state he wondered if the attempt on his life was connected to what he had learned earlier from Peter Lawford. He had no idea then and in 2021, with all the hindsight time provides, he still doesn't know. Still, he wonders.

What happened in the following months would make him wonder even more about events and his experiences within LAPD intelligence. When he was able to leave the hospital, he was kept under guard by a heavily armed LAPD SWAT team at his home. Although the shooting was the main conversation topic for his family and friends, astonishingly, the attempt on the life of an LAPD intelligence detective did not make the evening television news or even the inside pages of the newspapers. His OCID colleagues blocked out all reporting of the event. To the outside world it was as if it had never happened. Rothmiller knew they could kill news as well as fake it and now it was happening to him. The one thing OCID hated was publicity. His outfit never made arrests as legal proceedings would bring attention, involve lawyers and, much worse, journalists.

The lethargic *Los Angeles Times* dominated the city's press narrative and were totally unaware of OCID's activities as was its much livelier competitor, the *Los Angeles Herald-Examiner*. The television journalists, with their minds more dedicated to hair and make-up, were no bother either. OCID blanked them all. No spotlight on the way that particular division went about their business was permissible.

Mike Rothmiller had a tough time recovering from his injuries, especially the damage to his back and leg. And the daily cocktail of nearly a dozen pain killers and other drugs didn't help. Within days, he received a call from the LAPD Medical Liaison supervisor who instructed him to file a worker's compensation claim. He grudgingly followed the order and made a claim when all he truly wanted to do was to go back to work at OCID. To his bewilderment, it met with immediate hostility – and *he* had been the one shot at.

For the next eighteen months, the detective played cat and mouse with his own department who disputed his claim. They ran all manner of interference, disrupting his and his family's lives and unleashing a torrent of their dirty tactics. Two members of OCID were caught burglarising their home and attempting to kill their four-month-old puppy. The police force openly tried to intimidate his attorney and doctors, and illegally wiretapped his home telephone. LAPD placed dozens of threatening calls to their home and put them under surveillance. During the worker's compensation trial, LAPD was severely reprimanded in open court by the judge 'for wilful suppression of evidence, falsifying statements and evidence, and obstruction of justice.' Shortly afterward, LAPD unsuccessfully attempted to intimidate the judge in his chambers. Then, on February 28, 1984 – for Rothmiller an especially Orwellian 1984 – a court ruled against Big Brother declaring he had been 'investigated and harassed' for nearly two years by the LAPD because of his claim.

Later, OCID decided to falsely claim their one-time colleague was now a mobster and convinced the IRS to conduct an extensive audit of his family's personal taxes. The IRS audit found they were in complete compliance. LAPD called Nancy's office and told her boss that Mike had just been killed in a road accident. While Rothmiller was out of town and Nancy was at work the local police claimed they received two disturbing 911 calls from their home. Although the Rothmillers lived 50 miles away from Los Angeles, inexplicably, two members of OCID *just happened* to be parked steps away from their home. With local police standing by, the OCID detectives broke through a bedroom window and entered their home activating the alarm system. Somehow, the two detectives knew how to deactivate the alarm. The alarm system had been installed by Rothmiller and an OCID colleague who knew how the system operated. The two detectives spent roughly an hour rummaging through their home before leaving. The following day, Rothmiller's attorney demanded to hear a recording of the alleged 911 calls but the police claimed that a system malfunction had failed to record *just those calls*. What OCID didn't know was that an LAPD officer lived just a few houses away, witnessed the entire event and identified one of the detectives. Years later, one of the good guys in OCID provided Rothmiller with the names of those two OCID detectives.

Judge Gabriel L. Sipos found the LAPD's misconduct so despicable and unjustified he awarded Rothmiller an additional 50 per cent under labor code 132a (1). His $25,000 award almost paid his legal fees. Later a police retirement board denied him a medical pension for his permanent injuries. LAPD's conduct reinforced what he already knew; LAPD could be as ruthless and underhanded as any criminal organisation. Even though all the acts of misconduct and the criminal actions of a few OCID and Internal Affairs [IA] detectives were reported directly to Chief Gates, he demonstrated his power when he waved his hand and every act was overlooked. Nobody faced criminal charges or any discipline for their misconduct.

Over the ensuing years, while Gates was still chief, LAPD continued the harassment. OCID secretly monitored Rothmiller's broadcast and business career. Years later, a few senior OCID detectives contacted him and said the actions were undertaken on the orders of Chief Daryl Gates, and one detective gave Rothmiller portions of the dossier OCID established on him.

The detective told him: 'Gates was terrified you'd become a whistleblower, and that would take him and the department down. They had to take you out.' Eventually, the honest OCID detectives provided him with all the names of those involved in the LAPD's campaign of harassment.

After Rothmiller won the legal battle, LAPD offered him a position in the Juvenile Narcotics Division. Having survived the ruthless LAPD gauntlet, he said: 'No thank you…' In off-the-record conversations, two investigative reporters told him they believed at least one member of OCID was involved in planning the assassination attempt on him. Was it all because of the Lawford interview? Being a former OCID detective, Rothmiller cannot completely dismiss that possibility. Since LAPD was willing to unleash dirty tricks on one of their own, what chance did a hapless Marilyn stand during a time when LAPD had no restraints?

Mike Rothmiller did the unexpected – he got on with his life after a distinguished career in law enforcement, working across US Federal and State agencies and with American and international intelligence services. In total, he served for ten years with the LAPD including five years as a deep undercover detective in OCID.

After he quit the department, Rothmiller began a hugely successful career in broadcasting, business and as a bestselling author. In 1992, he published a book titled *LA Secret Police: Inside LAPD's Elite Spy Network* [Pocket Books, Simon & Schuster] which revealed the inside story of his time in the force. His book became a *Los Angeles Times* and *New York Times* bestseller. It was his revelations about corruption, racism, false arrests and police brutality which devastated the worlds of politics and policing. So much so that, in 1992, the newly appointed LAPD

Chief of Police Willie L. Williams – who replaced Chief Daryl Gates – ordered both offices of the LAPD's OCID be closed and padlocked. Williams then posted 24-hour uniformed officers and police IA Division detectives to guard the entrances to 'maintain the integrity' of the secret files. In the book, co-written with Ivan Goldman, Rothmiller made brief mention of Marilyn Monroe's death and that he had read her diary. Immediately he was overwhelmed by media requests to tell more. He refused, other than to make a couple of non-committal comments. [Yet, since then he has been regularly sought for interviews and reflections, and has been cited as a source – often for just saying 'hello' on the telephone – in several books purporting to reveal all the facts.] In his long career, Rothmiller has encountered all manner of deception and atrocity, but he remains most concerned by his investigation into the death of Marilyn Monroe. The psychological and, in some cases, physical harm she suffered at the hands of those who were accepted as being good, righteous, honest and trustworthy, amplified the unease he felt about this abuse of power. Powerful men exploiting vulnerable women is not a scenario which has changed much in the decades since Marilyn died. He regards our conclusions in this book as the rich and important culmination of a lifetime of inquiries which will hopefully achieve legal redress, posthumously in some cases, and correct the fabricated history about the death of Marilyn Monroe and about those who used and killed her. It should stir the conscience of many.

Following the publication of the book 1992, the former Los Angeles Mayor, Sam Yorty [1961–1973], and former LAPD Chief Thomas Reddin [1967–1969], separately contacted him and asked what happened to Marilyn Monroe. Tom Reddin told him that OCID openly lied to him on several occasions while he was police chief. He said that on his first day as chief, February 18, 1967, he called OCID and asked a lieutenant if they had files on Marilyn Monroe and the Kennedys. He was told they did and the new and enthusiastic Chief Reddin ordered them to be brought to his office that afternoon. Later that day in Reddin's office, the captain of OCID said the lieutenant had been mistaken, they had no files. Rothmiller knew this was a lie. During their conversations he explained to Reddin and Yorty what he knew and suspected about the death of Marilyn Monroe.

Others, like former LAPD Sergeant Jack Clemmons, contacted Rothmiller to help his inquiries, his personal quest to prove the truth. Rothmiller did not know Jack Clemmons from his days in OCID or even recall his name. It was only when Clemmons reminded him that he was the first cop on the scene of Marilyn Monroe's death that this unexpected contact made sense. Both men knew there was more to know and wanted to find it. After Rothmiller checked out what Clemmons told him on the phone was true, they arranged to meet and did so regularly until Clemmons' sudden death in April 1998. Clemmons contributed valuable intelligence, front-line primary knowledge of the crime scene and fascinating insights into the unknowns.

What also helped Rothmiller's inquiries was the earlier publication of JFK mistress Judith Exner's *My Story* [Grove Press, 1977]. Her book was a major contribution to the dismantling of the Kennedy's Camelot legend. It opened up for scrutiny the subject of President Kennedy's sex life, something that had been way off-limits when he was alive, when, even in the 'New Age' 1960s, there remained a dignified respect for the Presidency. Now, JFK was publicly linked with Hollywood actresses and many other women. After her death, renowned newspaper columnist Earl Wilson quoted Marilyn Monroe on her relationship with JFK: 'I think I made his back feel better.' That was one of the remarks Mike Rothmiller read in more definitive detail in her diary. Yet, whatever he learned in her writings, and her massive OCID file, was constantly offset by those pushing the Kennedy legend and the counter-intelligence.

The mystique was created from day one of the JFK Presidency; when the Kennedys got the keys to the White House, the power it granted overwhelmed them despite getting there by a much slimmer mandate than expected. They believed they could do anything they wanted with good haircuts, winning smiles and all that global power. They behaved like their money, which was only a generation or so removed from its source. So, stopping the interference of a Hollywood actress, famed and adored but not the international icon she became after death, was not an enormity in their global agenda compared to toppling governments or killing foreign leaders. That Kennedy grandeur and influence may have faded since a Democratic Party fundraiser at Madison Square Garden when Peter Lawford introduced Marilyn Monroe to sing *Happy Birthday, Mr. President* to JFK on May 19, 1962, but it still wielded power and often successfully.

Mike Rothmiller, because of his knowledge and investigations involving the Kennedy family, was invited to discuss the groundbreaking film *Chappaquiddick* by American broadcasters in 2018. The movie received solid reviews and was a drama stripping away confusion – a Kennedy trademark – over the mysterious events surrounding the death of intern Mary Jo Kopechne, 28, after Ted Kennedy drove his car off that now infamous bridge on July 18, 1969. The two had attended a summer party at which Kennedy and five other married men entertained six single women ['boiler room girls'] who had worked on the Presidential campaign of his brother, Robert Kennedy, in 1968. Kennedy, then 37, skidded his Oldsmobile into Poucha Pond in Chappaquiddick. He left Mary Jo to drown as he fled the scene infamously complaining: *'I'm not going to be President.'* He did not report the car accident until ten hours later. The film depicts how a team of nine men worked cynically to salvage Ted Kennedy's political career.

The 2018 cinema release of *Chappaquiddick*, which delves into the aftermath of her death in a *#MeToo* drama about a powerful man in politics trying to spin a potentially career-ending scandal, was one of the reasons Mike Rothmiller believed the time was right for him to reveal the truth about the death of Marilyn

Monroe. It seemed that, finally, the protective shield around the Kennedy clan was collapsing in face of the truth. There was reported pressure from associates of the Kennedy family to suppress the film which showed Ted Kennedy as a man more concerned about his political career than the life of a young woman. Byron Allen, the film's executive producer, said: 'Some very powerful people tried to put pressure on me not to release this movie.' The film's director John Curran said in 2018: 'This is a story that happened 50 years ago and the fact this is a sacred cow we should not speak about was odd to me, and in itself became a motivating factor. I was angry; we weren't allowed to confront the truth.

'As an analogy, if all the women who worked under [Harvey] Weinstein [the disgraced and indicted Hollywood mogul] just kept sticking to "He's innocent," imagine the outrage in light of the evidence contradicting that?

'The Kennedys remain a powerful force. I guess it's the equivalent to the [British] Royal Family. There's something about that in America even today. From the Kardashians to the Trumps to the Clintons, we seem to embrace families as some kind of idealised version of ourselves.'

Yet, there is no time limit on revealing the truth. Just as there appears no limit on the appeal of Marilyn Monroe and the need to discover what really happened to her. She lives longer after life than many others manage in real time. The fascination with her endures even with those that weren't even born when she was alive – fan mail still arrives from eight to eighty-year-olds. Cinematographer Jack Cardiff said that she 'glowed' on screen. Her possessions are treated and valued like Rembrandts. Edward Meyer, vice-president of Ripley's Believe It Or Not museums who bought the dress she wore to sing for President Kennedy in 2016 for close to five million dollars, said after the purchase: 'This reminds the world why Marilyn Monroe remains an icon. We believe this is the most iconic piece of pop culture that there is. I cannot think of one single item that tells the story of the 1960s as well as this dress.' The 1999 Christie's sale of Marilyn memorabilia remains a landmark and in the reportage of that, where prices soared above reserves, there are stories like that of her pet poodle's tag and license sold for $63,000. [Frank Sinatra gave her the poodle. She called it Maf, short for Mafia.]

It's often been suggested the Mob wanted her dead. She and Sinatra were certainly acquainted with members of the criminal underworld. No matter how hysterical the claims were, how elaborate the theories over how she was assassinated, how outlandish they seemed, they were never totally dismissed. And there have always been question marks over her death. With time and study, Eunice Murray, a grandmother who had been placed as Marilyn's housekeeper by her psychiatrist Dr. Ralph Greenson, came to be seen as a slightly sinister Mrs. Danvers type, and the Dr. Greenson that emerged was not *Dr. Kildare*. It was the poltergeist of the mystery, who had truly done what, moved this, hidden that, which invoked the camaraderie of paranoia. From the start, there was always a strong belief that her death was no accident. There was not so much fingers of suspicion being pointed, but handfuls of indictments being shaken at whoever appeared in the frame, no matter how short was their cameo. Much was suppressed. Shortly after her death, former FBI agent Frank Capell's short book *The Strange Death of Marilyn Monroe* was published in 1964. The book linked President Kennedy and the Attorney General to both intimacy and skullduggery with Marilyn Monroe. FBI chief J. Edgar Hoover, alerted by his erstwhile agent, bought up many of the now rare copies and used the information to taunt Robert Kennedy. For so very long the stories remained stories, although they became more volatile packages of innuendo and speculation. There had always been ample evidence of JFK's advocacy of the medicinal power of glamour, the pursuit of which was hidden for many years, especially by his loyal Secret Service protection squads.

Believers *and* debtors protected the Kennedy Presidency and, later, its legacy. Anything was allowed in order to do that. It was a culture which was emphasised when the Kennedy family first won the White House; it was, for them, intoxicating. It was walking on water time. They were young and keen and even had a shorthand language, something they spoke among themselves. Of all things, they were lauded most for *style*. They could do anything they wanted. Yet, cognitive thought instructs that there are always consequences and time will always tell.

With all this knowledge, Mike Rothmiller had a new assignment. He wanted to clear up loose ends and confirm and collaborate, to investigate the way he'd been trained. It took time, and it took care. Even with a truth discovered, those involved deny what they have done as easily as they previously forgot what they believed. He had more questions for, whatever you discover, there is always more to learn and, most of all, to understand. The big question was why. Indeed, obvious – but why go so far? Why take such a crazy risk? Forget the morality of it; just why? And how? And, just as staggering a puzzle, how could an act of such enormity be concealed and kept such a fiercely guarded secret for so many years? Who had the ability and the means? Yet, guile has a time limit too. Skeletons rattle. JFK had been reckless in his affairs with Marilyn and Judith Exner and talked with both of them by telephone from the Oval Office. Transcripts are said to exist of those conversations, those with Marilyn reportedly 'sexually explicit', but the tapes themselves were either removed or tampered with before being placed with other documents in the control of the Federal archive in 1976. There had been more than a dozen years – ample time – for the tapes to be screened. It was the accepted way to cover-up misdemeanours and felonies.

Such was the power of the Kennedy myth, that overwhelming efforts have been routinely made over the years to head off any possible taint on the Kennedy White House. When William Manchester presented the manuscript for *The Death of a President* [Harper & Row, 1967], the book he'd written at the request of the Kennedy family, he was asked to remove sections which spoke against the image of the Kennedy 'style'. One objectionable section described the President's habit of wandering around in his underwear before bed. And a list of the contents of Jacqueline Kennedy's purse the morning after the assassination. It identified something The First Lady had kept secret for her one thousand days with that title – her cigarettes. There were many people keeping secrets. LAPD Chief William Parker's much younger brother Joe recalled hearing about some racy goings-on involving the Kennedys and Hollywood starlets. 'I don't understand how that could be true,' he remarked. His more clued-in brother explained: 'Joe, you don't hear anything about what's really going on.'

To get an understanding of what did go on, what happened to Marilyn Monroe, is to understand the desperation to protect the Kennedy image and also the culture of Hollywood where many of the risks were taken. It was a world of corruption and favours. A world of debauchery and deceit by protagonists and witnesses who *did* know better.

It has taken Mike Rothmiller four decades after that pivotal interview with Peter Lawford to feel safe enough to tell the whole story, the truth of what happened to Marilyn Monroe. He was and still is nervous about revealing what he knows, for death chased and teased him shortly after his interview with Peter Lawford, a concern even if happenstance was all it was, for he will never be totally sure.

He still takes precautions, keeps his findings and documentation in safe places, looks over his shoulder and under his car, but for myriad reasons, and with the blessing of his wife Nancy, decided it was time the world knew what he discovered. He says with confidence, 'If I presented my evidence in any court of law, I'd get a conviction.'

For so many of the players, in some strange, supernatural way, tragedy has multiplied by the years, few have truly escaped from flirtations with or membership of the Kennedy Camelot. There is no statute of limitations on the crime of murder in the state of California. Neither is there an end to the legend of Marilyn Monroe.

# PART TWO

## Meet The Gang

*'Mr. Schultz is showing me the world; he is like a subscription to the* National Geographic Magazine *except the only tits I've seen are white.'*

— **The eponymous 'Billy Bathgate' on his gangster-world mentor 'Dutch' Schultz in E.L. Doctorow's novel, 1989.**

# IV: LA Confidential

*'Fasten your seat belts; it's going to be a bumpy night.'*
— Bette Davis as Margo Channing, *All About Eve*, 1950.

When William Parker became the 42nd chief of the Los Angeles Police Department on August 9, 1950, Marilyn Monroe had discarded her model-starlet image and was being considered by some who mattered as 'a serious actress'. Both would have a turbulent relationship with Hollywood, and both would leave their own indelible mark on the world. They were their own people, strong but still dependent on the diligence and duty of those around them. Neither truly blamed anyone else for subsequent misfortune. Marilyn (24) had a dozen years of global stardom ahead of her and Parker (47) had sixteen years until his sudden death, in office as America's most powerful policeman.

By the end of 1950, Chief Parker had quite a file of information on Marilyn Monroe and her extraordinary collection of friends. Marilyn had gone into the OCID files not because the movies were taking her seriously but because so many 'people of interest' to the LAPD were. And had been for some time.

By then, this shapely blonde 'bombshell' wasn't just on screen; she was at Ciro's on Sunset Boulevard in West Hollywood or at the Mocambo providing extra special glamour for the nightclubs and spicy copy for the gossip columns. Sometimes her crowd moved around the Sunset Strip and would find themselves in Sherry's, Sneaky Pete's or another spot favoured by other, more threatening, nightlife. It was not long after the war, and the people with money were those earning well in the town's business, working at the studios or in the affiliated trades. The others with 'new' money were the mobsters, and with *laissez-faire* abandon, they spent it in the nightclubs mixing with the movie crowds. Chief Parker didn't like gangsters. So, by association, Marilyn came to the attention of the LAPD intelligence squad. She was one of many young women then whose names and photographs appeared in the files held on the established players in town. For her, this was the genesis of a Pandora's box.

Marilyn was that particularly rare being, a Hollywood actress who had been born and raised in Tinseltown. The story of her early life is confused by misinformation, much of it from Marilyn herself. Throughout her life she gave various versions of events including a grandmother who did or didn't try to suffocate her and a foster father who may or may not have raped her. She never knew her father and throughout childhood she would pretend Clark Gable was and hung his picture alongside one of Abraham Lincoln on her wall. Her birth was recorded at 9.30 a.m. on June 1, 1926, in the charity ward of Los Angeles General Hospital. Her father was named on her birth certificate as Edward Mortensen but he never featured in her life, hence the elevation throughout her life of movie star Gable and others as replacement fathers. Her mother, born in 1902 as Gladys Monroe, became Gladys Baker from her first marriage which produced two children, and then Gladys Mortensen from her second. At the time of her second daughter's birth, she was a popular, single woman working as a cutter and paster of film negatives at Consolidated Film Industries in Hollywood.

Time and amateur psychology have obscured the mental health of the 24-year-old Gladys but archive accounts by those who knew her paint her as shaky and unstable in everything but her work which she was good at and enjoyed. She was sexually attractive and generous with her favours, which led to competing claims in later years about who was Marilyn's *true* father. Stan Gifford, Gladys' supervisor at Consolidated Film, was named by her and believed to be so by Marilyn – depending on her mood. However, in times long before DNA, there was and is no certainty.

Sex was everywhere. There were many young girls following Hollywood dreams but, as always, there were only so many roles on camera. Off camera, there were ever so many opportunities. This was F. Scott Fitzgerald's Jazz Age, the 'Roarin' Twenties', and as morals dropped, hemlines went up and inhibitions vanished with the intake of cocaine and heroin. The movie industry was coming into its own in the mid-1920s, and those who befriended Gladys were, like her, film fans. She wore the make-up and the fashions of the actresses she watched on screen. Yet, fantasy only went so far. Gladys found reality heavy going.

It was for propriety that she listed her second husband Edward Mortensen on her daughter's birth certificate [Marilyn's death certificate states *father unknown*] but spelled it, 'Mortenson', adding to decades of error about Marilyn's antecedents. There are many theories on why Gladys called her daughter Norma Jeane, but the most probable is that she named her after a girl she looked after when she was working as a nanny rather than screen legend Norma Talmadge. It was also the fashion of the day to give girls two first names.

So, we have 'Norma Jeane Mortensen' sometimes known as Norma Jean Baker, the daughter of a fragile 24-year-old mother very much part of the Hollywood machine. In 1927, Norma Jeane was advisedly placed with foster parents, Albert and Ida Bolender, in Hawthorne – a small city a bus trip south-west of Los Angeles. The Bolenders made extra income through fostering children and had strong Christian values and rules. Gladys lived with them for a time too, but work forced her to find accommodation in Hollywood proper.

She'd visit Norma Jeane at weekends, and that went on until 1933 when Gladys bought a small home in Hollywood for her and Norma Jeane; lodgers helped pay the bills. It was ideal but only for a short time as Gladys' delicate mental health turned into a serious breakdown which was diagnosed as paranoid schizophrenia.

Marilyn Monroe was seven and a half years old when her mother was moved from being cared for in a Hollywood rest home to the Metropolitan State Hospital in Los Angeles County, a group of buildings in the City of Norwalk surrounded by high-security fences and landscaped with neat lawns, palm trees and bougainvillea to disguise the anguish of those inside. Gladys was mentally off-kilter for the rest of her institutionalised life, and for much of her grown-up life, her daughter obsessed over her own mental health.

Marilyn became a ward of the court and was bounced around further foster homes. On September 13, 1935, she was aged nine and was admission No. 3463 at the Los Angeles Orphans' Home in Hollywood. [She later said orphanage life was traumatic: 'I felt unwanted. I didn't like the world around me because it was kind of grim, but I loved to play house. It was like you could make your own boundaries.'] Her mother's friends watched out for her, and she moved from the orphanage in 1937. Then in September 1938, she came into the care of the aunt of one of Gladys' closest friends.

Ana Lower was a Christian Scientist who lived in Sawtelle on the westside of Los Angeles and with her life calmed down for Norma Jeane and she started to attend Junior High School. However, because of Mr. Lower's ill health, she was bumped on again and moved in with her mother's friend Grace Goddard in Van Nuys in the San Fernando Valley. When Mrs. Goddard's husband, Doc, got a new job out of state they couldn't take the almost sixteen-year-old Marilyn with them. So the teenager found her own solution: she married the boy next door, James Dougherty, on June 19, 1942, a little more than a couple of weeks after she became legally of age to do so. Dougherty was 21 years old. Norma Jeane became a housewife and quickly grew bored. It was a miserable set-up. Her factory worker husband joined the Merchant Marines the following year, and she moved with him to Catalina Island, a ferry ride from Los Angeles' San Pedro port. After America entered World War Two in December 1941, Jim Dougherty was posted to the Pacific and South East Asian war zones in 1944 and Marilyn went to work at a munitions plant in Van Nuys. His absence gave his wife time to develop her skills in how to conquer people's affections, especially those of men. She wore bright cherry-red lipstick, fitted sweaters and short skirts.

A photographer, David Conover, working for the army's movie unit and looking to glamorise the war effort, turned up at Norma Jeane's factory and chose her as one of his models. Norma Jeane liked the attention and moved on from factory worker to model eagerly for Conover and a string of other photographers. When she signed a contract with the Blue Book Model Agency in the summer of 1945, she felt 'emancipated'. She was happy to display her body in provocative poses, to wander around without underwear, to emphasise the curves her outfits were clinging to and she was an enthusiastic indoor-nudist.

This was the start of the legend but also the beginning of her years as a sexual toy in the after-dark Hollywood game of pass-the-starlet. She was too top-heavy for a fashion model, and with her brown hair now blonde she was ideal for pin-up work. Her work got her noticed and featured on more than 30 magazine covers within a year. Soon, she was being measured against established Hollywood actresses like Rita Hayworth and Lana Turner. Did she have 'it'?

Ben Lyon was the talent director at 20th Century Fox studios, working for the dictatorial Darryl Zanuck. Lyon and his wife, Bebe Daniels, became household names in Britain throughout the 1950s with the radio and television series *Life with the Lyons*. He knew his actresses and had starred in the 1930s in *Hell's Angels* with, the original platinum blonde, Jean Harlow. On July 17, 1946, agent Helen Ainsworth arranged a meeting for him with her client, Norma Jeane Dougherty, and afterward Lyon announced that it was, 'Jean Harlow all over again.'

As the studio's talent manager, he arranged a screen test in expensive Technicolor, so his 'discovery' would look and perform at her best. It was to be a non-speaking test – to see if she was as sexy on film as she was in printed material. Ben Lyon knew he had to get the test past Darryl Zanuck and brought in make-up wizard Alan 'Whitey' Snyder. Norma Jeane wanted the make-up done her way, and Whitey Snyder obliged, just as he would oblige her for the rest of her life as her personal make-up artist and once more after her death. The model make-up she insisted on was too much for the movies and Marilyn had to wash it off. Norma Jeane snapped at Whitey, but her nerves jangled, and her teenage stutter returned. Whitey talked her through the moment: she did not have to speak, just look gorgeous.

She did, and all at the test were enthusiastic, but when Zanuck – the powerhouse who helped create the Hollywood studio system – saw it, he was not convinced. So Norma Jeane's agent, Helen Ainsworth, dropped a story to the gossip columns that Howard Hughes, mogul, and owner of RKO Studios, was interested in signing Norma Jeane Dougherty. It was the wrong verb, but Hughes was indeed interested. Zanuck didn't like to lose out, and Norma Jeane contractually became Marilyn Monroe at 20th Century Fox on August 24, 1946. She wasn't enthused by her professional name – Ben Lyon provided the Marilyn, her mother's maiden name supplied the Monroe – but that was the way of Hollywood. She was given a seven-year contract on $75 a week, with a salary review every six months, and any money earned outside of Fox through television or photographic work was kicked back to the studio. Any similarity to indentured servitude was totally intentional. The studios ran the players – and the town.

Marilyn won small roles in three films [*Scudda-Hoo! Scudda-Hay!, Dangerous Years* and *Ladies of the Chorus*] but was more sought after as a 'photo opportunity', Some of the least hysterical reportage about this time is by anthropologist, Hortense Powdermaker. Her research became a book, *Hollywood, The Dream Factory* [Secker & Warburg, 1951]. It contains some startling remarks when set against the 21st century #MeToo movement:

'While the bed may be and sometimes is the way to secure a test or a bit part, this is the end unless the girl has some objective qualities which would tend to make her success as an actress probable. However, very few girls realise this. The majority say "yes" very easily to men at the studios, some for a combination of reasons including career ambitions and sex desire, others purely for ambition, only very few just for pleasure, and still fewer because of emotional involvement.

'Many believe and act on the myth, jumping into bed with anyone on even half a promise of help to stardom. It is probable that more men have to refuse girls who make advances than the other way around.

'In Hollywood, sex is regarded as a means of getting ahead, a form of excitement and fun, a function of power, a biological act. Far more rarely is it associated with love or affection or giving meaning in human relations.'

It was into this world that Marilyn Monroe wiggled. For wiggle she did through the 20th Century Fox studios, parading at lunchtime through the commissary with all the other girls seeking attention and the big prize – stardom.

There is a story of one Fox executive entertaining Mike Cowles, the publisher of *Look* magazine, and telling him: 'We have a new girl on the lot with something unusual. Instead of sticking straight out, her tits tilt up.' Cowles appeared bemused, and the unnamed studio man called for Marilyn to be sent to his office. When she appeared, smiling, he lifted her sweater to prove his point. Marilyn never stopped smiling.

She became available around town which was very much a boys' club. There would be card parties, and women would decorate the homes or the clubs where poker was played, sometimes for money but often for fun and beers. The men played cards but the girls were always there. The producer Sam Spiegel [*Lawrence of Arabia*, 1962, *The African Queen*, 1951] was a gambling fanatic and a regular at illegal 'chemmy' [*chemin de fer*] games in London and at the Paris casinos. In Marilyn's early Hollywood days, he held weekly games at his home in Beverly Hills. Spiegel, known as 'the velvet octopus' for having his hands all over young girls, always had plenty of his favourites around. Marilyn was sometimes one of them. The omniscient writer and card player Budd Schulberg, scion of the studio system, offered acute testimony:

'[Spiegel] was an inspired pimp. Women were looking for acting jobs, and it was a knee up the ladder.'

Indeed, Marilyn became proficient at oral sex, so much so that the stories of her abilities became somewhat legendary. Of course, fellatio was practical in that it avoided pregnancy, but also it was intimacy without *intimacy*. As she became successful, Marilyn was asked about the best thing fame had brought her and she replied, 'I'll never *have to* suck another cock again.' In her diary, read by Mike Rothmiller, Marilyn complained it was the one act JFK demanded most from her: 'He always wants me to blow him.'

That was later. Now, it was a man called 'Pat' DiCicco who, in the curious carousel of Hollywood, became important in her life. She didn't know then, and nor could anyone, how prescient of her future life and death, this handsome man was. Pasquale 'Pat' DiCicco was a former bootlegger, a former pimp, friend of 'Lucky' Luciano (the co-creator of the modern American Mafia) and cousin of James Bond film producer Albert 'Cubby' Broccoli. When Marilyn met him, his current incarnation was as a film agent. He was also leader of the Hollywood 'wolf pack' which had no links with and, most certainly, none of the rules, of the Boy Scout movement. DiCicco had the advantages of charm and money. The personality was apparently from his mother. The source of the cash was less obvious but presumedly from his mobster connections or his work tempting starlets into the arena of billionaire Howard Hughes.

DiCicco's legend was irrevocably linked to the tragedy of Thelma Todd, his first wife. Marilyn had heard the story several times for it was part of Hollywood history. Yet never did she associate it with herself. Like Marilyn, Thelma Todd, from Lowell, Massachusetts, wanted to be a movie star. She made it, aged 21, from small-town beauty queen and pin-up into Paramount Studio's Stars of Tomorrow Acting School. There was one snag. Thelma – blonde, bountiful, funny and certainly having that special star quality – liked to eat. At first, diet pills helped, then amphetamines washed down by good Prohibition-era booze. She looked the part – and got plenty of them, working with Laurel and Hardy, Buster Keaton, and appearing in *Monkey Business* and *Horse Feathers* opposite the Marx Brothers. She was an instant star and gained a reputation as a wisecracking comedian – the 'Ice Cream Blonde' – but she could do drama, too. She showed that in the 1931 original screen version of Dashiell Hammett's *The Maltese Falcon*, playing Iva Archer, the discontented wife of Sam Spade's murdered partner. [Bebe Daniels, wife of Ben Lyon, co-starred as Miss Wonderly.]

In the vivacious Thelma, Pat DiCicco saw a stunning, very funny and needy woman. She saw her fantasy man. They eloped to Prescott, Arizona, on July 18, 1932, but as husband and wife were a disaster. DiCicco enjoyed other women and kept his business affairs quiet, while she mixed her tranquillisers – jumping into boxes of pills and bottles of booze and pulling the stoppers after her. She had so many car smashes Paramount Studios ordered her to have a full-time driver.

Officially, her marriage ended on March 3, 1934 – by then she'd made 70 movies – with Thelma citing cruelty and incompatibility, which DiCicco did not object to within court proceedings. She became friends with the director Roland West and involved with Lucky Luciano. She enjoyed the Mafia man and the endless supply of drugs he provided. Luciano catered for an all-around need.

Roland West offered Thelma a business deal, as well as care and attention. He opened a seafood restaurant in a three-storey building only a pedestrian bridge away from the beach at 17575 Pacific Coast Highway, Castellammare, between Santa Monica and Malibu, which became Thelma Todd's Sidewalk Café. One floor up was their private nightclub, named Joya's, where a select group of the Hollywood crowd could gamble privately. There was a bandstand and a dance floor. Thelma was the attraction, even on the drinks menu: Thelma Todd Knockout – $1; Thelma Todd Milk Punch (gin base) – 45 cents; Thelma Todd Rickey – 45 cents. Minus the Thelma glamour, it was: Gin Fizz – 35 cents.

The actress had an apartment at the top of the building, but she had nothing to do with running what was quickly a popular hot spot at the beach. She was the show. And the Mob wanted part of it. There was pressure on Roland West regarding the restaurant business – who would supply napkins, food, drink, laundry services – and also directly from Luciano, who wanted to open a proper gaming room in the upstairs club. Thelma Todd rebelled. She put the picture of Mob extortion together and told them that if they didn't leave her alone, she'd take her complaints to the district attorney. Oh, but this was 1930s Hollywood, a mirror of the one Marilyn joined, and District Attorney Buron Fitts was connected. Two of Luciano's men worked in his office. So when Thelma Todd made an appointment for a meeting with him on Tuesday, December 17, 1935, simply dismissing her didn't seem like it would be a problem.

But it was. Thelma knew a lot just from being around DiCicco and Luciano, and the district attorney couldn't just ignore her: she was too high profile and would make a lot of noise. He couldn't prosecute the Mob, as that would be prosecuting himself. And he'd be dead before he got started. It would be much simpler for all concerned if Thelma Todd was the one who disappeared.

The evening before that conclusion was reached, Thelma, in a mauve and silver gown, a mink and a Crown Jewels starter kit, was driven by chauffeur Ernie Peters to a party at a former speakeasy, the Café Trocadero on Sunset Strip, given by British actor Stanley Lupino and his talented daughter Ida. Pat DiCicco had asked actress-director Ida Lupino if he could be seated next to his former wife but turned up late with actress Margaret Lindsay and all but ignored Thelma, who proceeded to get drunk and argue with him. They were in a cordoned-off VIP area – the Café Trocadero embraced the attractive concept of the 'velvet rope' behind which only beautiful people could party – but guests at the club had a good view of Thelma as she drank and laughed. She certainly wasn't acting suicidal.

Still, that was how it looked on Monday morning at 10.30 a.m., December 16, 1935, when her maid Mae Whitehead found her lifeless body slumped in the front passenger seat of her chocolate-coloured 1934 Lincoln Phaeton convertible in the two-car garage of the cliff-side mansion. The car's engine had been running. Thelma was in her evening gown.

Roland West had locked the restaurant at 2 a.m. Thelma had left the Café Trocadero just before 3 a.m. Limo driver Ernie Peters had dropped her at the Sidewalk Café at around 4 a.m.

The drink had put her choreography a little askew, but he said she had made it up the staircase to her apartment. The *Los Angeles Times* front page headline read: 'Body of Thelma Todd Found in Death Riddle.' If it sounds like a Raymond Chandler thriller, it certainly became part of one. Chandler was a neighbour, living in Pacific Palisades – his view over the ocean was one of the most spectacular in the world – and *Farewell, My Lovely* (published in 1940) contains many elements of the demise of 'Hot Toddy' as she was fondly known. The 'death riddle' proclaimed by the headlines became an ongoing debate. There was a simple explanation: given the time, the place and the ambitions of those with whom Thelma Todd was involved. She was in the way, and she was about to make trouble. And she was dead on deadline, exactly 24 hours before her appointment with District Attorney Buron Fitts. There were many theories. Her death certificate said she died from accidental carbon monoxide poisoning and the LAPD asserted that she had been running the engine to warm up the car or herself. There was an autopsy but, after the funeral, her body was quickly cremated, with the paperwork signed off by the District Attorney's office. And why not? Thelma had died accidentally. This left no opportunity to examine the body medically and give reasons for her broken nose, the blood coagulated on her face and splattered across her dress and body, or her missing teeth and two fractured ribs.

Many stories circulated implicating Pat DiCicco and Roland West in her death. There was a rumour about another lover and an intruder. But it came around to suicide again. Some who had primary information on the case maintain she was knocked out with a blow to the face, beaten and placed in the front seat of the car, where she was killed by the carbon monoxide, which turned her face crimson. That could have been done by any of the three men who had been present at a corner table at the Trocadero at the Saturday night party. The men were all known associates of Thelma's lover Lucky

Luciano. No one was ever arrested in connection with the death of the 29-year-old film star who never did get to testify about the Mob in Hollywood because no one required that either.

And as Pat DiCicco sat at the central card table at Sam Spiegel's only a few years later, he looked up and grinned over his gin rummy hand at yet another Hollywood hopeful, the blossoming Marilyn Monroe. DiCicco was impressed and, of course, could impress himself. He was tempted, explained somewhat by Groucho Marx, who against perceptions, knew much about such matters and said of Marilyn: 'She is Mae West, Thelma Todd, Theda Bara and Bo Peep all rolled into one.'

By then DiCicco had remarried and then divorced heiress Gloria Vanderbilt, who said he physically abused her. His connections were an advantage to Marilyn: he knew the men that mattered and linked Marilyn to senior executive at the William Morris Agency, Johnny Hyde. While she was making these Hollywood connections, LAPD's intelligence division were monitoring her and the friendships she was establishing.

Marilyn left 20th Century Fox in 1947 when her contract was not renewed, but through various 'friendships' she signed on a year later with Columbia Studios run by the monstrous Harry Cohn.

Johnny Hyde, aged 52, fell obsessively in love with 22-year-old Marilyn. Hyde, a regular at Sam Spiegel's 'boys nights out,' left his wife and proposed marriage to the girl with the, now, platinum hair courtesy of Columbia Pictures. Hyde sought perfection and supplied the cash for cosmetic, reconstructive work on her nose and jawline which were all on display with the rest of her when she posed naked for a set of nude photographs. Like cherry-red lipstick, it got attention. Which she wanted more than Johnny Hyde, whom she was fond of but did not want to marry.

Hyde negotiated a small role in a Marx Brothers movie [*Love Happy*, 1950] for her and his influence stretched to more work and more influential roles which ignited her stardom. Not too long after *The Asphalt Jungle* was released on New Year's Day, 1950, word about the shapely blonde who played a small but plot-important role in the ground-breaking heist movie [directed and co-written by John Huston who remained a forever fan of Marilyn's] was going around Hollywood. In the film, nominated for four Oscars, she wiggled briefly past the lustful gaze of the villain [Louis Calhern] and his appraising squeal of delight enhanced Marilyn's currency. She went on to cash that on October 13 that year when *All About Eve* opened and created even more of a fanfare. The Bette Davis led movie became as famous for its barbed one-liners as for its grand acting and directing achievements, and Marilyn benefited from that in her cameo as 'Miss Casswell' whom George Sanders' theatrical agent Addison DeWitt describes as 'a graduate of the Copacabana School of Dramatic Art.'

She was as glamorous as that Rio beach. This blonde 'bombshell' was what the 1950s wanted from Hollywood and, in return, what Hollywood wanted for their audiences, the servicemen returning from the Korean War and those who craved the undulating Marilyn Monroe but not to take home to mother. Female filmgoers wanted glamour and she provided that too, but she was by then absolutely defined by the way men looked at her and reacted to her. Zsa Zsa Gabor accompanied her husband [the third of nine] George Sanders to San Francisco to film *All About Eve* and booked on the flight with them was Marilyn. Zsa Zsa reported:

'I met Marilyn the first time in the commissary at Fox and noted she was extremely adept at wiggling her ass and batting her eyelashes. On the 'plane to San Francisco, I had the window seat, Marilyn the aisle – with George, appropriately, sandwiched in the middle. Marilyn spent most of the trip batting her eyelashes at George, who turned to me when we were alone and said, with a mixture of sympathy and pride, "Poor girl, she has it bad." I said in a fury, "George, don't flatter yourself, she's having sex with everybody."'

Well, *almost* everybody, it seemed from her many romances. The film's director, Joe Mankiewicz, although charmed by Marilyn's 'sort of glued-on innocence that I found appealing,' nevertheless regarded her as one of the loneliest people he had met. 'She remained alone. She was not a loner. She was just plain *alone.*' Bette Davis was quoted – in *All About Eve* Margo Channing mode – in reference to Marilyn: 'She's the original good time that was had by all.'

What mattered most from the two films for Marilyn and the eager Johnny Hyde was that *she* got attention. That it came from as many chancers as cheerleaders was, for the moment, irrelevant. She'd seen off considerable competition to play 'Miss Casswell' including from another young actress, Angela Lansbury, and she'd got to work opposite Bette Davis [it took eleven takes for one scene between them]. What was noted as an extremely dry martini of a movie was an astounding success, and so was she. Marilyn was gathering a formidable following. She was one to watch.

The Mocambo nightclub was hesitant to hire singer Ella Fitzgerald because she was black. Monroe telephoned the owner and said she would take a front table every night if they hired Fitzgerald. The deal went through. The jazz genius said she found Monroe to be 'an unusual woman – a little ahead of her times.' What was most unusual was that no strings were attached. It was a purely benevolent gesture. There were few of them in Hollywood. For many stars, actors, directors and stage performers, the incredible money they could and would command often had to be shared with the silent guys like Marilyn's friend Pat DiCicco and mobster Johnny Rosselli. Many of Hollywood's agencies, like the unions, had Mob interest if not control.

In December 1950, Johnny Hyde negotiated another renewable seven-year contract for Marilyn with 20th Century Fox but died, his weak heart giving out, a week before Christmas that year. Although devastated, Marilyn had other connections as Peter Lawford discovered after they met at his agent's office the next year.

They became friends and dated as a couple and in foursomes, but nothing developed sexually in their relationship. She couldn't understand that almost everyone with a heartbeat, male and female, hit on her in that way. Including Howard Hughes whom she'd been introduced to by Pat DiCicco. Hughes, then only borderline unusual and paranoid, was a man fixated by women's breasts and making money [he'd bought RKO Studios in 1948]. He became an instant fan of Marilyn. Young Lawford discovered this when he turned up to take Marilyn to the movies but was confronted by two refrigerator-large men, one of whom asked him what he wanted.

'I have a date with Miss Monroe.'

'She's not going out,' he was told.

'But I have a date—'

'Forget it. She's staying here tonight.'

Lawford deployed discretion. When he returned home, he telephoned Marilyn. 'What's going on?'

'It's Howard Hughes. He's jealous and won't let me out of the house at night… I'm his prisoner…'

Hughes was more controlling than the jealous type but, with his short attention span, the interest didn't last. He had girls scattered all over, in apartments and beach bungalows, all under the watch of his beyond-temptation troops, the Mormon Mafia.

Marilyn was 25 years old when she met Peter Lawford, who was 28. She was a rising star on contract to 20th Century Fox. Despite Darryl Zanuck's initial reservations, her future appeared limitless. In contrast, Lawford's prospects at MGM were as dismal as those of other contract players [he lost $2,000 a week that year when his deal was not renewed] as the studio's profits shrank with the popularity of television.

Three years later, Lawford's financial concerns ended when he married, on April 24, 1954, Pat Kennedy, daughter of the hugely ambitious and powerful Joe Kennedy, former bootlegger and the longtime lover of Hollywood legend Gloria Swanson. He befriended her brothers, John and Robert who, in time, would meet and enjoy Marilyn Monroe, drawing even more attention from LAPD Chief William Parker.

# V: The Gangster Squad

*'See, that's Federal property. This isn't. This is LA. This is my town. Out here you're a trespasser. Out here I can pick you up, burn your house, fuck your wife and kill your dog. And the only thing that'll protect you is if I can't find you. And I already found you…'*
— LAPD Lieutenant Max Hoover [Nick Nolte],
*Mulholland Falls*, 1996.

By the time William Parker took control of the LAPD, the force had become a praetorian guard, a self-policing organisation whose rules and pliable parameters had been established by Chief James Edgar Davis [1933–1938] for whom the then Lieutenant Parker had been a loyal supporter. As chief, Parker enforced the LAPD's paramilitary mindset which Davis had enforced up to World War Two. By then his protégé had become Captain Parker. He should have been a commander but had stumbled against the corruption allowed by the nepotistic make-up of the department. LAPD examinations and promotions were being bought and sold, but Parker didn't pay off so, although he ranked first on the lieutenant exams, he was placed at number ten for promotion. When he took the inspector-commander exams, the same thing happened.

But, being Bill Parker, he persevered and became Captain Parker when he put on another uniform as a military police major under General Eisenhower in command of all police and prisoner manoeuvres for the 1944 Normandy invasion. He had an exemplary war record and showed bravery beyond duty, especially under fire from a German Stuka dive bomber [a Junkers Ju 87]. For this he was awarded the Purple Heart and the *Croix de Guerre* by France and a Silver Star of Solidarity from Italy. Before returning to Los Angeles in November 1945, he reorganised [a euphemism for de-Nazifying] the police forces of Frankfurt and Munich.

Back home, it wasn't clear to him who the enemy was. He was a decorated war hero, but his position in the LAPD was obstructed by politics, red tape, and his superiors' fears and suspicions about themselves as much as the growing gangland and social problems of their rapidly expanding city. The orange groves, the wineries of Los Angeles County and vast acres of agricultural land now had houses, shops, and factories on them. The population had changed too. Ethnic groups had grown, but there were legal restrictions, covenants, and prohibitions on property ownership. Just as the Mocambo nightclub had been cautious about hiring Ella Fitzgerald, the singer Nat King Cole was forced to use a side or back entrance to night clubs he performed in. When he bought a home in Hancock Park, Los Angeles, his family were subjected to racial slurs, and a Ku Klux Klan-style cross was burned on their property. Marilyn's friend, Sammy Davis Jr., said that his talent allowed him to 'be insulted in places most Negroes can't get insulted.'

There was tension within and without the LAPD. There was corruption too, as much in City Hall as in LAPD which shared [until 1955] the same building at the corner of Spring and Temple [the mayor entered his office from Spring Street, the chief of police from Temple]. There was Hollywood and the power of that money and the brutal power of mobster Mickey Cohen who had taken over from Benjamin 'Bugsy' Siegel who had been assassinated in 1947. There were huge differences in the way people and communities were viewed and treated. It was delicate. The initial policing was not.

The LAPD had more scandals than bravery medals. When a civic-minded politician attempted a clean-up campaign, he was dynamited in his car and left the city minus his left arm. The rogue gene was present throughout the LAPD, which was why Sergeant Willie Burns, a former US Marine gunnery officer became the leader of the 'Gangster Squad' in 1946. This bunch of cops used a lot of fists and Tommy guns. As the 1940s became the 1950s, they could have stepped out of one of Howard Hughes' *film noirs* from RKO – with Robert Mitchum chasing William Bendix in a white suit and Jane Russell in a ripped blouse. The cops dressed like they were in the movies – or maybe it was vice versa – with fedoras, big, snappy ties and coats, cigars, guns and they had a certain swagger. Shortly after World War Two and the formation of the 'Squad', a mobster threatened Willie Burns' family. In retaliation, he and four of his men carried out a drive-by shooting on the mobster as he sat in his new Cadillac. Each of them emptied 50-round cartridge drums from their Tommy guns into the car. The mobster survived and came around the next day. There had been a 'misunderstanding.' Which was what Burns did not want with his new team. He wanted them crystal clear on their mission. When he got his first recruits together, he pointed to the Thompson gun on his desk and explained that was to be the weapon of choice 'to keep down these gangster killings and try to keep some of these rough guys under control.' With their machine guns, they'd get a carrying case – it was the double of a violin case, so they were cumbersome. They also couldn't be left in a car – the 'Squad' had to keep them secure. Officers slept with them under their beds. The 'Squad' didn't so much have an office as a series of parking lot meeting points. They'd ride four or five to a car in their broken-down Fords. They would still appear on the duty rosters of their divisions because the 'Squad' didn't officially exist. They were *intelligent* intelligence officers. The goal was to get the hoods out of the shadows and into the sunshine and out of southern California – and to specifically stop the infiltration of LA by the East Coast Mafia. The officers came extra-large, tall and muscled. They were former jocks and war veterans, and the image of dumb cops for hire was theirs to dispel. They all had to know what they were in for.

It was sometime later, through Grand Jury testimony and affidavits given in court cases, that the full throttle of the pandemonium the 'Gangster Squad' caused among the Hollywood Mob *and* the LAPD, became known. The East Coast Mafia were no nickel and dime agents. They wanted at least 30 per cent of the show – any show. The movies, the gambling, the sex, drugs and other vices, interests or perversions – they could all turn a profit. As always, it was about money. When the mobsters extorted landmarks like the Mocambo and the Brown Derby at Hollywood and Vine, the owners, worried about what might happen to their business and their families, could not refuse. A handful of the most hardened cops, mainly former Marines, were instructed to 'beat the shit' out of any uninvited East Coast mobster coming to Los Angeles. They would wait at the downtown train station, greet the mobster as he stepped off the train and promptly escort him to an isolated warehouse or suitable motel room where a significant beating would be administered. Once the chief's message had been adequately delivered, they'd drive the mobster back to the train station and toss him on the next train headed East.

Jack O'Mara, another member of this ghost squad of detectives would take mobsters up to Mulholland Drive which has the best views out over the Hollywood Hills and the San Fernando Valley. 'We have a little heart-to-heart talk with 'em,' he recalls, 'emphasise the fact that this wasn't New York, this wasn't Chicago, this wasn't Cleveland. And we leaned on 'em a little, you know what I mean? Up in the Hollywood Hills, off Coldwater Canyon, anywhere up there. And it's dark at night.' In that darkness, 'Mad Jack' would put a gun to their ear and say: 'You want to sneeze? Do you feel a sneeze coming on? A real loud sneeze?' O'Mara saw the squad as a detergent as much a deterrent. He called their work 'wiping off the dandruff'.

It wasn't just out-of-towners who got the treatment. Fred Otash – who was to become an informant for Mike Rothmiller and a pivotal player in the story of the death of Marilyn Monroe – handed some out to local mobsters too. As an LAPD officer, he was in a black and white when he saw Johnny Stompanato, lover of actress Lana Turner, and gangster Mickey Cohen's number one gun, driving down Sunset Strip. He told his partner to pull alongside Stompanato. He wound down his window and when they got alongside the hoodlum, pointed a shotgun at him and shouted, 'Now you've had it, you motherfucker...' Otash, the renegade, recalled later with much amusement, 'When Johnny saw the shotgun, he ducked, losing control of his new Cadillac. It went over the curb and down the hill of Sunset. He could have been killed.' Stompanato complained and Otash was mildly ticked off.

Captain James Hamilton, Bill Parker's confidant, explained why the 'Gangster Squad' was necessary: 'Our main purpose is to keep anyone from getting too big. When we get the word that someone has 'juice' and that he's trying to 'fix things', and thinks he can, then we're after him. We're selfish, damned selfish. Because we know that that's the kind of guy who's going to wreck your police department if he can. And we're going to stop him. One way or another.'

Yet, there was also a changing mood in Los Angeles. Words like 'respectable' and 'civilised' were being mentioned, and in the same sentences. Some cops were more roguish than most members of the 'Gangster Squad'. It wasn't difficult for them to be unscrupulous, to look the other way, to accept a gratuity to forget. This practice was not so much venal but traditional in certain police circles at that halfway point of the 20th century. There was something of a game at times.

Part of the 'intelligence gathering' involved planting listening devices – multiple, multiple bugs – without a fuss. Or a warrant. When they listened in on Mickey Cohen, they heard him complaining about his staff and customers being rousted at Michael's Haberdashery. Sergeant Willie Burns' wife later received a bouquet of flowers shortly after that eavesdrop. It was a funeral arrangement. Mickey Cohen – who only wore his suits twice and then sold them as new in the store – was telling the 'Squad' he knew he had been bugged. It was an upsetting gesture.

There were more parties interested in getting Mickey Cohen out of the way. Cohen married the Hollywood studios freelancer dance instructor LaVonne Weaver in 1940 – he got his pre-wedding blood test in his bookie's shop – and nine years later they were living at 513 Moreno Avenue which cuts down from Sunset Boulevard to Wilshire Boulevard in Brentwood, close to where Marilyn Monroe spent her final months. It is a smart address and was outfitted with automatic security lights. Cohen was arriving home to have dinner with his wife and the 'connected' actor George Raft. The floodlights flashed on as he came into his driveway and a gunman opened fire. Whatever they say about fish in a barrel, the shooter couldn't hit anything but the Cadillac. Cohen drove off and returned home bleeding from shattered glass – but alive. George Raft said he looked 'a little mussed up,' but the gangster insisted on supper – Raft's favourite of New York strip steak, rare, followed by LaVonne's apple pie.

Death sneaked a little closer to Cohen on July 19, 1949. He had dinner with Artie Samish [a powerful political lobbyist in Sacramento] and put on a sparkling show dripping with bodyguards, starlets and members of the press who knew he was always good for a headline. The Los Angeles County Sheriff's Department had rousted Cohen and his men on gun charges.

They were checked so often that they did not carry weapons. The California State Attorney General's Office, along with Special Agent Harry Cooper, was protecting Cohen [because of the Mob's connections] following the previous attempts on his life. After dinner, the crowd headed for Sherry's at 9039 on West Sunset Boulevard. By 3.30 a.m., Cohen felt he might go home. Sherry's owner and Cohen's friend, Barney Ruditsky checked out the parking lot. It appeared clear. Two of Cohen's crew went to get his Cadillac. A valet brought round, Cohen's lieutenant, Frankie Niccoli's Chrysler. At 3.50 a.m. the gunfire arrived in a smooth Remington crackle and blast from a .30-06 calibre rifle. The laughing partygoers fell to the ground. The evening's favourite blonde, Dee David, twisted her ankle in the melee. The indefatigable newspaper columnist Florabel Muir ran toward the source of the gunfire to find her story and got a blast of shotgun pellets in her backside as she turned away from the continuing onslaught. Hoodlum Nebbie Herbert was riddled with bullets. Agent Cooper was staggering chaotically, waving his revolver and holding his bleeding gut. Mickey Cohen, with his right arm bleeding, used his good one to get Cooper into the Chrysler. How the relatively short mobster got the broad-shouldered, six-foot Cooper into the car was, he said at the Hollywood Receiving Hospital, 'mind over matter.' Cooper survived. Cohen had a bullet-torn shoulder. Nebbie Herbert died in hospital. It was open season on who was responsible. Killers like the Los Angeles' Mafia Don, Jack Dragna and Jimmy 'The Weasel' Fratianno were mentioned as well as 'big' Frank Costello, boss of the Luciano Family from the East Coast.

A prescient Florabel Muir suggested the LAPD might have had something to do with it. Her theory was supported by forensics. Amid the detritus of the armed ambush were used shotgun shells that were regular LAPD issue. The subsequent stand-off between Mickey Cohen and the cops turned into a mess for the authorities. It was indicative of the world that incoming Chief Parker was to patrol and control.

The LAPD vice squad rousted Cohen's henchman Harold 'Happy' Meltzer for illegal possession of a weapon – a revolver they themselves had planted on him. Cohen was telephoned by Sergeant Elmer Jackson of the LAPD Administrative B Vice Squad and told that $5,000 would make the charge – and the gun – go away. Cohen retaliated by appearing at Meltzer's trial with taped evidence of the blackmail, extortion and pays-offs between the vice squad and Brenda Allen, the undisputed queen of Hollywood prostitution, who had 148 'pleasure girls' on her books at the service of the movie business elite and special cops. Madam Allen's lover was LAPD Sergeant Elmer Jackson. She soon turned on him saying he and other vice officers took pay-offs. The scandal stretched from the mayor's office to the chief of police. Finally, a Grand Jury investigation was ordered. It led to the resignation in summer 1949 of Police Chief Clemence B. 'Jack' Horral and a group of other officers were indicted for perjury. Sergeant Willie Burns took early retirement from the 'Gangster Squad'. In a panic, the civic leaders appointed William Worton, a World War Two Marine Corps major general, to replace Horral. General Worton went full on – he wanted active intelligence, information, and analysis of it to offer predictions of impending criminality within the LAPD. It was a modern approach, modelled on the army's intelligence service, and used wiretaps and surveillance. Worton [he was limited by City Charter to a one-year tenure as an outsider and not a sworn policeman] appointed Bill Parker as deputy chief and head of the Bureau of Internal Affairs, aka the 'corrupt cop hunting department'.

Parker saw the need for tactics and intelligence, and understood that information could be as valuable as any other weapon. The intelligence division already had massive files on politicians, on the activities of almost all serving police officers and other 'parties of interest'. It was, he decided, part of his and the LAPD's future. Detective Con Keeler, one of the original 'Gangster Squad' who had worked with Parker before the war, warned that Parker was not someone to take any nonsense. He'd police the police much more than the mobsters. When Parker became chief in the summer of 1950, Keeler's fears that the 'Squad' might be closed down were proved wrong. Chief Parker told them to put their 'toys', the Thompson sub-machine guns, away and start thinking because the tactics were changing. He wanted the 'Squad' to be a better version of Hoover's FBI. He enlarged the unit to nearly 40 officers and placed his most trusted ally, Captain James Hamilton, in charge. It was renamed the Organized Crime Intelligence Division [OCID] and the files they had begun compiling two decades earlier were to expand and become more than information – maybe not water into wine, but potent material. The power of the chief of the LAPD was underestimated. On the East Coast they say, with amusement, that when they made America, they tipped it on its side and all the nuts rolled into California. Still, it has to be said that the ambitious – from the gifted to the grifters – have always landed in the state and most often in Hollywood where dreams are mass manufactured. If you have the ability to watch and listen to all these people, an awesome power base of information can be created. And with this, events, like a sensational death, can be kept under control – and the narrative can be yours to manipulate.

Parker had learned about the power of information from his early mentor, Chief James Davis, who had established an intelligence detail in the 1930s supervised by Acting Captain R.A. Sears. Back then it was rough and tumble stuff with more bruises than brains deployed. It all changed when Bill Parker, a man appropriately born in Lead City, South Dakota, and raised in Deadwood City, took over. Upon accepting his position, he made some remarks that rather shook up his officers:

'There are wicked men with evil hearts who sustain themselves by preying upon society. These are men who lack control over their strong passions and, to control and repress these, evil forces have been established. Sometimes wicked men elude the detection devices of the selection process and find their way into the police service. Their evil acts, when discovered, cast disrepute upon the entire force. I will strive to make this department the most respected police force in the United States.'

Not many officers liked Bill Parker, but all were aware of his determination and skills. Aged 47, his brown hair receding, his Spanish eyes always questioning – he was a chilling presence. He had a disarming intelligence, and had seen the worth of having friends in high places and the right connections during the war and in his climb to the top LAPD job. He was convinced that knowing more than the other guy was the way to get, and stay, ahead. There were few he trusted. One of the first was the 24-year-old Daryl Gates who became his driver, bodyguard and a lifelong admirer. Parker didn't have many allies in law enforcement. His many speeches on law and order had attracted the jealous interest of the FBI's J. Edgar Hoover who wanted just one top cop in America – himself. Other national figures were slightly more benevolent toward him and of this new age LAPD.

America was changing and so were its politicians and, as always, its organised crime networks. As gangland became corporate, the authorities had to combat it in kind. The changes to both sides were evident in downtown Los Angeles in November 1950, when the Senator from Tennessee, Estes Kefauver, came to Hollywood. He was the head of a cumbersomely titled operation, the Special Senate Committee on the Investigation of Syndicated Crime in Interstate Commerce. It was no surprise it came to be known popularly as the Kefauver Committee. The committee held hearings in fourteen cities, including LA, with witnesses that included major crime bosses. The hearings were televised and became more popular on American television than *The Red Skelton Show*, and madcap Lucille Ball's *I Love Lucy*. It was a lesson in the power of television to create political stars. And, as Richard Nixon would discover, blunt judgments.

The ever polite, slow-spoken Kefauver was an ambitious Senator from Davy Crockett's state and had an Abe Lincoln look and a folksy, frontiersman way about him. He would peer through his big, horn-rimmed spectacles at the strange bunch of characters who appeared before him as he and his committee crisscrossed the country. Americans had never seen anything like it. The Cold War and Communists seemed so far away. They could be chased away. Now here on their doorstep was organised crime, something called 'The Mafia' – a parade of gamblers, thugs, hoodlums, crooked cops and caricature criminals, sweating and tapping their fingers nervously, under the bright lights. Every word was recorded, and every movement seized by the television cameras. These were guys talking in broken, Runyonesque English, and guys who couldn't count to five but were taking the Fifth Amendment, like the Mob's important pay-out man Jake 'Greasy Thumb' Guzik who didn't want to 'criminate' himself. Viewers were mesmerised day after day. In bars and cafés with televisions, workers gathered voyeuristically. Shops and offices nationwide piped in all-day radio broadcasts covering the hearings. The American public were finding places to get this insight into crime, and the other booming post-war economy in America, illegal gambling. The hearings were an exciting eye-opener into the dark secrets of a criminal organisation, a deadly group with Sicilian antecedents, that FBI director J. Edgar Hoover had told them didn't exist. It existed now in the public consciousness, as it always had in reality. Chief Parker was much keener to talk about it than J. Edgar Hoover. And his enemies were very aware of it. The evening before Parker was due to testify before the Kefauver Committee, his intelligence chief, Captain Hamilton received an alert that gangland operators were going to attempt to assassinate the chief that night. Parker told Daryl Gates to take a different route to the evening meeting he was speaking at. He also allowed his wife Helen to travel with him: she sat in the back seat with a loaded shotgun on her lap. Extra security was provided, and the evening and the following day's testimony went without trouble.

There was a chill, something of the night about William Parker. Before he went into television and established himself by creating *Star Trek,* LAPD Sergeant Gene Roddenberry had worked with Parker and said he modelled Mr. Spock on him. That Parker would not be intimidated was a serious positive for an up-and-coming politician and crime-fighter, Robert Kennedy, the brother of Washington star on the horizon, Jack Kennedy. Bobby Kennedy was following the Kefauver Committee hearings with expectancy. He sensed that Parker peed ice-water and he liked that. Parker was in the business of being proactive, stopping trouble before it occurred.

Kefauver had dished out subpoenas from New York to New Orleans and from Detroit to Los Angeles, and his lawyers always arrived ahead of the committee. They were often met with disdain in places, but they just did things their way. In New Orleans, the sheriffs said they did not exactly enforce the law when it came to gambling and prostitution in the parishes of Louisiana. 'Diamond' Jim Moran, the owner of La Louisiane Restaurant in New Orleans, saw the television coverage as a marketing opportunity and testified at the hearing that his establishment, which had rows and rows of illegal slot machines, served 'food for kings'. In St. Louis, the city's unsettled police commissioner said he couldn't recall any details of his financial status before becoming a public official. The city's betting commissioner James J. Carroll refused to testify on television, stating that it was an invasion of privacy. Kefauver warned Carroll that he'd be cited for contempt by the Senate, but Carroll refused to answer any questions, walking jerkily around the courtroom. Finally, he sat down. Did he know [Luciano Family boss] Frank Costello? Never met the man. Mickey Cohen? 'I have no recollection.'

The hearings on the West Coast drew the largest audiences recorded in daytime television. It wouldn't be long before Chief Parker's nemesis, and Hollywood's most notorious hoodlum, Mickey Cohen was called to speak. But first, in the downtown courtroom of the federal building, the senator listened to other mobsters insolently respond to his questioning with 'I don't remember'. Al Smiley, an associate of Bugsy Siegel who was there the night he got shot, refused to explain why, after Siegel's untimely death, he had routinely shuttled back and forth between Houston and the Beverly Club, the casino near New Orleans controlled by New York's Frank Costello. Smiley's reward for these mysterious services was 'a small piece of property.' What kind of property? 'Well, it may have had a few oil wells on it.'

Mickey Cohen turned up late for his showtime. At 9 a.m. on a January morning in 1950 when he was due at the federal building, he was still in bed. When he was alerted by committee investigators, he said he had to take his time dressing as it was 'like going to a Hollywood premiere'. As a witness, he was a star. He wore a brown suit, a cream shirt and brown tie. As he wasn't bothered about his timekeeping he wasn't bothered about the truth and he lied. Disassembling was the duty of the day. He had *never* muscled, bribed, pistol-whipped or strong-armed anyone. Prostitutes? Perish the thought. Corruption and bribes? What a dreadful suggestion. Where Cohen came unstuck was over questions about his income. His lifestyle didn't match it. He'd borrowed the money, he claimed. It wasn't a convincing answer. The paradox was that there was a certain honesty about him – who expected the truth from a man who, even in his Sunday best, looked like a rolled-up carpet?

When the Kefauver Committee reached New York in March, the proceedings were broadcast to dozens of stations across the country. The city was obsessed: Broadway theatre and cinema audiences dwindled for eight days as the Mob put on their show – a carnival of criminality, scandalous and wonderful all at the same time. It was theatre, tragedy and comedy, dark Jacobean and Shakespearean slapstick, the *Lemon Drop Kid* and gunsels like Sam 'Golf Bag' Hunt who were more sinister than the comedy of their names.

The engaging Longy Zwillman had helped one Governor of New Jersey get elected and offered $300,000 to aid another; all he wanted in return was to choose the Attorney General, the state's lawmaker. Zwillman, the founder of Murder, Inc., was one of the first major underworld figures to launder his profits from gambling and prostitution in Hollywood studios. The Mob wise man, who'd compromised Hilton dynasty patriarch Conrad Hilton by linking him with mobster Arnold Kirkeby and washing cash through the Kirkeby-Hilton Hotel chain, felt he was being generous. He could have asked to choose all the legislature.

Chief Parker and the Kennedys followed every moment of the New York hearings. The *Los Angeles Times* called the testimony 'the greatest show television has ever aired'. *Life* magazine reported that: 'The week of March 12, 1951, will occupy a special place in history. People had suddenly gone indoors into living rooms, taverns, and clubrooms, auditoriums and back-offices. There, in eerie half-light, looking at millions of small frosty screens, people sat as if charmed. Never before had the attention of the nation been riveted so completely on a single matter.'

Post-war foreign policy was cumbersome, the potential Communist takeover of China was a worrying threat and the readjustments in Europe as it recovered from war were viewed through a myopic lens. So law and order was a helpful domestic issue to focus on. And people were watching. The ratings were a historic high for this new medium of communication and television had arrived as a political force. Could it get any better? Oh, yes it could. When the pantomime opened in Washington D.C. onstage came Virginia Hill one-time paramour of Bugsy Siegel and gangster aristocracy, wearing a mink cape, silk gloves, a large hat and oozing Hollywood presence. She sashayed into the US Courthouse in Foley Square and told the guys in suits about other guys in suits, 'the fellas', who gave her gifts and money. But as to how those men came into their money, she didn't know 'anything about anybody'. She admitted she and Siegel fought after she punched out actress Wendy Barrie in the lobby of the Flamingo Hotel: 'He told me I wasn't a lady,' she said, in a way that questioned why anyone would think that about her. Like all her evidence it was combative. There was never a doubt that the leading lady of the Kefauver Follies was Virginia Hill. Committee member, Senator Charley Tobey from New Hampshire was mightily challenged as to how Miss Hill 'made ends meet'. Senator Tobey asked why so many men gave her money and presents: 'Why would they do it?' Virginia Hill evaded the question. The Senator kept repeating it. He was especially intrigued as to why Joe Epstein, an ageing bookmaker in Chicago and a man old enough to be her father, provided her with regular payments. Tobey persisted.

'Why? Young lady, why?'

'You really want to know why?'

'I really want to know why.'

'Senator, I'm the best goddamned cocksucker in America.'

In addition to this talent, Hill's most gratifying skill was moving money around the world without detection for the executive mobsters. Outside the hearing she was confronted by Miss Marjorie Farnsworth of the *New York Journal American*. Miss Farnsworth got thumped in the face with a vicious right hook. An intrepid man from the *New York Times* tried to intervene and was kicked in the shins. Virginia Hill marched out onto Foley Square, chucking a comment over her shoulder and back at the aghast Press corps: 'I hope a fucking atom bomb falls on y'all.'

Watching the proceedings on television, the young Bobby Kennedy was appalled. Yet, Hill had a strange effect on Walter

Winchell, newspaper columnist, staccato broadcaster and friend of and tipster for J. Edgar Hoover. He pondered on the effect of reality television: 'When the chic Virginia Hill unfolded her amazing life story, many a young girl must have wondered: who really knows best? Mother or Virginia Hill? After doing all the things called wrong, there she was on top of the world, with a beautiful home in Miami Beach and a handsome husband and baby!' Bobby Kennedy wasn't having any of that. Crime would *not* pay. He began establishing his credentials as a campaigner against crime, and municipal and national government corruption. It was a dangerous area.

The Kennedys also learned a political lesson about the power of national visibility from the Kefauver Committee proceedings. The hearings made Estes Kefauver so popular he sought the Democratic Party's Presidential nomination in 1952 defeating the incumbent, Harry S. Truman, in the New Hampshire primary following which the sitting President abandoned his campaign for renomination. Kefauver lost out to Adlai Stevenson who went on to lose the election to Eisenhower and his Vice President Richard Nixon. Yet, four years later, Kefauver was still a major player and enough of one to concern John F. Kennedy who was campaigning to be Democratic Presidential nominee Adlai Stevenson's running mate in the 1956 race. That August, as JFK campaigned, Bobby Kennedy announced his government committee was investigating America's biggest, most influential and powerful trade union, the Teamsters Union. The questions were all about the Mob and the Teamsters' quarter of a billion dollars pension fund. It was helpful publicity. Although Adlai Stevenson's favoured choice for Vice President was Senator John F. Kennedy of Massachusetts, he decided to let the delegates themselves choose and Kefauver was nominated for Vice President. That ticket was wiped out in an Eisenhower-Nixon landslide and the Kennedy Brothers said they'd know better next time.

By November 1956, Bobby Kennedy, chief counsel of the Senate Permanent Subcommittee on Investigations, frustrated in his fight against organised crime, looked to the one police department who had cleaned up their city – the LAPD. He arranged private talks with Chief Parker and Captain James Hamilton. He flew to Los Angeles with a former FBI agent and lawyer, Carmine Bellino, who he recruited a year earlier as his most trusted staff member. According to Howard Hughes' right hand man, Robert Maheu, Bellino also worked for Joe Kennedy Senior as a 'personal secretary'. Bellino specialised in dealing with organised crime and corrupt trade union officials, knowing everything that was going on but closeting information and actions. It was a style he recommended to the Kennedy brothers. On this trip to Los Angeles, to keep things secret, Bobby adopted an alias, Mr. Rodgers. It was not the only time he would use it.

# VI: American Dreams

*'Just the facts, ma'am, just the facts.'*
— Jack Webb as Sergeant Joe Friday, *Dragnet*,
December 16, 1951.

It was on that American election year visit in 1956 to California that the Los Angeles Police Department, or more specifically the Organized Crime Intelligence Division of the LAPD, became part of the Kennedy machine. It would become a powerful source of information for Bobby Kennedy, through wiretaps, bugging, surveillance and bedroom and boardroom gossip. He and Captain James Hamilton were ideological twins. Chief Parker was rather proud and protective of them. For the Kennedys, there was also the blowback from the fame of the LAPD which had become the best-known police department not just in America but, increasingly, thanks to *Dragnet* on television, around the world. The department was very much in partnership with the producer-star Jack Webb who called on their expertise, especially that of the intelligence division. Captain Hamilton was a regular consultant and Chief Parker was thanked by name at the end of each episode when Webb's Sergeant Joe Friday had cracked the case. J. Edgar Hoover [who got his own show, *The FBI*, in 1965] hated it. Almost as much as he hated Parker and feared he was after his job. Until then, Hoover and his companion Clyde Tolson were often seen in southern California, in the sun in Palm Springs, at the Del Mar horse racing track and with the stars in Hollywood. That stopped when Hoover thought it more politic to lower his profile. Chief Parker, relishing the power a more celebrity status offered, stepped into the vacuum. Profile *was* important. But so was keeping secrets. And helping friends.

The LAPD moved their headquarters to what became Parker Center, an eight-storey glass and steel building known as the 'The Glass House', at 150 N. Los Angeles Street. Chief Parker and Captain Hamilton did have sensitive information stored there but the important material was kept in secret off-site locations. Off-the-record operations were also discussed and sanctioned off-site.

Captain Hamilton had pointed Bobby Kennedy toward the corruption in the Teamsters Union in Portland, Oregon, and opened their files on organised crime. One memo recorded the bugging of a suite at the Conrad Hilton Town House Hotel in Los Angeles. Three members of the Chicago 'Outfit' were heard telling Jimmy Hoffa that he was going to be the next president of the Teamsters Union. There was an ongoing partnership between Captain Hamilton and Bobby Kennedy in his role as counsel to the McClellan Senate Committee investigations into organised crime in the American labour market. Bobby Kennedy became a lifelong supporter of the

LAPD. Following the Kefauver Committee hearings, he had confronted J. Edgar Hoover and asked him to produce dossiers on the hoodlums named. None were forthcoming. Bobby Kennedy reacted: 'The Bureau didn't know anything really about these people who were the major gangsters of the United States.' He and his investigating team turned to the Narcotics Bureau but got even less help. So, he called on his friends in Los Angeles. The bond between Captain Hamilton and Bobby Kennedy became stronger and Chief Parker became their regular sounding board. Bobby Kennedy began to consider creating a national intelligence information HQ – based on the OCID – to help the good fight against crime and corruption.

Yet, when do you cross the line? How far do you go to help friends? Captain James Hamilton didn't hesitate when he got a call from Jack Webb. Webb had established himself on radio, where he introduced the *Dragnet* concept, and in 1947 married the then showgirl and about to be singing star [*Cry Me a River*] Julie London. Some years later they had two children and a rambling suburban home in the San Fernando Valley over the hill from Hollywood, but Webb wanted a divorce. His work was overwhelming him but, in fact, it was the actress Dorothy Towne [the soon-to-be second Mrs. Webb who had recently appeared in a *Dragnet* episode] doing the overwhelming. Webb was terrified about how much of his money London would get. He asked the OCID chief to 'bug her' to show evidence of wanton expenditure. Webb was great for PR, but Julie London was no hoodlum or drug dealer. Yet Hamilton didn't question the morality and took on the job personally. He put electronic wizard, Bert Phelps to work. Phelps had concerns:

'I was asked by the captain to go with him to Jack Webb's place just off Ventura Boulevard in Encino. He and his wife were having all kinds of battles, they were going through a bitter divorce and when we got there a private detective was there and wanted to bug the rooms for Jack Webb. Now, why the captain brought me there for a civil situation, I felt very uncomfortable. They asked me for my opinion and what should be done and I told them. I said: "Whatever the captain wants me to do, OK." It happened and he got the evidence. Jack Webb and the captain were very close. I think it was "scratch my back, I'll scratch yours."'

It was something of a one-way scratch. In the files, Mike Rothmiller discovered that Chief Parker and Captain Hamilton had 'sat on' some of the sensitive information gathered in the bugging of Webb and Julie London's home. It was for use 'when needed'. What information they did release to Webb's divorce lawyers did not mitigate his payout and Julie London got $150,000 cash, the same amount in *Dragnet* shares and $21,000 a year in financial support. Yet, Webb still believed he owed a favour and, of course, friends help each other. Webb went before the California State Assembly's Judiciary Committee with Chief Parker to boost the case that the police needed a free hand in their investigations. He produced an episode of his show titled *The Big Ruling* in which Sergeant Friday gets information about a heroin shipment, finds the contraband but has no warrant so the drug smugglers go free. 'Who's better off?' Webb asked television viewers and politicians. What Webb didn't know was that his ex-wife's secrets had joined the huge file OCID had on him and other members of his cast and production company. Along with files on several members of that Judiciary Committee.

A file was also being compiled on the arrivals and activities of Jack and Bobby Kennedy who were regular visitors to the home of their sister Pat and their brother-in-law, Peter Lawford, at 625 Palisades Beach Road [Pacific Coast Highway] right on the ocean front in Santa Monica, California. Built on 30-foot high 'stilts', to disdain and be safe from the aggressive Pacific surf, the house had a long, welcoming living area with French windows leading out to balconies and views across the sea to the horizon over which Japan was all but the next stop. Closer, off the sun deck, was Sorrento Beach where on a cool night you could lie on the sand and stare at the stars and vice versa. Everyone was young, beautiful and healthy and the playground – the house was originally created for Louis B. Mayer with thirteen mirrored bathrooms – was always ready for a close-up. This was the high end of the emerging new American dream. The beach parade was a regular excitement for surfers, a sunbathing Angie Dickinson, Pat Lawford tossing a volleyball to a barefoot Marilyn Monroe – beautiful people against a clear California sky, images from the idea's notebook of a good public relations man. At this moment, the link between America's political and Hollywood centres was comfortable, and so were the crowd in the social swirl of the Kennedy clan in Palm Beach, or the Sinatra clique in Palm Springs.

Where the exact blame lays for the mess this became is a confection too rich for most. There were so many factors but indisputably Marilyn Monroe got in the way of too many people. Her connections – through Pat DiCicco and mobster Johnny Rosselli – with organised crime figures, are in the OCID files. But her fame has obscured some of that particular legend. She was quoted as saying: 'I am good, but not an angel. I do sin, but I am not the devil. I am just a small girl in a big world trying to find someone to love.'

From the decades of reportage since her death, it is clear that Marilyn feared her own links with insanity through her mother and her grandmother, Della Mae Monroe, who died in a strait jacket. Amateur psychologists, and several professional ones, argue that she dressed up as Marilyn Monroe to escape the possible madness of remaining Norma Jeane. No matter the 'why', she took the leading role in what became a gothic fairytale. By 1953, she was most certainly 'Marilyn Monroe the movie star'. For

Fox, she'd starred in *Niagara*. The thriller, a *noir* but filmed in Technicolor, was the studio's biggest success for years. Marilyn was now the one thing that Hollywood adored above all else – someone who made money. There was more to come: her next two films that year, *Gentlemen Prefer Blondes* with Jane Russell, and *How to Marry a Millionaire* with Lauren Bacall and Betty Grable, made even more cash. It is at these high points that stars are cocooned: no one wants them flying free. Especially the one now declared the sex symbol of the Western world. Moviegoers loved Marilyn Monroe. She became shorthand spelled out in spotlights for glamour and fashion. But the Hollywood she existed in was ruled by men in suits who didn't like being questioned or confronted, especially by women. Marilyn wasn't afraid of making a nuisance: 'When you're famous you kind of run into human nature in a raw kind of way. It stirs up envy, fame does. People you run into feel that, "Well, who does she think she is, Marilyn Monroe?" Which is kind of difficult when you *are* Marilyn Monroe.'

Although Monroe had officially become 20th Century Fox's 'greatest asset alongside CinemaScope', her contract had not changed since 1950, meaning that she was paid far less than other stars and couldn't pick and choose her roles. Her efforts to make 'serious' films were thwarted by Darryl Zanuck who preferred this particular blonde to make frothy comedies and musicals. Marilyn's 'serious' cause was not helped by appearing on the cover, and as a stapled centrefold [from a 1949 set of nude photographs], of the first ever *Playboy* magazine, published in December 1953. Zanuck was a beast and when Marilyn refused another musical comedy, *The Girl in Pink Tights,* co-starring with Frank Sinatra, Zanuck suspended her from Fox on January 4, 1954. Ten days later she married an American legend, one of baseball's all-time greats, the loping Joe DiMaggio. No one could keep Marilyn Monroe off the world's front pages. Eventually, Zanuck bowed to her stardom and granted some of Monroe's demands for more control and more money, but she remained wary and scared of what Zanuck and Fox Studios truly thought of her. She wanted to be cocooned, to be protected. She had a lifelong attraction to men who could take her away from herself, take her away from the pain, to the point where it often became seriously desperate. American hero Joe DiMaggio had that role for the moment, but competition was always around. A great athlete, but like so many of them, he was selfish, concerned about his health, his prowess, his abilities and his image. The 'Yankee Clipper' wanted a wife for himself, not a sex symbol he would have to share with the entire world. He wanted to display Marilyn in his arms but keep them closely wrapped around her.

Senator John F. Kennedy, who would appear as a leading man in Marilyn's life shortly, was similar to DiMaggio in his demands from a woman. JFK required unrestricted female attention. In a remarkable book, *A First Rate Madness* [The Penguin Press, 2011], Nassir Ghaemi of the Tufts Medical Center in Boston, revealed an explanatory study of what, in essence, made Kennedy sex-mad.

'Kennedy's hyper-sexuality was not limited to his Presidential years, but also occurred in his college and Congressional years, before and after marriage. JFK always had a high sex drive, probably related to his hyperthymic temperament, and later strengthened by libido-enhancing medications [anabolic steroids and amphetamines]. When Kennedy combined procaine [injections] with other agents that produced euphoria, like amphetamines and steroids, they all augmented one another, increasing his energy and libido further.' It concludes that Kennedy used 'more drugs than he needed' which provided him with a 'manic like enhancement of his physical and sexual energy.' That is the scientific stuff.

One of JFK's early girlfriends, Harriet Price, whom he dated during his time at California's Stanford University in 1940, was convinced the future President's womanising was him simply following his father's example. He thought and could get away with it according to her testimony in distinguished academic Fredrik Logevall's landmark biography, *JFK: Volume 1: 1917–1956* [Penguin-Viking, 2020]. But it was his use of amphetamines and steroids including an oral testosterone in later years that increased his libido and led to an enhancement of his sexual energy. Kennedy had a severe case of Addison's disease which weakens the immune system. He was given last rites on four occasions and at thirteen he almost died from appendicitis. In college, he suffered a back injury playing football, but he was born with one leg slightly longer than the other, so he had back problems even before the football injury but his back issues would plague him for the rest of his life.

In the diary held by the OCID and seen and copied by Mike Rothmiller, Marilyn writes of an encounter with the President where she remembers him 'taking a blue pill' and giving one to her. She also writes: 'John and I made love in the pool.' She offers no location for the pool. In his book, Nassir Ghaemi recounts how JFK used the White House swimming pool for sexual encounters including ongoing affairs with Judith Exner and Mary Meyer [the sister-in-law of *Washington Post* editor Ben Bradlee], a White House intern and two secretarial staff blondes identified only as 'Fiddle' and 'Faddle'. Ghaemi also claims that unknown women 'presumed to be prostitutes' were regulars at the swimming pool which, for whatever reason, was filled in by Richard Nixon when he later became President.

Ghaemi forcefully suggests that Kennedy's drug use, and the control of it, led to distinctive episodes during his term in office – which he calls simply 'the good' and 'the bad'. The less successful – or the bad –was most certainly from 1961 to 1962 when, it is argued, his judgment was not at its best. Also, a difficult time to be dealing with Fidel Castro, the Soviet Union's Nikita Sergeyevich Khrushchev *and* Marilyn Monroe, all of whom were equally consistent in troubling him. [The following is, with Marilyn's spelling of Khrushchev's first name, a brief comment from her diary that Mike Rothmiller copied: 'Niketa is a horrible man and must be stopped. He doesn't like John and John doesn't like him. I'm scared there will be a war.'] President Kennedy had inherited Castro and Khrushchev, but Marilyn he had pursued as Senator Kennedy. Peter Lawford, pivotal as he was to be in this story, was the matchmaker.

Lawford was a complex man, and like Marilyn he had a confused and difficult childhood – nomadic but with money – from his aristocratic English heritage. He was the only son of the decorated soldier, Lieutenant-General Sir Sydney Lawford and the cantankerous Lady May Lawford. Young Lawford wasn't decisive and he wasn't brave. He scared easily which would later play an important role in tragic events. When his family arrived in Los Angeles, he recalled that, 'My mother was very keen that I meet the right people, and movies seemed a logical way.' He was young, good-looking and charming and of that trio it was his charm – a willingness to help and to be of service – that opened the doors. At fifteen, he landed his first credited role in *Lord Jeff* [1938]. *Son of Lassie* [1945] made him a leading man ['The dog didn't like me'] and a man about town. Lawford became involved with movie star Lana Turner who was also friendly with the other Hollywood movers and shakers, Mickey Cohen and associates. A sixteen-year-old Elizabeth Taylor enjoyed her first screen kiss with him in *Julia Misbehaves* [1948] and she admitted that Lawford was her first big crush. He married Patricia Kennedy at St. Thomas More's Church in Manhattan [the Kennedys could not use St. Patrick's Cathedral as Lawford was not a Roman Catholic] on April 24, 1954. Lawford had made many movies, but there was a noticeable absence of star names at his wedding. Actress Marion Davies, the lover of the manipulative newspaper baron William Randolph Hearst who had died in 1951, was there at the invitation of Kennedy patriarch, Joseph Kennedy.

The senior Kennedy had tried to sabotage his daughter's marriage to Lawford and told anyone who would listen: 'If there's anything I'd hate more for a son-in-law than an actor, it's an *English* actor as a son-in-law.' That remark did not intimidate his daughter, but it did intimidate Lawford. Whether it was awe at the money and power or simply that he felt out of place, he was constantly fearful of and obedient to the Kennedy men.

Months after his marriage, in July 1954, Peter Lawford 'connected' the elder of his new brothers-in-law with Marilyn Monroe at a party hosted by agent Charles Feldman. When she was introduced to Senator Kennedy, he employed a tired line: 'Haven't I met you someplace before?' She took the question at face value and said possibly she had when he'd stayed out in Hollywood with the actor Robert Stack [*The Untouchables*]. Marilyn was at the party with her husband of six months, Joe DiMaggio, but the baseball hero was a reluctant guest. He didn't like Hollywood and he most certainly didn't like the Hollywood people who gathered around his wife. It didn't take long for DiMaggio to get hot under the collar. He got more and more upset as JFK stared at his wife for much of the evening. The partygoers were intrigued and, although the gossip was whispered, it roared around the room. It proved a volatile mix. Marilyn was delighted by the attention ['He couldn't keep his eyes off me'] but DiMaggio kept urging her to leave, taking her by the elbow and leading her toward the door. Finally, and reluctantly, she went off with her husband leaving her smile and telephone number behind with Kennedy. He telephoned Marilyn the next day. Joe DiMaggio answered, heard Kennedy's voice and hung up on him. 'I guess I shouldn't call at certain times, huh?' Kennedy asked Marilyn the next time they met.

Later, in October that year, regular visitors to Kennedy's hospital room, where he was recovering from spinal surgery, noticed a Marilyn Monroe poster. She was wearing blue shorts and standing with her legs spread well apart. The image was taped upside down on the wall above Kennedy's bed. Young women he called his 'cousins' paid visits and his wife Jackie was attentive. During his recuperation she invited Grace Kelly, star of *High Noon* [1952] and *Rear Window* [1954], to dress up as a nurse and feed him. He failed to recognise her and the future Princess Grace left, complaining: 'I must be losing it.' Marilyn's poster stayed in place.

Marilyn's 'connection' with John Kennedy became an 'item' in the OCID files if not the gossip columns. It also made her apprehensive around Peter Lawford. When they were seen in public together they seemed good friends, fellow actors moving in the same circles. But after she met JFK at Charles Feldman's party [after her death the official line was JFK and Marilyn first met in November 1961, at Lawford's Santa Monica home], Marilyn herself said she was scared of Lawford. She spelled out her fears in a note in a 1956 diary – an expensive, green Italian book with careful engraving – which is quoted in the book *Fragments* published in 2010. There is no way of telling if the entry was made in 1956 or added by her to the diary at a later date. What the diary has for certain is impressive provenance. Along with her personal effects, Marilyn left an archive of poems, letters, scribbled notes, recipes, and other paperwork to her acting teacher Lee Strasberg who died in 1982. His widow and third wife, Anna Mizrahi Strasberg, received more than $13 million when she sold the majority of Marilyn's personal items at Christie's in New York in October 1999. Anna Strasberg later found two boxes of written material which comprise the bestselling *Fragments* which on publication was announced as a 21st century sensation. One of the editors, Stanley Buchthal, was a family adviser to Anna Strasberg and the estate of Marilyn Monroe. It was suggested in *Vanity Fair* magazine, in November 2010, that her writings are a comfort to her fans who 'still want to rescue her from the taint of suicide,' and more evidence for those convinced, like Mike Rothmiller, that she was murdered. One note, eerily prescient, talks of her fears about Peter Lawford – that he might poison her. The same note mentions 'Jack', who, it is suggested in *Fragments*, is dancer Jack Cole who worked with Marilyn on *Gentlemen Prefer Blondes*. But this is if you believe she didn't meet JFK until 1961. We know now she had met the then future President well before. The brief note is a goosebumps-inducing look inside her mind:

> '… the feeling of violence I've had lately about being afraid of Peter he might harm me, poison me, etc. why – strange look in his eyes – strange behavior (sic)… nothing really in my personal relationships lately have been frightening me – except for him – I felt very uneasy at different times with him … not in the way I love & respect and admire Jack [the name not clear in the original] …'

Marilyn kept her concerns confined to her diary. Hollywood stars were not allowed to have fears or troubles, and they were distant from their public. 'Paparazzi' wasn't yet in the dictionary. *The System*, that is the studios, ran things. When names like Marilyn Monroe appeared in films it was an occasion, when they appeared in print or on television it was orchestrated.

As it was on Manhattan's Lexington Avenue on September 15, 1954, when Marilyn was making Billy Wilder's *The Seven Year Itch*. The filming of the movie, in which she becomes her neighbour Tom Ewell's sexual fantasy, was based at the 20th Century Fox studios in Hollywood but, for publicity, the filming of one particular scene was organised 'live' and in public. In what became a landmark Hollywood image, Marilyn posed on a subway grate with air blowing up the skirt of her Travilla-designed white dress. Watched by a crowd of around 2,000 people, the dress whirled over her head and she glories in the legendary moment. It's been interpreted in many ways. That moment was Marilyn showing the world how to relax about sex and showing what a free spirit she was. In truth, it was a remarkable and globally successful publicity stunt.

The image is regarded as iconic but so was William Travilla's dress which, faded from white to ecru, sold for $5.6 million dollars in a 2011 auction of actress Debbie Reynolds' collection of movieland memorabilia. The one person who didn't like the dress was Joe DiMaggio. His increasing jealousy and possessiveness had worsened the tensions in their marriage. He hated her sex symbol image; she knew it was making her a movie star. DiMaggio watched the air blowing up the skirt scene being filmed in New York and several accounts say there were shouts and screams [he slapped her around] heard from their hotel room that evening. The next day they flew together, silently, to Los Angeles, the next month Marilyn filed for divorce after nine months of marriage to the sporting hero. Most knew it was truly over when DiMaggio was banned by Daryl Zanuck from 20th Century Fox studios. For Zanuck, who had dismissed the early Marilyn, she was now the star of the picture that would be one of the world's biggest commercial successes of 1955.

It was the end of another American fantasy but the start of another mess for Marilyn with repercussions for her and everyone around her. By November 1954, she was living a block south of the Sunset Strip in the Brandon Arms Apartments at 8338 De Longpre Avenue. She was living alone and planning to take off to New York 'to be taken seriously'. DiMaggio remained obsessively jealous and hired Sunset Strip private detective Barney Ruditsky and his partner Phil Irwin to 'watch' [what today we'd call 'stalk'] the activities and movements of his former wife. OCID detectives also had been watching Marilyn because of the many people she associated with.

On October 27, 1954, Marilyn and Joe's divorce became final. Florabel Muir, now recovered from her ordeal at the Mickey Cohen shoot-out, was reporting for the *New York Daily News* and presented a revealing portrait of the demise of the marriage.

The Marilyn-DiMaggio partnership had seduced the world and the international media were caught up on every word of testimony from the divorce proceedings. Florabel knew more than most as she was being fed information from her sources within the LAPD and other 'unofficial' detectives. A hard-edged reporter, she captured the emotions of the day:

'Marilyn Monroe won an uncontested divorce from Joe DiMaggio today after sobbing that Joe was "cold." He was "indifferent" and terribly "moody" too, Marilyn testified, when all she wanted was love. Once he wouldn't talk with her for ten long days, she said, and "when I tried to find out what was the matter with him, he would say: "Leave me alone!" and "Stop nagging me!" A man sitting next to me said out loud: "That guy must be nuts." A woman on the other side remarked: "She isn't telling the whole story." Marilyn's five-minute testimony was packed with emotion. She sighed. Her voice broke twice. Once it was in a sob. She brought a handkerchief toward her face, but there weren't any tears to wipe away. She tilted her head slightly forward and directed her little words to Judge Orlando H. Rhodes. The judge seemed quite interested when Marilyn said Joe was indifferent to her. Dressed in somber black – a two-piece, black silk, faille suit with half-plunging shawl collar, black straw hat tilted back on her head, and white gloves – she was asked right off what her name was. "Marilyn DiMaggio," she told her attorney, Jerry Giesler. "You mean Norma Jean, don't you?" "Oh, yes," she said. Then she plunged into her story of how Joe had spurned her charms during their eight and a half months of marriage. "I expected to find love, warmth, affection and understanding in my marriage," she said. "Instead, I found complete indifference and coldness." Marilyn said she even offered to give up her acting career, "but he was indifferent to that offer too." Not once did she refer to Joe by name.

"I was not permitted to have any visitors in the house without an argument. I don't think we had visitors more than three times during our marriage."

'Once, Marilyn said, Joe permitted someone to come into their big house "when I was sick, but all during the visit there was great strain." She didn't say who the visitor was. Marilyn said Joe's coldness and indifference affected her health and "I was under the care of my doctor quite a bit of the time."

'Marilyn's business manager, Mrs. Inez Melson, corroborated her story. She said when Marilyn tried to give Joe warmth he would push her away and said, "Don't bother me." [Inez Melson had been introduced into Marilyn's life by Joe DiMaggio, to "keep an eye" on his wife and to report back anything untoward. She continued as Marilyn's business manager following the divorce.]

'She swore that before Joe and Marilyn broke up in late September – they lived under the same roof for a week, he downstairs and she upstairs – Joe told her: "I know I am wrong in my approach to coldness and indifference. I regret it but I cannot help it."'

Yet, ignoring he was abusive, Joe DiMaggio had convinced himself his wife had left him for someone else. Why else? He was jealous of Marilyn's career and wanted her to give it up and settle down with him. He was jealous of the attention she received from other men, a curse for a man married to an international sex goddess. He was, he would admit, insane with jealousy. Nine days after her marriage was officially over, on November 5, Marilyn drove her white Cadillac convertible to visit a friend at a small apartment building nearby in West Hollywood. The private eye contacted DiMaggio who was drinking with Frank Sinatra at Patsy D'Amore's Villa Capri on McCadden Street in Hollywood. [When it moved in 1957 to a better location on Yucca, one block north of Hollywood

Boulevard, Sinatra used it as an HQ to plan support for JFK's Presidential campaign.] Hollywood columnist Jim Bacon was there that evening and gloried in recalling how Sinatra, who'd been intimate with Marilyn, had waved him over, but he'd declined after seeing how upset DiMaggio appeared. With, given retrospective irony, some brass neck, Sinatra sympathised. He agreed that Marilyn was most probably seeing one of her 'many, many lovers'. A few more drinks, and they agreed to call the private investigators and catch Marilyn with her lover in a photograph. This incongruous gang gathered at the corner of Waring and Kilkea in West Hollywood at midnight and with an axe burst through the front door and into the wrong apartment. Instead of Marilyn, the private detective turned his camera flash on Florence Kotz, 39, a secretary and in curlers and confusion. She was also screaming. Sinatra, DiMaggio and the private eyes ran for it. Blinded by the flash, Miss Kotz couldn't identify anyone, and the raid was written off by the police as a thwarted robbery, until the publication of the September 1955 edition of *Confidential* magazine, which reported DiMaggio and Sinatra as a couple of idiots in a story titled 'The Real Reason for Marilyn's Divorce'. Chief Parker, who had no time for Sinatra and his underworld connections, never admitted to having anything to do with leaking the truth about the 'Wrong Door Raid' to the magazine. Of course, that would have been done by Captain James Hamilton, who in the OCID files, had even more access to information than *Confidential,* which enjoyed a circulation of nearly five million readers, if not the direct means to share it.

The studios didn't like the trouble caused for their stars by magazines like *Confidential.* They saw their stars as investments – their moneymakers – and they were being threatened by the salacious revelations. When more and more imitation scandal magazines started to emerge, the studios put pressure on the government to intervene.

California Attorney General Pat Brown, and father of future Governor Jerry Brown – both of whom are the subjects of bulging OCID files – put *Confidential* and its editors, along with the many imitation publications that had sprung up, under scrutiny over their reporting in a series of prominent hearings in 1957. The exposé on the 'Wrong Door Raid' would be a key example. It ended in a hung jury but not before Chief Parker had some fun. Pat Brown, who became California Governor in 1959, set up a State Senate Investigating Committee looking into how stories were leaked to magazines like *Confidential*. Sinatra was invited to testify but, when he refused, Chief Parker had a word with Captain James Hamilton. Sinatra, one of the world's most popular entertainers, was 'just another Los Angeles citizen' to Chief Parker. He had a subpoena served on Sinatra at 4 a.m. in the bedroom of his Palm Springs home by three uniformed policemen. Sinatra responded: 'It was a good thing I was asleep or I might have gotten a gun.'

'It seems to me that somebody is trying to take the spotlight away from the real issue in this matter,' said Chief Parker, who by the time of the Grand Jury in 1957 had given up drink. He'd gone cold turkey for health reasons and Daryl Gates said that from then on 'he was a real mean son of a bitch'. Sinatra was just another buzzing and irksome insect in Parker's pragmatic world. Sinatra said he would sue Chief Parker and Captain Hamilton, but wisely his lawyers advised that could open him up to many other questions he might not want to address.

Instead, Sinatra hired LAPD policeman and 'Gangster Squad' veteran turned private detective, Fred Otash, to prove that he had not lied about his role in the farcical raid. He testified under oath that he had been outside the apartment building but had not entered the apartment. This conflicted with other accounts. DiMaggio said he and Sinatra were at the Villa Capri all evening. Detective Phil Irwin said they had *all* burst into the apartment adding: 'Almost all of Mr. Sinatra's statements were false.' Sinatra asked the jury: 'Who you gonna believe? Me or a guy who kicks in doors for a living?' His celebrity rather than the plausibility of the testimony won the day.

The unanswered question was *who* gave the story to *Confidential*? Phil Irwin said there were only four people alive who knew all about the details of the raid: 'That was me, Ruditsky, Sinatra and DiMaggio. I didn't tell and Sinatra and DiMaggio wouldn't. That leaves Ruditsky.'

There were connections. There were *always* connections with OCID. DiMaggio's private detective, Barney Ruditsky, was the owner of Sherry's when Mickey Cohen escaped the assassination attempt there in the summer of 1949. He had also permitted – if he had a choice – the OCID to use his office there for their wiretapping operation on Hollywood madam Brenda Allen which brought the house down on many of Chief Parker's police predecessors.

Marilyn Monroe was invited to attend the Senate hearings but, as an innocent party, [Marilyn had been at the home of her friend, Sheila Stewart, as her ex-husband and Sinatra burst through next door] there were no legal demands on her. She was working in London filming *The Prince and the Showgirl* with Laurence Olivier at the time. She'd changed her professional outlook. Box office wasn't enough for Marilyn. She wanted to be taken seriously as an actress and, shortly after divorcing DiMaggio, left for New York. There she encountered the playwright Arthur Miller. She had met Miller before through the director Elia Kazan whom she'd been introduced to at one of Sam Spiegel's card parties. In 1952, Kazan had controversially testified as a witness for Senator Joe McCarthy's House Committee on Un-American Activities ruining the careers of supposed Communist sympathisers and was never forgiven by many.

Miller was also under suspicion for alleged 'Communist sympathies' and was under investigation by the FBI. His 1952 play *The Crucible* suggested the Salem witch trials as a metaphor for

McCarthy's hounding of some Americans. Marilyn's association with Miller meant that J. Edgar Hoover opened a file on her. It was much thinner than that held out on the coast by the OCID. Fox Studios, with whom Marilyn had entered into a seven-year co-production contractual arrangement, panicked that she might get blacklisted like so many had because of McCarthyism. But she was adamant about her involvement with Miller. Miller was called a Communist and subpoenaed to appear before the House Committee on Un-American Activities on 21st June 1956. Marilyn married him five days later. J. Edgar Hoover's favourite columnist and friend Walter Winchell said: 'America's best-known blonde moving picture star is now the darling of the left-wing intelligentsia.' Other publications were equally aghast. *Variety*'s headline was 'Egghead Weds Hourglass'. Another noted that it was 'the most unlikely marriage since the Owl and the Pussycat'. Marilyn had converted to Judaism for Miller and, two days after a civil wedding, they had a Jewish ceremony. As with so many things in her life, Marilyn was committed to her new husband.

Bobby Kennedy was also committed. He was pursuing his anti-gangland campaign with some gusto and the help of the LAPD. He was becoming a regular in Los Angeles. As was his older brother. The Kennedys, both of whom had inherited the penchant for extramarital excursions from their controlling father, had their comings and goings to southern California logged by the OCID. Peter Lawford was an active enabler on JFK's 'hunting expeditions' for women in Hollywood. The details of the Kennedys' risky behaviour are extraordinary, and that they got away with it is bewildering, for everything went on under the ever-watchful eyes of the LAPD spook squad. The OCID monitored, they noted, they transcribed, and they filed. The OCID sent detectives to the East Coast to monitor the meetings between John Kennedy and Marilyn Monroe.

On July 17, 1952, Chief Parker revealed at a meeting of police chiefs in Richmond, California, that he had 10,000 dossiers on what he called 'major criminals' in America. He implied that was the FBI's job but that they weren't doing it. What he didn't disclose to his colleagues – or to J. Edgar Hoover's special agent Robert J. Abbaticchio, from San Francisco, who had infiltrated that meeting – was that he also held more than that number of 'non-criminal' dossiers. [When Mike Rothmiller first joined OCID he calculates there were between 20,000 and 25,000 *non-criminal* dossiers.] Knowledge of others' sins gave Parker more power. These files held the astonishing stories about Peter Lawford, his Rat Pack friends, the Kennedys and their women. They noted John Kennedy's trysts with June Allyson, Gene Tierney [Tierney said later of JFK: 'Gifts and flowers were not his style. He gave you his time, his interest. He knew the strength of the phase, "What do you think?"'], Jayne Mansfield, Eva Marie Saint, Yvonne De Carlo, and many others who wanted a sprinkle of Kennedy stardust. It was a sexual merry-go-round. Part of that heavily male-dominated culture of the time was that men often passed around their 'conquests', like sharing a tip about a new restaurant. One FBI file records details of 'sex parties' in the suite kept at the Carlyle Hotel in New York by Mrs. Jacqueline Hammond, the divorced wife of the former US Ambassador to Spain. The report, sent directly to J. Edgar Hoover [now released through the Freedom of Information Act], says Mrs. Hammond had 'considerable information' about the upmarket orgies. Hoover, mesmerised by the sex lives of others, read the names of those who had 'participated at different times' which included, in report order: 'Robert F. Kennedy, John F. Kennedy, Teddy Kennedy, Sammy Davis Jr., Mr. and Mrs. Peter Lawford, Frank Sinatra and, Marilyn Monroe.' Peter Lawford's name had a telephone book of mentions in the FBI files but the inclusion of Pat Kennedy Lawford raised eyebrows. She was on the radar of FBI surveillance but previously there had been no indication, circumstantial or otherwise, of her involvement in such gatherings. The FBI certainly did not have the scale of information that was held in the OCID files which recorded and kept every detail even while protecting the Kennedy brothers. Still, there were greater surprises to come.

# PART THREE

## Too Hot To Handle

*'There was a desert wind blowing that night. It was one of those hot dry Santa Anas that come down through the mountain passes and curl your hair and make your nerves jump and your skin itch.*

*'On nights like that every booze party ends in a fight. Meek little wives feel the edge of the carving knife and study their husbands' necks.'*
        **— Raymond Chandler, *Red Wind*, 1938.**

# VII: Some Like It Hot

*'Real diamonds! They must be worth their weight in gold!'*
— Marilyn Monroe as Sugar Kane Kowalczyk,
*Some Like It Hot*, 1959.

Many have attempted and a few have arguably come close to explaining the conjuring act going on inside Marilyn Monroe's head, but it is clear that she was much taken, often giddy and sometimes drunk on her own desirability. It was potent and led her life, but nothing was as faithful to it as the movie cameras. They always made her look a star and offered no critical whiplash which was why her commitment to Arthur Miller only went so far. She'd thought becoming a serious, dramatic actress would boost her confidence, but it just made the scaffolding around it all the shakier. She could put on the costume, the pout, the persona of Marilyn Monroe with precision – she'd invented her – but was increasingly overwhelmed by her ambition to be taken seriously. Marriage to Miller had provoked more intellectual curiosity than cachet for her, and her disappointment at that only caused more damage to the union.

When she met up with Senator John Kennedy her confidence, her *seriousness*, was boosted beyond the fiction of her imagination. He – goodness, *they* – talked of world events. In her diary and still married to Miller, she notes: 'John called, he wants to see me again. He'll have me picked up and taken to the hotel.' That hotel was the Carlyle on East 76th in New York, watched by the OCID but overlooked by the FBI. John Kennedy, as well as Mrs. Jacqueline Hammond, had constant access to a penthouse suite. Marilyn and JFK continued to meet throughout her marriage to Miller. She and Miller shared their time between their farmhouse in Roxbury, Connecticut, and her Manhattan apartment which was where Marilyn would go if John Kennedy was in town. The Carlyle Hotel, eighteen blocks from her East 57th apartment, was seen as neutral and therefore 'safe' territory. Her diary, copied by Mike Rothmiller, indicates she felt she was in love with JFK and that her love was returned.

She was sure Hollywood loved her too. She decided to deal with those who truly *wanted* her. Pragmatically, in her marriage to Arthur Miller, she was the one earning the big money. She returned to Hollywood in July 1958, for what was to be, for many, her most memorable film, *Some Like It Hot* [1959]. The movie is often cited as one of the best ever made but it had Marilyn-style difficulties. [Director Billy Wilder who had looked after Marilyn on *The Seven Year Itch* said of his great success: 'Anyone can remember lines, but it takes a real artist to come on the set and not know her lines and yet give the performance she did.']

Returning to Hollywood was also a reunion of sorts with Peter Lawford and the beach crowd who went to his home for weeknight dinners and weekend frolics, when she'd see Judy Garland or Lauren Bacall [single after the 1957 death of Humphrey Bogart] and, sometimes, Jack and Bobby Kennedy. In the Lawford crowd any Monroe-Kennedy connections were not alarming. Nor were they exclusive.

Marian Collier Neuman who appeared with Marilyn in *Some Like It Hot* was a showgirl in Las Vegas before moving to Hollywood and the film industry. She said in 2019:

'In those days, in the 1950s, everybody fucked Frank Sinatra. I did. Marilyn did. It was part of the life. Frank and Peter Lawford liked to party, liked the girls. They always wanted lots of girls. Marilyn was around the parties and then she was a star.

'Nobody thought a lot about the sex: it was like brushing your teeth, something you did. Marilyn just wanted to be looked after and that was a sure way to get a man to put his arms around you. Still, and don't let anyone tell you different, she was a tough cookie. There was a purpose to all she did and that was all about getting her own way or her own man. The consequences of her actions were of no interest to her. You come up the hard way like we did and no matter how much they polish off the rough edges there's still a lot of grit underneath. I don't know who killed her but she'd no more commit suicide than I'd cut off my leg with a blunt knife.

'While we were making the movie there were lots of times Marilyn was in her dressing room taking "private" calls and much was made of it being about her acting "coach" or something like that. But she was taking calls from her men. There were always men. That kind of wattage, that glow, will attract, it will always do that.

'The Kennedy boys were known as swingers around town and Jack Kennedy was just a good-looking boy then, a young politician who wanted to get on. That he wanted to get on with Marilyn wasn't hard to figure.'

Marilyn's make-up man Whitey Snyder said the problem with Marilyn was she hated confrontation with men and having to say 'no'. In an interview [with Douglas Thompson on November 11, 1989] he said that on the set of her films, and he worked on them all, she had to 'cope with everyone from the producer's best friend to the boy with a clipboard putting the moves on her. Everyone wanted a piece of Marilyn because that's what she was selling: she was promoting Marilyn the commodity rather than the person. Two very different things, one was human while the other was manufactured. I put the make-up on the manufactured one. I think she often went off with men so as not to disappoint them; it was easier all around to say "yes" and get on with it.'

To the Rat Pack, and some of the others around Peter Lawford and his wife, the affair between John Kennedy and Marilyn was another example of a Kennedy 'trophy fuck' but her diary, and the longevity of their liaisons, tells a different story. For him, there was the excitement of the risk, as it was with Judith Exner, but Marilyn also brought something else he craved, something many overlook. She brought behind-the-scenes endorsements in the powerful and persuasive form of celebrity. He was attracted to the appeal, the glitter of attention and he accessorised his personal charisma with it. He campaigned on it and it shone in the reflected magnetism.

Studying the history, what remains remarkable is his arrogance. In the late 1950s, Senator John Kennedy was preparing to make a run for the Presidency of the United States, but was seen in restaurants with his hand up Marilyn Monroe's skirt ['He went red when he realised I wasn't wearing panties,' she noted] and making suggestive remarks to one of the world's most famous faces, in public. That his aides and guards remained tight-lipped appears extraordinary today.

It *was* a different world, a sexual carnival, a prurient game being played out, but with secret cameras clicking and tape quietly recording in utility vans and other disguised vehicles all across Los Angeles and elsewhere. Peter Lawford's Santa Monica beach home was under a 24-hour watching and listening order. Whatever happened or was communicated inside was recorded. How could such supposedly smart people not know they were being watched? Possibly, they felt secure, they were being watched over by professionals who knew the rules of silence, not to risk problems and their jobs. One OCID report never made public, until now, had JFK climbing out of a window at the Lawford home, jumping over a fence, and getting into a car with Angie Dickinson and driving off north toward Malibu on Pacific Coast Highway.

Marilyn didn't own centre stage with JFK. Judith Campbell Exner became very much her rival for John Kennedy's time.

Exner grew up in Pacific Palisades which looks south across Pacific Coast Highway to Peter Lawford's beach home. Aged 18 in 1952, she married actor Bill Campbell who said [in a 1976 interview with Douglas Thompson] that his bride quickly came to believe she was 'missing out' by marrying so young. They separated in 1958, and a year later she began an affair with Frank Sinatra which ended, as had his fling with Marilyn, when he tried to get her to take part in a threesome. Still, Exner remained part of the entourage. Sinatra introduced her to John Kennedy in Las Vegas in February 1960, at The Sands hotel, where he was filming *Oceans 11* [1960] with a familiar selection of friends: Dean Martin, Sammy Davis Jr., Joey Bishop, Peter Lawford and Angie Dickinson. Exner said she and Kennedy 'clicked' and the only doubt she had in their sexual relationship was that he constantly demanded she 'service' him orally. Marilyn makes the same complaint in her diary.

What might be termed a curved ball, was pitched into the situation when Sinatra introduced Judith Exner to Sicilian-American, Sam Giancana, the Mafia leader in Chicago. She was also involved with the Mafia's 'Hollywood Mr. Fix It', Johnny Rosselli, the associate of Pat DiCicco and a former lover of Marilyn. As Exner embarked on an affair with Giancana, Chief Parker's helicopter – the first bought by an American police force – was stretched to keep up with all the action. There was just so much for the OCID to record. California State authorities and the Federal Bureau of Alcohol, Tobacco, Firearms [because of gambling licenses] were also closely involved and concerned but, to protect the Kennedys, Captain James Hamilton deployed his own select teams to monitor them.

If the Kennedys were preparing for political battles, the LAPD were involved in constant skirmishes. With Chief Parker and Captain James Hamilton's encouragement, national law enforcement agencies gave their support to Bobby Kennedy's quest to crush the American underworld. J. Edgar Hoover saw that as his job and was angered by what he regarded as an encroachment on his fiefdom. This fact only encouraged the OCID to keep all information and the Kennedys to themselves.

The OCID files rated Marilyn as a potential source of insider information but J. Edgar Hoover had her filed as 'a Communist sympathiser'. They both had to deal with the real thing after President Eisenhower invited Premier Nikita Khrushchev to America in September 1959, and revealed the eleven-day trip would include one day and one night in Los Angeles. Locally, there was a panic – *The Russians Are Coming! The Russians Are Coming!* – and a protest rally was staged at the Rose Bowl in Pasadena. Chief Parker was in charge of the Soviet leader's security in southern California and advised the concerned citizens to receive Khrushchev in 'a state of aloof detachment'. Under Chief Parker's plan, there would be cops on alert at strategic points throughout the visit and the Communist leader would have no contact whatsoever with the good ordinary citizens of the City of Angels. Perish the thought. Marilyn had never been classed as ordinary. She was having lunch with Khrushchev. She happily agreed after Government aides told her that in Russia the United States was defined by 'Coca-Cola and Marilyn Monroe'.

Los Angeles Mayor Norris Poulson was miscast. He had been more comfortable in his role bringing the Dodgers baseball team from Brooklyn to Los Angeles a year earlier than he was welcoming the Soviet leader. Khrushchev's plane was taxied to an obscure corner of the airport and Poulson offered an ill-mannered greeting. It was the height of the Cold War, a terrifying time of fallout shelters and 'duck-and-cover' nuclear attack drills. A Soviet leader had never visited before and most Americans knew little about Khrushchev other than that he didn't have much hair and that a couple of weeks earlier his nation had landed a missile on the Moon, something which had raised reported UFO sightings throughout southern California. Khrushchev in Hollywood was another spectral spectacular.

Chief Parker had more secular concerns. Along with his official tour guide, Henry Cabot Lodge Jr., the United States ambassador to the United Nations, Khrushchev arrived in Hollywood with an invitation to visit 20th Century Fox Studios to watch the filming of the risqué Broadway musical *Can-Can*. Lunch would be provided in their grand commissary, the Café de Paris, where Khrushchev could meet the stars. Irony upon irony: fervent anti-Communists begged for one of the 400 lunch spaces available. Arthur Miller was urged to stay home because he was a leftist and much too radical to dine with the Communist dictator. Yet, Marilyn *had* to be there, and the studio instructed her to wear 'the tightest, sexiest dress she had'. 'I guess there's not much sex in Russia,' Marilyn said in response to the request. Marilyn arrived in Los Angeles a day ahead of Khrushchev from New York and moved into the Beverly Hills Hotel. It was there that she began the remarkable metamorphosis of becoming Marilyn Monroe with the help of Whitey Snyder's make-up and the requested tight, low-cut, patterned dress. Spyros Skouras, the president of 20th Century Fox, checked she was running on time: 'She *has* to be there.'

The Cold War was the hot topic. People were having nightmares about being fried alive by nuclear attacks. This was a sensitive time for global politics. And Marilyn Monroe *had* to be there. And she was. One of the bigger shocks of the day was that Marilyn arrived early. Waiting for Khrushchev to arrive, Edward G. Robinson sat at table 18 with Judy Garland and Shelley Winters. The legendary Warner Brothers actor puffed on his 'Little Caesar' cigar and smiled at Gary Cooper, Kim Novak, Dean Martin, Ginger Rogers, Kirk Douglas, Jack Benny, Tony Curtis and Zsa Zsa Gabor. Marilyn sat at a table with Henry Fonda. Debbie Reynolds sat at table 21, which was intentionally located across the room from table 15, which was occupied by her former husband Eddie Fisher and his new wife, Elizabeth Taylor, who had been Reynolds' close friend until Fisher left her for Taylor.

Hollywood's bedroom merry-go-round, all neatly chronicled in the OCID files, was of no concern to Chief Parker at that moment. He had his undercover men smothering the studio with their presence. He also had to diplomatically handle the men in ill-fitting suits and rather big rubber shoes, the Soviet cops who were travelling with their leader.

There were cops in the gardens, the toilets and under the tables. In the kitchen, LAPD forensic specialist Ray Pinker ran a Geiger counter over the food. ['We're just taking precautions against the secretion of any radioactive poison that might be designed to harm Khrushchev.'] Chief Parker and Captain James Hamilton prided themselves on missing nothing and anticipating and cleaning up any eventuality, no matter how inconsequential it seemed. The LAPD had seen to everything that day.

The Dodgers were playing a California derby game with the San Francisco Giants and the television sets around the room, placed there for the audience to watch Khrushchev's arrival, had their control knobs removed so nobody could switch the channel to the baseball game. Instead, they watched Khrushchev emerge from a limo and shake hands with Spyros Skouras. It was the friendliest moment of the day. Khrushchev's wife Nina sat with Frank Sinatra and told him and Bob Hope how much she was looking forward to visiting Disneyland which was a new wonder of the California world. She wasn't aware that an errant and ripe tomato had already crushed her hopes. During the motorcade to the Café de Paris, escorted by fifty LAPD motorcycle officers and controlled by Chief Parker, a protestor hit the chief's car with a juicy tomato. Parker decided there was too much of a threat for a trip to Disneyland in Orange County, a 30-mile unsecured drive out of his jurisdiction. As Henry Cabot Lodge Jr. ate his squab, Chief Parker suddenly appeared with a frown on his face like a worn saddle it was so ridden by the circumstances of the moment. He whispered: 'I want you, as a representative of the President, to know that I will not be responsible for Chairman Khrushchev's safety if we go to Orange County.'

'Very well, Chief. If you will not be responsible for his safety, we will not go, and we will do something else.' Khrushchev was annoyed his trip to the magic kingdom was cancelled and made that clear as he ended his post-lunch speech.

'Just now, I was told that I could not go to Disneyland. Why not? What is it? Do you have rocket-launching pads there? What is it? Is there an epidemic of cholera there? Have gangsters taken hold of the place? Your policemen are so tough they can lift a bull by the horns. Surely, they can restore order if there are any gangsters around. Then what must I do? Commit suicide?'

Spyros Skouras saw an answer to the difficult moment – Marilyn. He hurried to introduce her. Khrushchev shook her hand and looked up and down and up and down. Marilyn said he looked at her like all men looked at her. 'You're a very lovely young lady,' he said, smiling. Like so many men he was fascinated, fluent with his look and unashamed in his admiration. Her involvement, emotionally and sexually, with the man who only a short time later, on January 2, 1960, would formally announce his candidacy to be 35th President of the United States, was not mentioned. That relationship was at the forefront of Chief Parker's mind. His role to protect the Soviet leader was professional and political. The day after Khrushchev missed Disneyland, he was swift to praise the work of his department as 'one of the greatest examples of proficiency ever demonstrated.'

It was light work compared to dealing with the proclivities of the Kennedys. Too many knew about Marilyn Monroe and Jack Kennedy. She talked about it in front of reporters and publicity agents. In the digital days of social media and smartphones it is all but impossible to imagine how such a relationship – America's screen goddess and the nation's 'golden boy' politician – could remain hidden. The political climate of the time, combined with the infamous Kennedy tendency toward promiscuity, had opened up John Kennedy and his imminent White House candidacy to a critical vulnerability. Kennedy aides and associates, some looking for personal advancement, issued half-hearted warnings but also helped to make potential 'one-night stand' scandals vanish. Carmine Bellino, the Kennedy Mr. Fix-It, was called up when the threat of scandal got really serious. During the 1960 election campaign, Charles W. Engelhard, a South African diamond merchant, discovered that John Kennedy was having an affair with a nineteen-year-old student at Radcliffe University. Engelhard tried to employ a private detective in Boston to get photographs of Kennedy with the student. The detective refused and told Kennedy what was going on. In *The Dark Side of Camelot*, 1997, the author Seymour Hersh picked up on that and the Radcliffe student details her affair with the President.

During his 1990s investigations, Hersh talked to columnists and wire service reporters who had worked in Washington and Hollywood during the 1950s. They readily admitted, more than 40 years later, that they couldn't get stories about the JFK/ Marilyn relationship published. It was all behind closed doors. Doors kept very firmly shut out on the coast with the help of Chief Parker and his LAPD.

That secrecy wasn't deemed necessary for Marilyn's dalliance with Yves Montand in her cottage in the gardens of the Beverly Hills Hotel. She was co-starring with the married [to Simone Signoret] French actor in the aptly titled *Let's Make Love*. She wasn't enamoured with the project but had her contractual obligation to 20th Century Fox. Montand distracted her from the script. Rather than try to cover-up the affair, the Fox publicity machine used it in the marketing campaign for the film. Marilyn was 'hot'.

But Marilyn was soon to be so 'hot' that a conspiracy to eliminate her was orchestrated from the highest levels of government. When John Kennedy became America's President, it changed the world and was the beginning of the end for Marilyn's time in it. If, with hindsight, she was an early victim of the brutal culture #MeToo has exposed, she was also a victim of expediency. It all happened in such a rush. Events formed around her like clouds, clouds waiting to burst in a perfect storm. In July 1960, she was in the Nevada desert filming *The Misfits*, the last movie she ever completed. The Democratic National

Convention [DNC] was being held at the Coliseum stadium in Los Angeles. Wild horses weren't going to keep her away. Her marriage to Arthur Miller, who had written the script about a group of cowboys chasing Marilyn and mustangs, was another emotional casualty. She didn't like her husband any more or the movie. The marriage would be officially over when they finished filming. She was difficult on set which inadvertently made life difficult for her co-star, her 'father-figure' Clark Gable. She had become cosy with barbiturates.

Marilyn took a number of 'breaks' during the eight weeks of filming on location in Nevada and it was on one of those that Marilyn found herself in downtown Los Angeles under the watchful eye of the LAPD. Chief Parker had several consultations with Captain James Hamilton about the requirement 'to keep the lid on things' as Marilyn joined Kennedy's many Hollywood supporters at the DNC. The OCID had been told that Marilyn was 'under control' and was being helpful to the Kennedy campaign.

Parker was an Eisenhower man and, in any other circumstances, would be supportive of the Republican Presidential nominee Richard Nixon with whom he shared friends and supporters. J. Edgar Hoover feared that if Nixon won the White House then he might replace him as the head of the FBI with Chief Parker. Hoover was aware that Parker was also threatening from another angle by his close association with Bobby Kennedy. That connection was heightened, cemented, when Parker put the LAPD and all its power and glory behind Kennedy at the convention.

For the opening Sunday reception on July 11, 1960, John Kennedy [Jacqueline Kennedy, his wife, was heavily pregnant and did not attend the convention] along with Bobby, his wife Ethel, Ted Kennedy and his wife Joan, were escorted by fifteen white-helmeted, specially chosen policemen. In turn, this group were covered by thirty plain-clothes officers. The big Texan senator and soon-to-be Kennedy's running mate, Lyndon Johnson and his wife Lady Bird and their two daughters were left to look after themselves. Some 'Johnson girls' handed out long-stemmed roses as a band played 'Everything's Coming Up Roses'. As, for some, it was. The Kennedy campaign had asked for a specific LAPD officer to look after their candidate: Captain James Hamilton. It quickly became clear Hamilton needed support though – John Kennedy lost his suit jacket twice as adoring fans reached out to shake his hand and pulled away the jackets in their excitement. There were also moments of extreme anxiety when the strength of his supporters' enthusiasm became a physical threat, especially given Kennedy's lifelong physical vulnerability.

Kennedy was in a rigid back brace, fitted from crotch to shoulders. He had tried to become intimate with a woman at a California swimming pool during a final campaign trip before the Democratic Convention, but she'd dodged his pass and he had wrenched his already damaged back when he fell into the pool. The brace kept the President upright for his assassin's bullets on November 22, 1963. The story of the attempted poolside seduction emerged in the mid-1990s after decades of general and dubious discretion when it was told by the distinguished journalist and expert on the American Presidency, Hugh Sidey. He said that no one would have dared or even been allowed to print such a story at the time.

John Kennedy was guided beneath the eye-catching, hand-painted ceilings of the Biltmore Hotel on South Grand Avenue, where he was officially staying but never slept, through the public areas of the Coliseum by a police team comprising of Captain James Hamilton, Lieutenant Daryl Gates, trusted officers Frank Hronek and Marvin Iannone, and two OCID detectives, Archie Case and James Ahern. This was the Kennedy praetorian guard. It was quite clear that Chief Parker was in charge. Los Angeles was his city, and if anything untoward happened, he believed he was personally and totally responsible. 'We clean up our own mess,' was his standard reaction to problems. And his rules were to be followed, no matter who you were. Parker was rigid in this, as he was in his attitude and practice of policing. When he was told the Presidential candidate had pushed two LAPD officers out of a squashed elevator to make room for two of his aides, the chief called Bobby Kennedy and told him: 'You tell your brother if he ever puts his hands on a Los Angeles police officer again, I will pull it all. Do you hear me? All the security off the Democratic convention. All of it! Uniforms – everybody will walk off the job. Now you tell him that!'

Sensibly, the Kennedy brothers were accepting, albeit reluctantly so, rather than angry about Parker's reaction. His commitment to heavy security impressed the Kennedys and was one of the reasons his and his department's relationship with them, in particular Bobby Kennedy, flourished. There was mutual trust, a belief that together they were doing 'the right thing'. Still, Parker held some disquiet about the sexual shenanigans that Jack Kennedy indulged in, and the brothers' connections with Sinatra and his associates like Johnny Rosselli who was the perfect mobster for Hollywood. 'Handsome Johnny' could be anything anybody wanted him to be. He was attractive to women [as well as Marilyn, his lovers included Betty Hutton, Lana Turner and Donna 'It's A Wonderful Life' Reed] and men found him fun, good company and a generous all-round nice guy. He was also a facilitator. He was able to arrange the murder of 'Russian Louis' Strauss who tried to blackmail his friend Benny Binion the owner of the Horseshoe Casino in Las Vegas. He could get a girl a date with Frank Sinatra or Greta Garbo and vice versa. He worked with Howard Hughes and acted as his go-between with Grand Guignol characters like Mafioso Meyer Lansky and Moe Dalitz. He knew George Raft, one-time matinee idol and Marilyn's *Some Like It Hot* co-star, playing gangster 'Spats' Colombo. Parker despised him and the ethos he represented. Yet, his blind spot was the Kennedys. He was pledged to protect them no matter what.

During the Democratic convention, an OCID team monitored John Kennedy's movement from the Biltmore Hotel downtown over to the North Rossmore home of producer Jack Haley Jr. [son of The Tin Man in *The Wizard of Oz*, 1939] near the private golf course, the Wilshire Country Club in Hancock Park. It was where he had 'private meetings' with several women according to OCID files. Marilyn is not identified in these files as having visited Kennedy at Jack Haley's home. But she was with him during the first 72 hours of the convention. On the second evening, she had dinner with him at Puccini's in Beverly Hills, known in the day as 'a lasagna joint' on South Beverly Drive and owned by Frank Sinatra and Peter Lawford. It had a private upstairs room for après–dinner entertainment. The next morning, July 13, 1960, Marilyn and John Kennedy were together, wet from the shower, at breakfast at Peter Lawford's house out on Palisades Beach Road.

It was a similarly well-scrubbed John Kennedy, the clean-cut candidate, who accepted the Presidential nomination in front of a cheering and flag-waving crowd of supporters at the Coliseum. He also announced that Lyndon Johnson, the Senate Majority leader, would be his running mate and the nominee for Vice President. Johnson on the ticket was not what Bobby Kennedy had wanted. His brother also wasn't keen, but it was necessary. JFK's personal secretary, Evelyn Lincoln, who worked for him before and after his election, said she was with John and Robert Kennedy in a suite at the Biltmore Hotel when they agreed to accept Lyndon Johnson. She heard them say that Johnson was blackmailing JFK into offering him the nomination with evidence of his sex life – his womanising – provided by J. Edgar Hoover. She said that Bobby Kennedy had argued against accepting Johnson but finally the brothers had agreed they had no choice but to do just that. In fact, the big, tall Texan won the Southern states for the Kennedy-Johnson ticket and tipped the outcome of the election. The Kennedys later acknowledged Johnson's role in their victory over the Republican's Richard Nixon, but they didn't have to like it. They swore not to be compromised again. Bobby Kennedy was fiercely protective of the Kennedy family and over the decades historians have spoken of his 'ruthless' streak. He could be 'cruel' and he could be 'mean'. In volume four of his triumphant biography of Lyndon Johnson [*The Passage of Power*, 2014], Robert Caro cites several examples of Bobby Kennedy's quick temper and violent nature. On the sports fields at university he'd be 'spoiling – off the field as well as on – for a fight, often a senseless fight.' Caro reports of one incident in a bar in Cambridge, Massachusetts, where Bobby Kennedy was celebrating his birthday. Another Harvard student, John Magnuson, was also having a party. When his friends began singing 'Happy Birthday' to John, the other birthday boy went over and hit Magnuson on the head with a beer bottle. Magnuson was taken to hospital for stitches to a nasty wound. Bobby Kennedy never apologised.

Caro also quotes the American commentator Anthony Lewis, who was a Harvard contemporary of Bobby Kennedy: 'I didn't like him, I thought he was callow and tough.' Anthony Lewis recalled another fight involving Bobby Kennedy who thought a man was making light of comments regarding his late brother Joe Jr. and recalled that: 'Bobby would have killed him if we hadn't pulled him off. We had to pry Kennedy's fingers off his neck. It really scared us.' The Kennedys had each other's backs.

With the Democratic nomination won, any indiscretions, if made public, would sabotage a lifetime of family scheming to take control of America. Marilyn remained a beckoning temptation. The night of JFK's triumphant 'The New Frontier' acceptance speech, a huge party was organised by Peter Lawford out at his beach house. It was a jubilant summer night celebration, noisy, loud with squeals and slurred laughter. The partygoers were like kids on a spring break and there were groups of party girls, organised by Peter Lawford, in attendance. The next President of the United States and the world's most famous sex icon got lost in the crowd. Most eyes were on the naked girls or searching for Ross Acuna the barman hired at great expense from Romanoff's on Rodeo Drive in Beverly Hills.

Chief Parker's security squadron were on duty at the celebration. OCID detectives Archie Case and James Ahern were on hand and helped some revellers to their cars around 3 a.m. The team, led by Frank Hronek, saw and reported everything at the party to the chief and Captain James Hamilton. It was all filed. There is no notation saying John Kennedy or Marilyn left 625 Palisades Beach Road that night. Chief William Parker, that inspiration for Mr Spock of *Star Trek*, must have pondered as he read the reports just where the final frontier might be.

# VIII: The Usual Suspects

*'We stand today on the edge of a New Frontier – the frontier of the 1960s, the frontier of unknown opportunities and perils, the frontier of unfilled hopes and unfilled threats.'*
— John F. Kennedy, Los Angeles Coliseum, July 15, 1960.

The Kennedys had to win the Presidency, Marilyn her confidence, and they all had to do so as a malignant jigsaw of events pieced together.

There was a moment of serendipity. On the day Kennedy became the Presidential candidate it was made public that Frank Sinatra, Dean Martin, Hank Sanicola, [a friend and business partner of Sinatra's, and Paul 'Skinny' D'Amato [an associate of Chicago Mob boss, Sam Giancana and owner of The 500 Club in New Jersey, a front for illegal gambling] had applied for permission from the state of Nevada to take over the Cal Neva Lodge and Casino at Crystal Bay on the shores of Lake Tahoe. 'Skinny' [which he was] D'Amato was important in the life of the Kennedys. At the urging of Joe Kennedy this graduate of the Mob in Havana along with his lawyer, Angelo D. Malandra, had raised cash from felonious associates for JFK to fight and win the West Virginia Primary election.

Veteran gangster Elmer Renner out of San Francisco owned the Cal Neva but owed $800,000 in tax. When, on paper, hoodlum Bert Grober bought the place the tax man went after him too. Then Sinatra and his other saviours rode into town. What wasn't public knowledge was that Sam Giancana had a big silent percentage in the Cal Neva and that he had persuaded owner, Bert 'Wingy' Grober to sell the property at an extremely undervalued price of $250,000. The casino itself was no great moneymaker but it gave Giancana another hook in Sinatra who he wanted to stay close to John Kennedy.

With hindsight, you can see the perils of such a business. The canny Dean Martin saw them on the day. With the Mob all over the deal he pulled out fast. The supposedly worldly and cynical Sinatra had, for an often-drunk depressive, a rose-tinted view of this particular business. He was aware that Anthony 'Fat Tony' Salerno, the New York Mafia powerbroker, retained 'an interest' in the property and that Giancana was putting up the money. They were concerns of course, but Sinatra was certain that the seasonal resort could turn a healthy profit and that was how he'd 'sold' it to Giancana. Sinatra did have the contacts to make it a success. On opening night, the Kennedy patriarch, Joe Kennedy, was there. For him it must have been déjà vu. The Cal Neva was one of his 'love nests' during his nine-year affair with his secretary Janet Des Rosiers.

The US ambassador to the United Kingdom [from 1938 to 1940] was 60 when he began 'dating' the green-eyed 24-year-old who worked for him in Palm Beach, Florida. Now, he was back at the Cal Neva but this time he was with his Presidential candidate son and *his* extramarital 'date', Marilyn Monroe. With them, a little further out of the spotlight, were Johnny Rosselli and Sam Giancana. J. Edgar Hoover's FBI agents and OCID detectives were watching the Cal Neva from Tahoe's famously heavily wooded hills. It didn't offer much of a view.

What provided cover and some legitimacy, was that Sinatra had invited, at Clark Gable's insistence, not just him and

Marilyn but all the crew and cast of *The Misfits* to the opening night of the Cal Neva. It was part of an elaborate scheme to 'quieten down' Marilyn. Her affair with Kennedy the senator was one thing, an affair with a Presidential contender quite another. Bobby Kennedy had advised his brother to end the affair. But JFK dithered. There was no real romance, no future in it but it was fun at that moment. Marilyn, who took no comfort in the fact that they could have sex, but it had to be secret, turned to the pill bottle to soak up the hurt with barbiturates. She thought this was a 'love affair'. [There are several published accounts claiming that she became pregnant by John Kennedy and had an abortion. There is nothing in the OCID files or Marilyn's diary, seen by Mike Rothmiller, to establish this story but, if true, it would so clearly have devastated her even more. There is, however, a report in the OCID files that Marilyn later became pregnant by Bobby Kennedy and had an abortion.]

It was with this, the dismantling of her marriage to Arthur Miller and the somersaults inside her head, that when she returned to work on the set of *The Misfits* she became ill. Peter Lawford and a Kennedy family friend, Charles Spalding [who said he'd been sent to see her by JFK], found her at Westside Hospital in Los Angeles. She'd had her stomach pumped free of drugs and was being looked after by her psychiatrist, Dr. Ralph Greenson and an internist, Dr. Hyman Engelberg, both of whom Peter Lawford was to get to know well and become intimidated by. Rest and care saw her back at work on the movie by September. Her make-up expert Whitey Snyder, who got real-life close-ups of her face every day, said she looked 'great,' and the word he kept repeating in my interview with him much later was 'refreshed'. It was, as JFK had said, a new frontier. But there were ambushes ahead. They arrived quickly.

On November 8, 1960, America went to the polls, and John Kennedy became President-elect in the early hours of the next day. Marilyn had been indisposed and unable to vote.

On November 10, JFK announced to public and even insiders' surprise, that J. Edgar Hoover would stay in post as the director of the FBI. Hoover had too much on the Kennedys to be dismissed. Yet, wily Joe Kennedy had a caveat to that and urged the President-to-be to appoint his brother Bobby as Attorney General. As head of the Department of Justice he would then become Hoover's immediate boss. JFK reluctantly agreed and, in doing so, irritated Hoover even more. Captain James Hamilton sent his congratulations to Bobby Kennedy. Chief Parker sent his congratulations to the new President on the election victory, privately, a warmer letter of applause to Bobby Kennedy. Publicly he issued a statement: 'It has been the pleasure of my office to work closely with Bobby Kennedy during his period as counsel for the McClellan Committee. This opportunity to observe his philosophies in the law enforcement field has been most gratifying, and I expect increased levels of support for law enforcement at all levels.' Indeed, within days, the new Attorney General announced a war on the Mob. Captain James Hamilton sent his own congratulations to Bobby Kennedy. Privately, there was talk of Chief Parker leading a national task force against organised crime, but J. Edgar Hoover tied that up in red tape and discarded that particular policy parcel. Hoover held his public temper even when Bobby Kennedy insisted the FBI get Justice Department approval for all their directives and public relations announcements, but the animosity between the two men only heightened.

On November 11, Marilyn officially announced the open secret that her marriage to Arthur Miller was over. The hourglass had run out. By then, she had Patricia Newcomb, a Bobby Kennedy confidante, once again looking after her image and as such, by the mechanics of public relations, her divorce. The situation presented to the press was that the parting was of a 'friendly' nature. Marilyn didn't feel friendly about any of it and the media circus performing around the pending divorce made her more disillusioned.

Marilyn was dumbfounded by the death of Clark Gable on November 16. Told the news in the middle of the night, she couldn't find words to express her shock. Gossip column tittle-tattle that she'd helped cause his death by her antics on the set of *The Misfits* sent her into a sleeping pill bottle, pulling the stopper behind her. [Robert Mitchum revealed in an interview with the author that he informed John Huston, director of the film, that his demands for perfection and Marilyn's on set behaviour, had killed Gable. Huston told Mitchum: 'I believe you are correct.' John Huston confirmed this to me. Marilyn Monroe herself speculated that this might have been a form of subconscious revenge on the father who never declared himself to her.]

It was a wicked month that November 1960. There were ricochets. The new First Family-to-be were, of course, a national focus at that brief, shining moment. Not all the journalistic guns were spiked. Shots were fired. The columnist and humorist Art Buchwald sneaked an item into his newspaper report about the JFK/Marilyn love affair headed 'Let's Be Firm on Monroe Doctrine'. The column asked:

'Who will be the next ambassador to Monroe? This is one of the many problems President-elect Kennedy will have to work on in January. Obviously you can't leave Monroe adrift. There are too many greedy people eyeing her, and now that Ambassador Miller has left she could flounder around without any direction.'

Although a supposedly 'blind' item in a column, the message was clear to the cognoscenti in Hollywood and Washington. John and Bobby Kennedy had affairs of state to consider but, in many ways, Marilyn too was now an affair of state. She wouldn't settle, chasing around America, pinging back and forth from coast to coast, dragging all the folly and bad memories around with her. The impact of the Kennedy/Marilyn affair, witnessed by the unremitting OCID surveillance and filming and recording of Marilyn Monroe and the primary players in her life, was enormous.

The evening before his impassioned inaugural speech ['We shall pay any price, bear any burden, meet any hardship, support any friend, oppose any foe to assure the survival and success of liberty.'] there was a gala staged by Frank Sinatra at the National Guard Armoury, with familiar names like Jimmy Durante, Gene Kelly, Shirley MacLaine and Ella Fitzgerald. The one sour note was the forced absence of Sammy Davis Jr., who had been banned from the proceedings on the orders of Ambassador Joseph Kennedy because of Davis' recent racially-mixed marriage to Swedish actress May Britt. Afterwards, the new President went to Paul Young's restaurant for a late-night dinner hosted by his father. Among the guests was Paul 'Red' Fay Jr., a friend who'd served with JFK in World War Two and later became Under Secretary of the Navy. In his memoir, *The Pleasure of His Company*, Fay said his task that night was to escort Angie Dickinson. He recalled her 'wrapped in fur, standing all alone' with himself there to disguise Kennedy's date with Dickinson. The author has interviewed the actress three times and each time she most politely brushed away talk of romance but of Paul Fay's remarks said: 'He shouldn't have written it. It was too personal. It's an annoyance, but I have to live with it. They wouldn't believe me if I said it never happened.' With the Kennedys, it's always difficult to see the truth for clouds of smoke and the many mirrors that they surrounded their lives with.

For Marilyn, it was still show business. Ten days after the inauguration, she was at the premiere of *The Misfits* with her co-star Montgomery Clift, at the Capitol Theatre, New York. She subsequently attended hospital to undergo psychiatric treatment. Increasingly mentally disorientated, she was developing an increasing dependence on prescribed barbiturates. With her mind clear, she most certainly knew more than most about

American foreign policy. Her diary recounts that JFK discussed hugely sensitive issues with her after he became President. But she didn't learn everything.

During the early weeks of the Kennedy Administration, medical treatment for Marilyn was ongoing. President Kennedy wanted to put a man on the moon and win the 'space race' with Moscow but his main mission was to end the problem of Fidel Castro in Cuba. Castro had embraced Moscow and shut off America. CIA officers and White House staffers reported that both the President and Bobby Kennedy were adamant that the way to deal with Castro was by assassination. Marilyn wrote twice in her diary about this: 'John told me about Castro and he must be stopped.' The second read: 'John does not like Fidel C and said he will be gone soon.' CIA officers testified in the years which followed that President Kennedy wanted to have 'executive action capability' to deal with Castro, and by inference, any other foreign leader who was deemed worthy of murdering. Kennedy Library documents and testimony indicate that long before the Kennedy Administration planned what became the botched invasion at the Bay of Pigs on the south coast of Cuba on April 17, 1961, arrangements were being made to assassinate Castro.

One of the earliest and most influential accounts of the Cuban missile crisis was written by Robert Kennedy who was a member of the Executive Committee of the National Security Council [ExComm] which advised the President during the crisis. In his book, *Thirteen Days* [published posthumously in 1969 and never out of print since], Bobby Kennedy portrays himself as playing a leading role in the deliberations [a White House aide, who read the manuscript in 1964, shortly after JFK's assassination, remarked: 'I thought Jack was President during the missile crisis.' Bobby, who was then campaigning for the US Senate, replied: 'He's not running, and I am.'] In death, the Kennedy brothers, especially JFK, achieved near-canonisation in a disproportionate weighing of legend and achievement. This has become more apparent with the release of classified information and previously unknown tape recordings of deliberations.

Author Martin J. Sherwin in his book *Gambling with Armageddon: Nuclear Roulette from Hiroshima to the Cuban Missile Crisis* [Knopf, 2020] maintains everything *anyone* has claimed about Bobby Kennedy's own conduct during that crisis is now called into question. The book highlights Kennedy's judgment, especially his lack of it in a crisis. Bobby Kennedy and other members of ExComm boasted that 'their careful consideration of the challenge, their firmness in the face of terrifying danger, and their wise counsel steered the world to a peaceful resolution of a potentially civilisation-ending conflict.' Martin Sherwin debunks the official narrative of the thirteen days, writing that, 'Nothing could be further from the truth. The guidance JFK received was, for the most part, lousy. Some of it was loony. Had he heeded ExComm's "wise counsel," chances are I would not be writing this, or you reading it. As the President told a friend not long after the crisis ended, "You have no idea how much bad advice I had in those days."' Most of that advice came from his brother. 'Oh, shit! Shit! Shit!' the 'levelheaded' Attorney General screamed when he was told that Moscow was putting missiles in Cuba: 'Those sons of bitches Russians.' Another intriguing revelation made by Sherwin in 2020 questions Bobby Kennedy's prized moral high ground. On day one of the missile crisis, he suggested America 'should sink the *Maine* again or something' to give a pretext for invading Cuba. [The sinking of the USS *Maine,* a United States Navy ship, in Havana Harbour in February 1898, was a catalyst for the Spanish–American War that April.]

A year after Sherwin's book was published, the extent of Bobby Kennedy's suspect judgement was emphasised in *Nuclear Folly: A New History of the Cuban Missile Crisis* [Allen Lane, 2021]. It is a prime example of time as the detective. Author Serhil Plokhy reveals, through newly available Russian and KGB archives, that Khrushchev interfered with the 1960 American election, attempting to help JFK defeat Richard Nixon. During the election campaign the Soviet President arranged meetings between Kennedy campaign manager Bobby Kennedy and a KGB agent, Yuri Baruskov. Plokhy, a Harvard University history professor, notes of RFK's contact with the KGB: 'meetings in which today's parlance would qualify as nothing less than collusion.' In his significant book Plokhy argues that the Cuban crisis is the closest the world has ever come to nuclear wipe-out, one folly after another.

The Bay of Pigs was a fiasco. British authorities had supplied intelligence to the White House and the CIA that the anti-Castro sentiment was dismal but that was ignored. Cubans, who had been trained up by the CIA, were no contest for Castro's men who'd had years of revolutionary arms experience and recent help from their Moscow friends. Afterwards, Bobby Kennedy was even more intent on 'getting rid' of Castro and, with the President, applied supreme pressure to get that job accomplished. As such, he came in contact with the experienced CIA agent William Harvey who was in charge of doing just that. Harvey is reported in government documents to have met with a CIA scientist to discuss viable poisons for killing Fidel Castro.

Veteran British intelligence agent Peter Wright, who became known as 'The Witchfinder', published Spycatcher, his sensitive and revelatory book in 1987 despite attempts by the UK government to ban it. In the book he details his hunt for Moscow 'moles' in British intelligence. He recounts that he was approached by William Harvey at a secret conference in Maryland about 'the Cuban business.' He said that Harvey wanted to discover improved 'delivery mechanisms' for poisons which would be deniable or even undetectable. In later government inquiry testimony, Mafia operative, Johnny Rosselli, said Harvey gave him CIA-made poison pills at a clandestine meeting in New York and approved the 'hit list' to include Che Guevara and Raul Castro.

Christopher Hitchens, the late and often contrarian author and journalist, picked up on this aspect of the Kennedy

Administration in the *London Review of Books* [February 19, 1998]:

> 'Having made or bought the friendship of mobsters like Sam Giancana and Johnny Rosselli, the Kennedys seem to have acquired quite a taste for the quick fix of murder. How closely this was related to their simultaneous pursuit of sexual thrill and cheap glamour is good material for speculation. That there was some connection is hard to doubt; Kennedy's best-documented affair was with Judith Campbell Exner, who was simultaneously entwined with the Mafia chief Sam Giancana, who was himself involved in the attempts to murder Fidel Castro. Ben Bradlee [the late editor of the *Washington Post* and *All The President's Men* alumnus] has told us of his horrified astonishment at finding that Ms. Exner knew all of the secret telephone numbers for contacting the President out of hours. Anyway, orders were sent out from the Kennedy White House that Patrice Lumumba in the Congo, Rafael Trujillo in the Dominican Republic and Ngo Dinh Diem in South Vietnam were, with a bare minimum of "deniability", to be taken off the chessboard. In some way, this was rationalised as a demonstration of manly toughness in a dangerous world. Both brothers were addicted to the accusation that anyone who had any scruples was inviting another 'Munich', and one remembers the enthusiasm of their terrible father for that pact – not because he was pro-Chamberlain so much as because he was pro-Hitler.'

The CIA's counter-intelligence obsessive leader, James Jesus Angleton, was as concerned about what his President was disclosing in pillow talk as he was about who he wanted eliminated. Angleton 'listened in' through the wiretaps placed at the homes of Peter Lawford and Marilyn by Fred Otash, one of his many off-the-record assets. Otash worked for the CIA while officially employed by the LAPD and for many years afterwards. Marilyn, by April 1961, had moved permanently back to Hollywood and was in and out of the arms of Frank Sinatra. Sinatra, who had once commiserated with lovelorn Joe DiMaggio, romanced Marilyn and shared with her his Rat Pack lifestyle. Peter Lawford was always around for her to have a drink with, and he made himself a friend. By then, Marilyn relied on him. Yet, she *depended* on and saw more of Dr. Ralph Romeo Greenson, the Beverly Hills psychiatrist based at 465 North Roxbury Drive, just around the corner from his colleague Dr. Hyman Engelberg at 9730 Wilshire Boulevard, who also was very present in her life in the summer and winter of 1961. Dr. Greenson was visiting Marilyn almost every day – at $50 a visit – and trying to help her to break her sleeping pill habit just as Dr. Engelberg was writing prescriptions for even more drugs to get her to rest and sleep. No wonder she said she got confused. Dr. Greenson was fashionable – patients included Vivien Leigh, Tony Curtis and, revealingly, Frank Sinatra – and one of the original 'couch jockey' psychiatrists in post-war California. Psychoanalysis and Beverly Hills were perfect partners.

Dr. Greenson, born in Brooklyn, New York, on August 20, 1911, graduated from the University of Bern in Switzerland having worked with Wilhelm Stekel, an eccentric practitioner and known as the 'most distinguished' follower of Freud. Hypnotism was one of his treatments. Dr. Greenson also had success treating soldiers returning from war for post-traumatic stress. He employed the 'truth drug' sodium pentathol but, in many cases, it wasn't a cure but a haphazard relief of the symptoms. Nevertheless, he was regarded as a pioneer in these in-vogue treatments and lauded in Hollywood as a status symbol – 'You *must* see Dr. Greenson.' He and his wife Hildi lived in a Spanish-style home in Santa Monica, near to Marilyn who was living in the antiseptic Doheny apartments at 882 North Doheny Drive at the west end of the Sunset Strip [Sinatra's business associate Harry Ziegler was the manager of the building which was renowned for running on 'hot and cold blondes' and also 'love nests for love rats']. From now, Dr. Greenson, his wife and their hospitality were never more than a short phone call or drive away. It became convenient for many people and reasons.

Because, or possibly in spite of, Sinatra, Marilyn became more and more friendly with Pat Lawford the increasingly impatient wife of Peter Lawford. Pat Lawford would invite Marilyn out to the beach for the weekend and it would be relaxing. One midweek party at the beach house, monitored by OCID in October 1961, had Marilyn and Bobby Kennedy among the guests. The Attorney General had been to a meeting in San Francisco and had flown down privately to spend time with his sister and friends. One of Bobby Kennedy's aides said that around that time there had been 'several parties' at the beach at which Marilyn and Bobby had been together and danced. One report, not in the OCID files, said they were spotted dancing intimately at a political fundraiser at the Beverly Wilshire Hotel in Beverly Hills. This was comparatively sedate behaviour.

If Peter Lawford issued an invitation to a party it often meant his wife was back East at the Kennedy family home at Hyannis Port. He arranged what he called 'party time' with strings of girls, often prostitutes, available for any sort of fun. Marilyn felt affronted to be invited but she usually turned up, often leaving if the sexual activity got too hot. Author Lois Banner [*Marilyn: The Passion and the Paradox*, 2012] quotes Sinatra's butler, George Jacobs, saying his boss called the Lawfords' beach house 'Hi-anus-port'. She reported that Bobby and John Kennedy were known 'gropers' around the party girls in the later part of 1961. The Kennedy Brothers were now the President and the Attorney General of the United States.

Chief Parker was discomforted when he read the OCID reports and the transcripts from the Fred Otash recordings. He also knew he was not the only one seeing the information from Otash – affectionately known as 'Mr. O' to the clients he didn't rip off. In the third week of November 1961, the OCID files are not clear on the exact date, President Kennedy attended a fundraising dinner in Los Angeles. He spent the night at the Lawfords' beach house. Marilyn was there. Otash reported: 'Yes, we did have [Lawford's house] wired. Yes, I did hear a tape of Jack Kennedy fucking Monroe. But I don't want to get into the moans and groans of their relationship. They were having a sexual relationship, period.' This wasn't information America was ready for. No matter how brazen they had been before, Kennedy was President now and this didn't fit his clean-cut, all-American-boy White House image. It was avoided rather than denied as much as there are those who do not want to accept that Rock Hudson was gay.

It was Fred Otash, a nightcrawler in Hollywood moving about the city in a Cadillac with a driver, who first got the revelations about Hudson into the OCID files. He wasn't quite the knight errant Hollywood private eye of Raymond Chandler's world. He smoked four packs of unfiltered Camel cigarettes and got through most of a quart of imported Scotch most days. So he enjoyed the accoutrements to fit the fictional image but struggled with the upright morality of doing the right thing. Mike Rothmiller liked him and regarded Otash as a rascal but a very useful one. He became one of his useful informants during his time with OCID. A Hollywood vice cop turned freelance 'eyes and ears for the stars' he was a towering man, a proud 6 feet 2 inches tall, a muscled 220 pounds and with a charisma; he was screenwriter Robert Towne's inspiration for Jack Nicholson's detective Jake Gittes in *Chinatown* [1974]. He died at his West Hollywood apartment on October 5, 1992, and the thing that would have most surprised him in his life was that it ended from natural causes. After his death, a transcript was found amongst his files of a 1958 confrontation between Rock Hudson and his then-wife Phyllis Gates, about Hudson's closeted homosexuality. Otash knew where Judy Garland kept her drugs and had evidence of James Dean shoplifting. His reports confirmed John and Bobby Kennedy both had a sexual relationship with Marilyn. If there

*Picture Credit: Silver Screen Collection/Hulton Archive via Getty Images*

An early and rare tranquil day with her mother Gladys for the three-year-old California girl Norma Jeane Baker on the beach at Santa Monica, 1929.

*Picture Credit: Jill Brady/Portland Press Herald via Getty Images*

The wedding day smiles of just turned sixteen-year-old Norma Jeane and James Dougherty, 21, on June 19, 1942, vanished quickly and the marriage ended in 1944.

Dynasty — The Kennedy Clan present and correct at the April 23, 1954,
New York wedding of Peter Lawford to JFK's younger sister Patricia.
L-R: JFK, Jean Kennedy, the bride, patriarch Joseph Kennedy Senior, Robert Kennedy.

Hollywood, 1956: Kennedy protector
LAPD Chief 'Whisky Bill' Parker and
*Dragnet* creator and star Jack Webb
famous for asking: 'Just the facts ma'am.'

Mike Rothmiller's OCID boss
and LAPD Chief [1978-1992]
Daryl Gates who led dubious
investigations into the death of
Marilyn Monroe and the inquiry
into the assassination of RF.

*Picture Credit: Bettmann via Getty Images*

Brothers-in-law and partners in crime, Peter Lawford and RFK at the 'Happy Birthday, Mr President' celebration for President Kennedy on May 19, 1962, ten days before his 45th birthday proper.

*Picture Credit: Cecil Stoughton/The LIFE Images Collection via Getty Images*

Bobby Kennedy, Marilyn Monroe in her Jean Louis dress, and President Kennedy share difficult conversations at the Madison Square Garden birthday after-party.

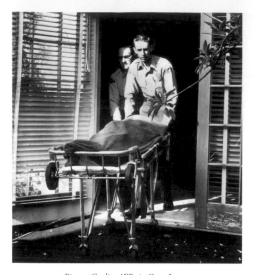

The cover-up conspiracy was already in place as Marilyn Monroe's body was taken from her bedroom at Cursum Perficio on Sunday, August 5, 1962.

The man who knew the secrets: Mike Rothmiller's police informant, former LAPD cop, CIA and FBI contact, wiretap specialist, and Hollywood private eye, Fred Otash.

As the world heard of the death of Marilyn Monroe on August 5, a panicked Peter Lawford telephoned his brother-in-law, the President, at the White House.

Mike Rothmiller's notes from Marilyn's diary secretly held within the labyrinth of the OCID coded filing system.

*Picture Credit: Mike Rothmiller Collection*

In these astonishing diary notes, Marilyn compares the merits of her two lovers, the President of the United States and his brother, the US Attorney General.

*Picture Credit: Mike Rothmiller Collection*

Marilyn, in these notes from her diary, bemoans the selfish sexual demands of the President of the United States.

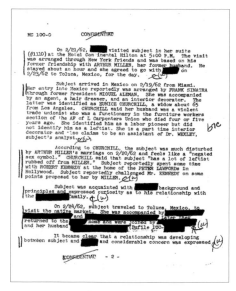

*Picture Credit: Mike Rothmiller Collection*

Marilyn was under constant FBI surveillance and was watched on her shopping trip to Mexico to buy furniture for the Spanish-style Cursum Perficio.

PERFORMANCE EVALUATION REPORT

| SEMI-ANNUAL | TRANSFER | SPECIAL | PROBATION/PROMOTION | SEPARATION |

NOTE: Supervisors completing this report shall refer to the Performance Evaluation Report Guidelines For Supervisors, Form 1.78.2.

| NAME - FIRST, MIDDLE | | SERIAL NO. | CLASSIFICATION | GRADE | DIVISION, AREA OR BUREAU |
| JTHMILLER, M. | | | Det. | I | O.C.I.D. |
| DUTY ASSIGNMENT (E.G., SENIOR DET) | JOB CODE | PERIOD COVERED | FROM: | | TO: |
| Field Investigator | 071C | 6 MONTHS | 11-1-81 | | 4-30-82 |

CHECK-BOX EVALUATION SECTION (Items 1 and 2). The below categories of employee performance consist of various sub-factors (e.g., Initiative). The employee should be evaluated in each of these sub-factors as follows:

Strong [+]    Competent [ ]    Needs Improvement [-]    Draw line through sub-factors not observed, e.g., PLANNING SKILLS

In making the evaluations of each category listed below, supervisors are to evaluate the employee's performance at or in the assignments during the preceding six month period, and compare that performance to that of other employees in the same class and in similar assignments.

1. DUTY PERFORMANCE (ALL EMPLOYEES)

| | | | | | | | | | UNSATISFACTORY PERFORMANCE | SATISFACTORY PERFORMANCE | PROFICIENT PERFORMANCE |
| | | | | | [+] INITIATIVE | | [+] TEAMWORK | | [ ] | | [X] |
| [+] RESPONSIVENESS TO INSTRUCTION | [+] PHYSICAL FITNESS | | ORAL EXPRESSION | [+] WORK QUALITY | | [+] ABILITY TO ORGANIZE | | | | |
| [+] JUDGMENT AND COMMON SENSE | [+] USE OF AVAILABLE RESOURCES | [+] RELIABILITY | | [+] PRODUCTIVITY | | [+] CARE AND USE OF DEPT. EQUIPMENT | | | | |
| [+] QUALITY OF PUBLIC CONTACTS | [+] THOROUGHNESS | [+] SAFETY SKILLS | | [ ] COMMUNICATION SKILLS | | [+] DRESS & GROOMING | | | | |

2. LEADERSHIP CAPABILITIES (ALL EMPLOYEES)

| | | | | [+] ADAPTABILITY | | [+] EFFECT ON MORALE | | [ ] | | [X] |
| [+] ACCEPTANCE OF RESPONSIBILITY | ADMINISTRATION OF DISCIPLINE/PRAISE | CONTACTS WITH SUBORDINATES | [+] DEMONSTRATION OF LOYALTY | | [+] PLANNING SKILLS | | | | |
| SUPERVISORY PERSONNEL ONLY: | | | | | | | | | | |
| [ ] EFFECTIVENESS OF DELEGATION | TRAINING OF SUBORDINATES | DNA EVALUATION OF SUBORDINATES | COMMITMENT TO AFFIRMATIVE ACTION GOALS | | | | | | |

NARRATIVE EVALUATION (This section is to be used to record specific and personal characteristics of this employee, which are not adequately covered in the check-box sections above. Any incident or circumstance causing a weak evaluation in any of the sub-factors in section 1 or 2 above must be described in this section.)

Det. Rothmiller's performance during this rating period has continued to be outstanding.

Rothmiller is thoroughly familiar with the policies and procedures of OCID and always conducts his investigations in a totally professional manner. Rothmiller is one of the most innovative detectives in OCID. He uses all the tried and proven methods of gaining intelligence information, plus he has implemented several new techniques which have been successful and highly informative. He has established international sources that will not only serve OCID, but other agencies as well.

Rothmiller and his partner are currently involved in several investigations that have international impact. An average detective would be staggered by the enormity of the investigations; however, Rothmiller and his partner have demonstrated they are capable of handling these sensitive investigations.

Rothmiller has established outstanding rapport with law enforcement throughout the country. He is held in high esteem for the quality of his work and the confidentiality with which he treats all the information he receives.

Rothmiller maintains himself in outstanding physical condition through a program of running and weight lifting. His personal appearance is always outstanding and he makes a favorable ... ... goals he meets.

Rothmiller is an asset to both OCID and the Department. With his background as a detective and field supervisor he is more than qualified for promotion to Detective II.

How can this employee best improve his/her performance?

Rothmiller has demonstrated his support of and compliance with Department policies and procedures. He should strive to ensure that his expressed opinions reflect an equally positive image.

APR 29 1982

*Picture Credit: Mike Rothmiller Collection*

Mike Rothmiller's glowing report card on his talents as a LAPD investigator.

*Picture Credit: Mike Rothmiller Collection*

President Bill Clinton thanks Mike Rothmiller after a briefing meeting in Houston. Texas, in 2000.

UNITED STATES DEPARTMENT OF JUSTICE
FEDERAL BUREAU OF INVESTIGATION

March 13, 1967

Re: Bernard B. Spindel

telephonically supplied the following information:

received a telephone call from an individual

maintained that because of antagonism between the FBI and Spindel, the FBI would probably not allow Spindel

said that Hogan, the District Attorney in New York, and the FBI have "bugged" Spindel's telephone line.

He also said that Senator Bobby Kennedy was present at the time Marilyn Monroe died and wanted to "get" Bobby Kennedy off his back could do so by listening to the various recordings and evidence concerning Bobby Kennedy's presence there at the time.

90 6 JUN 15 1972

92 8095-50

*Picture Credit: Mike Rothmiller Collection*

Hidden FBI and OCID files on Marilyn/Kennedy contain documents which say RFK was present when Marilyn died and there were wiretaps to prove it.

The ever present and dogmatic housekeeper/nurse Eunice Murray who finally admitted Bobby Kennedy was at Cursum Perficio the day Marilyn Monroe died.

Scapegoat psychiatrist Dr. Ralph Greenson and Marilyn's Dr Feelgood who, with his access to a pharmacy of drugs, has featured in all conspiracy theories.

Make-up man Whitey Snyder said Marilyn had 'always been afraid of death – or rather what happened after' and asked him to look after her body. She gave him this gold money clip inscribed: 'While I'm still warm, Marilyn.

was one person who knew almost all of Hollywood's secrets and possessed the knowledge, photographs and covertly recorded conversations from the telephone wiretaps and bugs he planted in homes and offices, it was Otash. A red filing cabinet vanished from Otash's apartment after his death.

Mike Rothmiller got to know Otash well as they worked together:'Fred was a fascinating man who was a master at earning a legal buck while also cautiously dabbling in the criminal world when it suited his needs. In 1959, he was convicted of conspiracy to dope a horse at Santa Anita racetrack. He knew too much. Behind the scenes, strings were pulled and the felony conviction was downgraded to a misdemeanour and, later, quietly expunged from his record. He served no time and got no fine. During his early years on the LAPD, he was a highly trusted and very proficient ass-kicker for the police department. Years later he was interviewed by Mike Wallace [the late CBS *60 Minutes* host] who introduced him as Hollywood's premier and the nation's highest-paid private detective. Fred's name carried weight with the entertainment industry movers and shakers. And, of course, with many of the country's unsavoury characters and politicians.

'Born into near poverty in 1922, he grew up in Methuen, Massachusetts. His mother was Syrian, and he inherited her dark wavy hair and olive complexion. At the time, Methuen was nearly 100 per cent Caucasian. As a result Fred, whose physical appearance was a little different from the other kids in his neighbourhood, became the subject of teasing and ridicule. Fortunately, being a big kid in a seedy area was a blessing to Fred. He had no choice but to learn the fine art of self-defence at an early age. He didn't bother with any form of martial art; he opted to be a real street fighter. 'He told me, "I learned to fight as a kid. Hit first, hit hard and kick the shit out of 'em." We were at Nate & Al's Deli restaurant in Beverly Hills. He grinned at me and took a sip of water before holding up a beefy clenched fist to emphasise the point. "And I didn't worry about kicking them when they were down. I just finished it. I always did. As a kid, as a Marine, as a cop, I always finished it."

'As Fred told it, he never lost a fight, and his fighting successes eventually earned his expulsion from high school. Not only did he need to win his fights, but he also had more significant dreams he needed to accomplish. Dreams of escaping poverty and making money. As a teen, he didn't know which path that would take, but he vowed to make it happen, with or without his fists. Eventually, he left home for a stint in the US Marine Corps. After his discharge, standing tall and strong, he was an ideal candidate for the Los Angeles Police Department. In those days, big ass-kickers were thought to be perfect cops, and, in many ways, they were.

'As an OCID detective and before meeting him, I read the extensive intelligence dossier LAPD maintained on Fred and his cronies. I immediately understood his potential value as an informant – on the surface, he appeared to be a living and breathing encyclopaedia with decades of secret, insider knowledge spanning Hollywood's scandals, crime and corrupt politicians of all stripes.

'His Hollywood clients list outlined within his OCID dossier was impressive: Bette Davis, Richard Nixon, Judy Garland, Errol Flynn, Peter Lawford, John and Robert Kennedy, Howard Hughes, Frank Sinatra and attorneys Melvin Belli, F. Lee Bailey, and many others. Scattered throughout his dossier was the secret work [primarily wiretapping] he performed for labor unions, the CIA, the FBI, OCID and high-profile Democratic and Republican politicians.

'Years earlier, Fred was hired by Peter Lawford to investigate a few of Lawford's business associates, and, with Lawford's approval, he bugged a few rooms in Lawford's beach house. Kept secret from Lawford's wife Pat, the bugging was done so Lawford could excuse himself from a meeting, go to another room and secretly listen to the conversation happening in his absence. It's an old tried and true business and government tactic. However – being Fred – he and his crew also secretly bugged the bedrooms and wiretapped Lawford's telephone so Otash could eavesdrop on Lawford and his guests at will. You must admire Fred's cunning business acumen for seeing the potential value in secretly installing his personal bugs and wiretap on Lawford's dime.

'Scores of movie stars, Hollywood's movers and shakers, and of course the Kennedys, all spent time at Lawford's beach house where they engaged in potentially embarrassing or even criminal activities. The knowledge of this was something that Fred could easily convert into large sums of cash. Fred understood very well that extortion of the rich and famous could be exceedingly profitable. But it could be exceedingly dangerous.

'When I pressed him on some sensitive details and relationships, Fred began to experience selective memory lapses. I asked how it came about that Teamsters' president Jimmy Hoffa also started paying him for his intelligence-gathering efforts aimed at John and Robert Kennedy during their visits to Peter Lawford's and eventually Marilyn's homes. He offered a convoluted, vague answer. He told me that one of his many questionable associates from Detroit contacted him and indicated the Teamsters Union wanted to retain his services for a West Coast investigation. He agreed and shortly after he received a sizeable cash retainer. He was placed in contact with an associate of Jimmy Hoffa who identified the targets and what type of information was desired. Hoffa was looking for the same information on the Kennedys which interested the OCID, the CIA and the FBI. Hoffa wanted embarrassing, career-ending blackmail material. In his roundabout way, he said that at first he hesitated when he learned the names of the targets –the Kennedys and Monroe – then he considered the amount of money being offered and reasoned since he had already installed bugs and a wiretap in Lawford's home, why not? I asked him how he came to be in the pay of the CIA and on this, he suffered a complete memory loss, but admitted that he believed his CIA contact worked with an OCID detective.

'OCID and the CIA working together was not unusual. During my tenure within OCID, I and many others had contact with CIA officers and agents. There were a few OCID detectives who were – for want of a better term – paid, part-time CIA operatives. Their work was supposedly secret, but nearly everyone in our unit knew about it. One senior OCID detective whom I considered a decent man, Lee Goforth, just happened to be a brigadier general in the army reserve. He told me: "I'm assigned to army intelligence. As a cop, I can legally do things the military and the Feds can't."

'From what I already knew, and later learned, I was able to fill in many of the blanks. It seems that Fred informed his OCID contact of Hoffa's request. OCID agreed not to interfere if Fred shared the information with them. OCID then brought the CIA into the circle who also agreed to pay for Fred's services. From OCID documents it appears Fred later contacted the FBI, knowing that J. Edgar Hoover would pay handsomely for the Kennedy information and safeguard him from any potential prosecution. The FBI did retain him and apparently paid Fred well. It was a bizarre tale, yet seemingly correct. It was Fred wheeling and dealing at his best. Just about everyone understood what he was doing, and if the information continued, he would be protected and paid.

'Fred confirmed his bugs and wiretaps at Lawford's home were in place for some time before Marilyn's death.

Installing the bugs and a wiretap in her home was very simple. Two telephone company technicians on his payroll disabled her telephone when she was out of town. The techs went to the house shortly afterward and informed the caretaker they were there to repair the phone. It was a natural and convincing cover. They spent several hours in the house installing bugs and wiretapping her telephone. It was a perfect operation. Marilyn never suspected a thing. It was then a simple matter of recording conversations, making copies and delivering the information to receive payment. Just hours after his men finished wiring Marilyn's home the telephone calls of her housekeeper were being intercepted. Fred could not recall the date that the first call between President Kennedy and Marilyn was intercepted and to the best of my memory this was not recorded in the OCID files. However the records do show that it was a call from Peter Lawford's home to Marilyn's home. Peter placed the call and briefly spoke with Marilyn before turning the telephone over to John F. Kennedy who was Lawford's house guest.

'After that initial recording, Fred said that his fee was no longer in question. The CIA, FBI and OCID paid him large sums of cash on request. Everyone was receiving what they wanted, except Jimmy Hoffa.

'Fred intentionally withheld most of the information from Hoffa. He knew the intelligence people would pay just as well plus they could provide protection. Also, he considered Hoffa a hothead who would have thrown him under the bus to destroy the Kennedys. Otash chose wisely.

'Otash recalled providing OCID and the other intelligence people with recordings of conversations involving either John or Robert Kennedy or conversations that mentioned the Kennedys. I had no way of verifying or disputing this claim. However, it would have been wise for him to include recordings of non-Kennedy related discussions to reassure the agencies that he was not withholding information.

'It was all a business for Fred. He did what he did for the money. If you paid him, he did what was requested. Whether it was listening in on the President or the Attorney General or monitoring starlets for Howard Hughes, it was all business. Yet, Otash understood that he could know *too* much.'

As it turned out, knowing *so much* and working for such an eclectic collection of acronyms and the firecracker boss of the Teamsters Union [ranked by Attorney General Bobby Kennedy 'as the most powerful institution in the United States other than the US Government'] kept Fred Otash safe, he knew too much about all of them and alluded to stashed evidence, in the increasingly more complex circumstances. Not everyone was so lucky as the second year of the Kennedy presidency loomed.

# IX: Big Brother

*'The Party told you to reject the evidence of your eyes and ears. It was their final, most essential command.'*
—*1984*, George Orwell, 1949.

It had been a constructive year for Chief William Parker of the LAPD. The political endorsement of his position and status as America's greatest lawman, and the enormity of his power, had justified not just his faith in himself and his inner circle but in his intelligence files.

Long before the movies coined 'keep your enemies close', the chief was doing just that. At the end of 1961, he had conquered efforts to discredit him by J. Edgar Hoover and a local political movement to have him removed as chief. The FBI director regarded the chief like an unflushed lavatory. He had been angered when Bobby Kennedy had called for a national crime commission [in his book *The Enemy Within: The McClellan Committee's Crusade Against Jimmy Hoffa and Corrupt Labor Unions*, 1960] but was way past furious when he learned that Chief Parker had given 'his personal friend Bobby Kennedy' the proposal. Hoover said it 'affronted his authority'.

Tom Reddin, LAPD Chief from 1968 to 1969, told Mike Rothmiller that when Robert Kennedy was Attorney General, he referred to Chief Parker 'as the greatest chief in the world'. Some Kennedy aides were concerned that Bobby Kennedy was 'infatuated with Chief Parker'. Historian Dr. Ed Schmitt echoed Tom Reddin writing: '[Bobby] Kennedy considers Parker the best police chief in the nation.' There was a mutual admiration, and the relationship was so good, a malleable ménage, that Bobby Kennedy consulted Parker and his drinks 'buddy' Captain Hamilton about counter-insurgency tactics in Latin America and particularly action in Cuba to effectively deal with Castro. [The Los Angeles Police Commission minutes from August 8, 1962, reveal that two LAPD OCID officers, Sergeant Jesus Mejia and Officer Hector Guevara, were recruited for the US Department of State's Agency for International Development and 'trained Latin American police forces to infiltrate leftist groups and prevent additional Communist revolutions in the region after Fidel Castro overthrew Juan Batista in 1959.']

The Kennedys may have loved Chief Parker but the black voters of Los Angeles, a growingly influential demographic, were far from enamoured. There were regular charges of police brutality made against the LAPD. Mayor Norris Poulson was nominally in charge of the police department, and therefore Chief Parker's actions. He was up for re-election and he was vulnerable. His opponent, Sam Yorty, saw an opportunity. Yorty had an eccentric political career behind him, being a tough anti-Communist and a Democrat who had supported Richard Nixon over JFK. In 1961, he was at a little bit of a loose end and ran against Poulson for the mayoralty. He was mocked for promising better local services like regular garbage collections and 'Trashcan Sam' became his moniker. He performed well on television though which was beginning to mean more than anything else. You could promise the world but if you couldn't do it effectively on television it wasn't a promise. Yorty's campaign was also given a huge boost by television anchorman George Putnam [the template for Ted Baxter on *The Mary Tyler Moore Show*]. Putnam was his on-air champion and allowed him to appear on his show night after night to make his pitch to voters. Yorty's campaign included targeted sniping at the LAPD. First, it was the Police Commission and not the chief but, as voter support grew so did the word that Yorty would kick out Chief Parker to appease his black constituency.

As he campaigned, Sam Yorty made it even clearer that a vote for him meant the end of Chief Parker at the LAPD. That was the deal, return him as Mayor and as he went into City Hall the Chief would be leaving. Norris Poulson countered on a law-and-order ticket while the chief did what he did best, gathered more information on Yorty. OCID files show he was followed and under surveillance by intelligence officers, even on public holidays like Memorial Day, May 30, 1961. That day a black teenager tried to sneak onto a merry-go-round at a fairground at Griffith Park and got into a fight with the attendant. The police arrived and it swiftly turned into a riot in which four cops were injured and several dozen black demonstrators were beaten and hurt. The next day, election day, with the riot splashed across the newspapers, the city went to vote, and the black community of south Los Angeles helped Sam Yorty to victory by 16,000 votes.

Well, they said, that was goodbye to Chief Parker. He'd had a good run. Lucky, really. The Kennedys would surely find something in Washington for him. Sam Yorty strongly suggested this would be the case at his first press conference as mayor of Los Angeles: 'It's perfectly obvious the police department was used to check the history, from childhood to current date, of everybody even remotely connected with my campaign and even my law clients. Chief Parker had to be aware of such activities. I will investigate these illegal activities in the department.'

'High noon' at city hall was heavily monitored by the press with the first private encounter between Mayor Yorty and Chief Parker following the election. Chief Parker was filmed going into the conference with a sombre look on his face and weighed down by a huge, bulging briefcase in one hand. The meeting went on for more than an hour.

When the two men emerged, they both appeared to have taken happy pills. They smiled and spoke positively to the reporters. Mayor Yorty had the 'utmost trust' in Chief Parker who would stay on as 'the best cop in America' with the mayor's 'total support'. At the meeting, Chief Parker had shown the new mayor the file that OCID held on him which had been expanding since 1938 when Sam Yorty was flagged as 'a radical liberal'. They had arrived at an arrangement. Chief Parker was going nowhere.

Marilyn Monroe's intimate arrangement with the Kennedys was more crowded because there were three people in it. Pat Lawford, a prime witness to much of it, didn't seem troubled but she had spent a lifetime watching her brothers chase girls and she had often assisted in finding, what she euphemistically called, 'dates' for them. Peter Lawford had his own excessive needs for drink and drugs and sex, but was nevertheless rather disquieted by events. It was nothing a couple of glasses of something couldn't dismiss from his mind though. They were part of the elaborate and high-profile cast of a national soap opera. Marilyn's role was as the gift-wrapped bundle in a game of pass the parcel by the men who surrounded her. Although, clearly, with hindsight, she was an abused victim.

Whether Dr. Ralph Greenson or any of his colleagues would have agreed is not known, but it appears that Marilyn was constantly grasping for a real chance at love. She didn't appear to be able to hold on to any physical or spiritual intimacy for very long. She lived her emotional life through others and wanted to hide herself in them. She doesn't seem to have been able to live as her authentic self. She needed a host. If she was rejected, the intensity of her reactions was erratic. She would alternately seek solace or vengeance.

Dr. Greenson and Dr. Hyman Engelberg balanced her between them with psychoanalysis and hypodermic injections [priced at $4, $6, $10 and $20 dollars]. Later more pragmatic arrangements were made, and Dr. Greenson arranged for Mrs. Eunice Murray to become Marilyn's housekeeper [it emerged years later that she was a qualified psychiatric nurse]. Murray would keep the apartment tidy and drive Marilyn to her appointments which now included meetings at 20th Century Fox where she was under contract to star in *Something's Got To Give*. Mrs. Murray kept her own apartment at 933 Ocean Boulevard in Santa Monica and rarely stayed overnight at the Doheny Drive apartment or at Cursum Perficio in Brentwood which Marilyn bought in February 1962, for $75,500. [The one-storey, Hacienda-style home comprising of four bedrooms and three bathrooms sold for $7.25 million in 2017.] She paid half in cash with the help of money from Joe DiMaggio [paid back after the probate of her estate] and took out a mortgage for the balance.

It was exciting – the first home she owned outright. It was L-shaped and the rooms were small but it had strong iron grills on the windows and felt solid and safe. Dr. Greenson was even closer now and his friend, the psychoanalyst Hanna Fenichel, was a neighbour at 12404 Third Helena Drive.

Of course, Peter Lawford was close too. He'd become an American citizen in time to vote for his brother-in-law as President – and he was still happy to help in any way he could. One way was to tempt the British actress Shirley Anne Field into the arms of President Kennedy. Shirley Anne Field was a young, emerging actress, who had co-starred with Albert Finney in *Saturday Night and Sunday Morning* [1960], with Laurence Olivier in *The Entertainer* [1960], and with Steve McQueen and Robert Wagner [a former boyfriend of Judith Campbell Exner] in *The War Lover* [1962]. She was publicising *The War Lover* with an appearance on the Johnny Carson Show in New York. With her were Zsa Zsa Gabor and Jimmy Durante. After the show she was told there had been a call from the White House asking about her. She thought it was a joke, her friend Dudley Moore, who was also in New York, was playing a prank. It wasn't a joke, as she found out a couple of weeks later when she had moved across America to Los Angeles.

She had been taking afternoon tea with Charles Feldman, Peter Lawford's agent who had hosted the party where JFK first met Marilyn Monroe. In interviews with the author in 2018 she said that a day or so afterwards: 'I received a call from Peter Lawford, and he invited me to a party he was having at his beach home. He told me his party would be the one I'd always remember. "Be sure to come," he said, "because someone very special would be there." That was all he said. Other than that, this special person would be the most attractive person I could ever hope to meet. I knew it wasn't just another Hollywood party when I was searched – frisked – by two security men. After an hour, and quite suddenly without any fanfare, President Kennedy was there. He walked over to me with two Marine guards on either side of him. He asked them to leave, and we talked. He said I was a difficult person to meet and I remembered the call after the Carson show. Oh, yes, he was chatting me up. That's why I was there, I'd experienced enough of that to know what was happening. Of course, I was flattered. With him close up he had a certain presence and he was very attractive and dynamic. I was a young girl and in awe.

'He leaned over as he was speaking and his head was only inches from my face. He said it was more comfortable for him to stand like that as he had a bad back from a war injury. He had to go, he said, but asked me to be a guest at a lunch party soon.

'On cue, the next day Peter Lawford called me and said I'd been a big hit with the President. There was going to be a big party the following month and he wanted me to be there and said the President would be. I was staying with a lawyer friend of my business manager in Malibu and he wasn't keen on me going to any Peter Lawford yacht parties with President Kennedy or anyone else: "You'd better take yourself seriously as an actress or you'll get a reputation as a party girl around town." I respected his advice.'

Shirley Anne Field went to an interview for a role in a movie. Marilyn went to the party. She should have been working at 20th Century Fox on *Something's Got To Give*. That movie project was cursed. Marilyn didn't want to do it but contractually it was important. She was being 'managed' now by Mickey Rudin, a short, aggressive man who spoke to people like he was controlling a wolf hound. Only he barked. Rudin prided himself on being Sinatra's mouthpiece and was a clever lawyer, nicer than he looked. His advice to Marilyn was legally sound, but she was also being 'guided' by Dr. Ralph Greenson and being injected with feel-good drugs by Dr. Hyman Engelberg.

*Something's Got To Give* should have been a feel-good movie both to watch and to make. A remake of *My Favourite Wife* [1940], the original had glided along with Cary Grant and Irene Dunne as a couple caught in a marital frippery involving a presumed dead wife and a remarried husband. Marilyn hadn't made a movie in more than a year. She had lost weight, so much time was set aside for wardrobe tests along with the rest of pre-production. The movie was to start filming proper on April 9, 1962, and Marilyn agreed with producer Henry Weinstein that she'd have time off to appear at President Kennedy's birthday gala on May 19 at Madison Square Garden.

She saw Bobby Kennedy long before that. On February 1, 1962, Peter and Pat Lawford hosted a dinner party for the Attorney General and his wife Eunice who were flying out from Los Angeles to begin a tour of the Far East. It's reported in files that at that party – Lawford's home was wired throughout – Marilyn asked Bobby Kennedy when he was going to fire J. Edgar Hoover. Bobby weaved an answer about it not being politically expedient at that time. There was much competition for his attention at the party. Natalie Wood sat nearby, but almost all his time was spent talking with Marilyn.

After the Kennedys left on their goodwill tour, Marilyn was due to arrive at the Fox studios to prepare for principal photography to begin. Before that, she had time to take a trip to Mexico, escorted by Mrs. Murray and Pat Newcomb who had taken on a role of minder as much as public relations adviser. Tequila, sunshine and the pushy gigolo charms of screenwriter José Bolaños ushered her into his arms as a distraction from shopping for furniture for her new home. It has been suggested that Bolaños was a CIA honeytrap but if that was so, it has been redacted in his CIA files. FBI files show the agency knew all about the brief affair, along with her meetings with supposed Communist sympathisers: something *for* the files, for you never knew when you might need something *from* the files. A freedom of information report has revealed that Mrs. Murray was the FBI asset forwarding information to J. Edgar Hoover.

Marilyn returned to California with Mrs. Murray, Pat Newcomb and José Bolaños. Joe DiMaggio had been keeping an eye on her welfare and was, as always, suspicious of new men in his ex-wife's life. He didn't like José Bolaños. Marilyn did and took him as her escort when she collected her Golden Globe award at the Beverly Hilton Hotel on March 5, 1962. With some encouragement from DiMaggio, [he was noted by OCID at Los Angeles International airport with him] José Bolaños returned to Mexico the next day.

So many people were telling Marilyn what was good for her. And who wasn't. Dr. Greenson tried to warn her away from Frank Sinatra but did not caution on the dangers of sleeping with the President *and* Attorney General of the United States. When the subject did come up in their psychiatric sessions, which Dr. Greenson taped, she says:

'Marilyn Monroe is a soldier. Her commander in chief is the greatest and most powerful man in the world. The first duty of a soldier is to obey her commander in chief. He says do this, you do it. He says do that, you do it. This man is going to change our country... It's like the Navy – the President is the captain and Bobby is his executive officer. Bobby would do absolutely anything for his brother and so would I. I will never embarrass him. As long as I have memory, I have John Fitzgerald Kennedy.'

This recording of Greenson's has Marilyn speaking in a stream of consciousness, but contains nothing disastrously harmful to the Kennedys. Yet, Marilyn, and it could have been so painfully obvious in the beginning, was going to be the ultimate collateral damage in terms of saving the Kennedy dynasty and legacy. Peter Lawford would also be critically wounded along with so many, many others by events. Mostly all caused by greed and egos and, to use that most efficient of British phrases, people being arses.

Sinatra, once again, was the biggest. And he was central to the mess that was being created. Peter Lawford was his conduit to the Kennedy White House but Lawford often irritated Sinatra with his British demeanour. He, Dean Martin and others were content to buy their mohair suits at Sy Devore's [Hollywood and Palm Springs] but Lawford insisted on Doug Hayward [Mount Street, London] making his suits. Sinatra kept Lawford around like a pedigree dog to elevate the mongrels yapping around him. Their friendship ended when Lawford didn't deliver President Kennedy to Sinatra's Palm Springs doorstep during a visit to California in March 1962. It was tumultuous, like a volcano going off, and following this the Kennedys dropped Sinatra out of their lives and future.

For decades, it was accepted that Bobby Kennedy cancelled his brother's stay in 1962 with Sinatra because of the entertainer's gangland connections. In 2018, the investigative and revisionist author Lee Server offered a different and convincing scenario in his biography of Johnny Rosselli [*Handsome Johnny: The Criminal Life of Johnny Rosselli, The Mob's Man in Hollywood*, Virgin Books,

2018]. Server, the author of distinguished biographies of Robert Mitchum and Ava Gardner [a one-time Mrs. Sinatra], questioned why, suddenly, the Kennedys would react so vehemently to Sinatra being friendly with Mob figures. It wasn't exactly news; it was all over the FBI and the OCID files. Server got a revealing answer from a Washington police source. It explained much about the events that took place that March – events involving most of the people surrounding Marilyn Monroe. Attitudes and agendas were changing. There weren't just political reasons but personal reasons for cleaning house. Debauchery, like all acts, had consequences. Peter Lawford had got stuck in the middle. He was given the assignment of informing Sinatra that his 'good friend' the President would not be his guest for the weekend.

Unfortunately, Lawford had asked Sinatra if Kennedy could stay with him some weeks earlier and an excited Sinatra had gone to huge expense, nearly one million dollars, and trouble to create, effectively, a White House wing with helicopter pad for the President's stay. Of the affair Lawford is widely quoted as saying: 'It fell to me to break the news to Frank, and I was frankly scared. When I rang the President, I said that Frank expected him to stay at the Sinatra compound, and anything less than his presence there was going to be tough to explain. It had been kind of a running joke with all of us in the family that Frank was building up his Palm Springs house for just such a trip by the President, adding cottages for Jack and the Secret Service, putting in 25 extra phone lines, installing enough cable to accommodate teletype facilities, plus a switchboard and building a heliport. He even erected a flagpole for the Presidential flag after he saw the one flying over the Kennedy compound in Hyannis Port. No one asked Frank to do any of this, but he really expected his place to be the President's Western White House.

'I made a few calls, but in the end it was [JFK's golfing partner] Chris Dunphy, a big Republican from Florida, who arranged everything at Bing Crosby's house for him. The Secret Service stayed next door at [Oscar-winning songwriter] Jimmy Van

Heusen's and Frank didn't speak to him for weeks over that one, but I was the one who really took the brunt of it. He felt that I was responsible for setting Jack up to stay at Bing's – Bing Crosby, of all people – the other singer and a Republican to boot. Well, Frank never forgave me. He cut me off like that – just like that.'

Sinatra didn't believe Lawford when he told him about the change of plan. He called Bobby Kennedy in Washington but got a chilled response. He attacked what he could. Lawford reported: 'Frank was livid. He called Bobby every name in the book, and then rang me up and reamed me out again. He was quite unreasonable – irrational, really. George Jacobs [Sinatra's butler] told me later that when he got off the phone, 'he went outside with a sledgehammer and started chopping up the concrete landing pad of his heliport. He was in a frenzy.'

President Kennedy tried to defend his brother-in-law. He telephoned Sinatra and said it was a security issue and all to do with the Secret Service. It was useless. With two exceptions, Sinatra never spoke to Lawford again: 'He cut me out of all the movies we were set to make together – *Robin and the 7 Hoods* [1964], *4 for Texas* [1963] – and turned Dean [Martin] and Sammy [Davis Jr.] and Joey [Bishop] against me as well.' To make the message entirely clear, Sinatra cast Bing Crosby in Lawford's role in *Robin and the 7 Hoods*. Lawford's 'divorce' from Sinatra, for that's what it was, precipitated even more problems with his real marriage.

Pat Lawford has always appeared a passive player in the events approaching the death of Marilyn Monroe, but what's revealed in Lee Server's biography of Johnny Rosselli shows her as much more pivotal. He reports on the testimony, under oath, of Washington detective and CIA asset, Joe Shimon who had dealt with the FBI, Sam Giancana, Johnny Rosselli and eccentric tycoons. He was also an associate of former FBI agent and Howard Hughes assistant Robert Maheu.

Details have been redacted, but what is generally interpreted from FBI files is that J. Edgar Hoover met with Bobby Kennedy on March 22, 1962. It was also accepted that they discussed, among other matters, JFK's affairs with Judith Exner, Marilyn and specifically the 'highly evidentiary' logged calls from Judith Exner to President Kennedy at the White House. They also talked about Sam Giancana the mobster – with whom JFK shared Judith Exner as a lover – and the Attorney General's campaign against the American underworld. Sam Giancana had stayed overnight at Sinatra's home in Palm Springs – they were business partners with the Cal Neva – and it was this connection which has, for so long, been presumed to be the reason why President Kennedy snubbed Sinatra's hospitality. Yet, Lee Server revealed evidence from Joe Shimon that on that day, Hoover presented Bobby Kennedy with audio tape from Sam Giancana's bugged telephones. Together Hoover and Bobby Kennedy listened to an extract in which Sinatra admitted to Giancana that he was having an affair with Pat Lawford. But the affair was not about love or even sex. Server writes: 'He was fucking the sister, Sinatra told Giancana, to get her to use her influence on the brothers. Sinatra made it sound like quite a sacrifice. He vowed he would "sleep with this goddamn bitch until I get something going."'

Malaria would be more welcome than Sinatra in the Kennedys' world after that. Peter Lawford, although desperately trying to conjure up ways to reconnect with Sinatra, was still very much on side with the in-laws. On the morning of Saturday March 24, he was up with a large Smirnoff and orange juice before he drove over to Marilyn's new home at Fifth Helena Drive in his Lincoln Continental. He was collecting Marilyn to transport her to meet President Kennedy in Palm Springs using Air Force One. She had been to the hairdresser that morning and was wearing a dark jacket, pencil skirt, a dark wig, heavy framed spectacles and carrying what she thought was a secretarial kit, a notepad and pencils. She was a new Presidential secretary.

Air Force One delivered the President and his entourage to Palm Springs earlier that morning and had returned to Los Angeles [LAX] to collect Marilyn and Peter Lawford. Marilyn found out on the journey that she was staying at Bing Crosby's estate and not at Frank Sinatra's. She was given a guest cottage on the Crosby estate in Thunderbird Heights, a private community in Rancho Mirage, the Springs' upmarket neighbour.

Among the White House staff was Mimi Beardsley an intern and regular lover of the President. She later became known as 'JFK's Monica' [Lewinsky] after she gave details of her affair in a book [*Once Upon a Secret*, Hutchinson Radius, 2011] after the long-running relationship was revealed following more than four decades of secrecy. Under her married name, Mimi Alford, she described in her memoir being told by the President to perform oral sex on one of his aides while he watched. He also asked her to 'take care' of his younger brother Ted, which she refused to do.

In the book she makes pertinent observations about the atmosphere and situation that weekend in Palm Springs. She was not there to have sex with the President. That weekend, that was Marilyn's chore.

'We headed out to Bing Crosby's house in Palm Springs, where a large festive crowd – many from the entertainment industry – had gathered to greet President Kennedy. I felt like I'd been admitted into some wonderful, secret club,' she wrote. 'But then the evening turned into a nightmare. Crosby's house was a modern, sprawling single-story ranch in the desert, and the party was raucous. Compared to what I'd seen in Washington, this was another planet. There was a large group of people, a fast Hollywood crowd, hovering around the President, who was, as always, the center of attention. I was sitting next to him in the living room when a handful of yellow capsules – most likely amyl nitrite, commonly known then as poppers – was offered up by one of the guests. The President asked me if I wanted to try the drug, which stimulated the heart but also purportedly enhanced sex. I said no, but he just went ahead and popped the capsule and held it under my nose.

'The President, with all his ailments, was accustomed to taking many medications and was reported to rely on amphetamines for energy. But he didn't use the drug himself that evening: I was the guinea pig. Within minutes of inhaling the powder, my heart started racing and my hands began to tremble. This was a new sensation, and it frightened me. I panicked and ran crying from the room, praying that it would end soon, that I wasn't about to have a heart attack. Dave Powers [The President's appointments secretary], bless him, ran after me and escorted me to a quiet corner in the back of the house, where he sat with me for more than an hour until the effects of the drug wore off. I didn't spend that night with President Kennedy. He was staying in a suite, now known as the Kennedy Wing, with its own private entrance on one side of the Crosby property. Was he alone? I do not know. For the first and only time since I met him, I was relieved not to see him − and fell asleep in one of the guest rooms.'

Marilyn was wide awake in the guest cottage when, with the President lying in her bed, she called her friend the actor Ralph Roberts who, when he 'wasn't working', made a living as a masseur. He had treated Marilyn with massages in New York and had flown out the previous November to base himself in Los Angeles when she settled back home. Roberts explained in later interviews that Marilyn called him and said she was 'arguing with a friend' about the muscle system and put President Kennedy on the phone with him. 'I was listening to these familiar Boston tones. I told him about the muscles, and he thanked me. I didn't reveal I knew who he was, and he didn't say.' Several people have reported seeing the President and Marilyn as an intimate couple that weekend but many more kept quiet for there were plenty of people around and there was no concerted effort to conceal the arrangement. There never appeared to be much effort to disguise such foolhardy behaviour which, if made public, would have decimated the Presidency of the

Roman Catholic and married father. The Kennedy family at that time was regarded by so many as saintly. For the American youth and the nation's liberals, John Kennedy was something of a god. A contemporary newspaper report has one 26-year-old man saying: 'We were so relieved to have a young, good-looking person in the White House after Eisenhower.'

On November 30, 1997, Thomas Powers, a Pulitzer prize-winning author and intelligence expert published a review of Seymour Hersh's *The Dark Side of Camelot* in the *New York Times*. In it, he picked up on the outrageous nature of the stories of the sex parties and the flagrancy with which the Kennedys flirted with ruin. Now, it makes you wonder when they had time to govern. Powers writes that these stories 'make poignant a remark to Hersh by Jackie Kennedy's personal secretary, Mary Gallagher, that the First Lady sometimes asked her to call the President's secretary to inquire whether his schedule permitted [her] spending the evening with him. But the President did not simply have affairs, according to Hersh. Several Secret Service men assigned to guard the President told Hersh he had a taste for bimbos, girls brought in off the street by friends acting as procurers; that he liked cavorting naked with such women in the White House pool, that friends often joined him, and sometimes his brothers Bobby and Teddy as well. The high point – or low point – of Presidential partying, Hersh writes, came in December 1962 at the Palm Springs estate of the movie star and crooner Bing Crosby. Secret Service men described to Hersh a night of drunken debauchery when state policemen guarding the front of the house thought the wild cries coming from the pool might be an invasion of coyotes. The women were introduced as stewardesses from a European airline, but who they really were the Secret Service men had no idea. This single tableau, including much I have not described, manages to cast a pale and bilious light over everything that's wrong with politics, sex, California, swimming pools, drinking after dinner and all else that slips out of control once men feel they are invulnerable.'

At the party at the Crosby house in March, guests found Peter Lawford wandering around outside the Crosby compound, confused after taking a production line of cocaine and indulging in the amyl nitrite, and wondering if anyone knew where the party was. Some of the guests thought he was trying to walk to Frank Sinatra's home.

Lawford was staying at Bing Crosby's house although he knew that would not help his case with Sinatra. He had asked to stay with Jimmy Van Heusen next door, but was told by the Oscar-winning songwriter: 'I know who your brother-in-law is but he doesn't sing songs.' It is never, Peter Lawford finally learned, all about you.

Marilyn thought it was. Especially after her weekend of lovemaking with the President of the United States who put her in the care of his brother Bobby for a Democratic fundraising event in Beverly Hills the following Monday evening before he and his entourage flew back to Washington. She now referred to Bobby Kennedy as 'the General'. He was very much on parade with her at the Beverly Hilton Hotel function which was also attended by members of the OCID who noted Marilyn and Bobby dancing happily. At one point of this peculiar triangle was Marilyn Monroe, fearful of inherited madness, anxious for attention and about her age [she was turning 36 on June 1, 1962] and grasping for self-confidence. She couldn't help herself. She couldn't say no to the Kennedys. She couldn't deny herself the chance of being someone else. Yet, everyone wanted Marilyn Monroe, the ultimate arm candy.

# X: Bobby's Girl

*'Everyone wants to be Cary Grant. Even I want to be Cary Grant.'*
— Cary Grant, 1974.

It was a kind spring evening on May 19, 1962, at Madison Square Garden when Marilyn Monroe appeared in a moment of pure theatrical Viagra. She shrugged off her ermine wrap to reveal herself clad in a skin-tight, rhinestone-encrusted gown that made her look almost naked. The Jean Louis custom-made, flesh-coloured design had more than 2,500 hand-stitched crystals, and was so snug fitting that Marilyn Monroe was sewn into it. When she appeared, she wasn't the only one holding her breath. She stepped up to the microphone and wished the President happy birthday in song, in a childlike, playful voice which has echoed her story and sadness ever since. It was blatant. The gossip columns loved it but were careful in their reporting. Still, that evening should have had alarm bells.

They were ringing long before Marilyn left Los Angeles. There had been delays on her film *Something's Got To Give* with script rewrites which forced the movie to push the start date for filming to April 23. Marilyn had visited New York on her free days and had picked up a cold either from her acting guru Lee Strasberg or from President Kennedy at a $10,000 a plate fundraising dinner she had attended in Manhattan on April 14. It had raised Marilyn's temperature and she phoned in a day before filming was due to begin to call off sick with a fever. As her temperature went up, her career was in free-fall. Director George Cukor was not a fan and the studio were not optimistic. Marilyn was being paid $100,000 while Elizabeth Taylor was getting one million dollars for that year's other particularly complex amusement, *Cleopatra*.

The studio sent Dr. Lee Siegel to see her, and he suggested filming would have to be postponed for four weeks, but George Cukor refused and started work filming around Marilyn's scenes with her co-stars Dean Martin and Cyd Charisse. When Marilyn was on set she complained of fever, headaches, chronic sinusitis and bronchitis. The film languished ten days behind schedule and was going over-budget. Not for a moment did George Cukor or any others imagine Marilyn would take time off to appear at President Kennedy's 45th birthday celebration although the trip had been approved by Fox executives. She was besotted. It could have changed so much if Marilyn had stayed focused on her work in Hollywood.

Despite threats of dismissal and a whole fandango of fuss, there was no stopping Marilyn. She contacted Bobby Kennedy about the lawyer's letter Mickey Rudin had been sent by the studio because he had 'all the connections'. She couldn't have known that by then the Kennedys' infatuation with her was turning into a fear of the consequences. Bobby Kennedy was being pressured by senior politicians and Kennedy supporters to cut Marilyn out of the event. The stories of their sex lives might not be in the newspapers, but the Washington press corps and the city's political constituency was speaking with some knowledge about the goings on. Strong pleas were made to keep her far away from events.

The pleas were all pointless. Marilyn knew how to make an exit. She left 20th Century Fox Studios not by car onto Olympic Boulevard but from soundstage fourteen and into the sky in a French, blue helicopter loaned by Howard Hughes. With her were Peter Lawford and the now ever-present Pat Newcomb. The helicopter coughed around the air for a matter of minutes before making its way along the coast to Los Angeles International airport where Marilyn would continue en route to a legendary if ultimately tragic evening where she would stand alone in a spotlight on a dark stage as the world watched her. Few knew what trepidation there was behind the scenes.

Peter Lawford had got her there, Bobby Kennedy wasn't happy she was there, and President Kennedy appeared guiltless. The First Lady had absented herself having heard a radio broadcast by columnist Dorothy Kilgallen announcing that Marilyn and a stunning dress were going to be the highlight of the evening for the 15,000 guests specially invited to the Garden – including Captain James Hamilton of the LAPD.

A live event is nerve-stretching at best, but this was hoping for a miracle. Marilyn, surfing on champagne and coffee, was preparing to wish a happy birthday, ten days early, to the President.

Peter Lawford, aristocratic in his dinner jacket, was looking off into the wings, waiting for a bright light and the moment that he could, at last, welcome 'the *late* Marilyn Monroe…'

When she came into the bright platinum spotlight her confidence was a veneer, painted on, much like her dress appeared to be. What followed were moments of absurd recklessness televised to the nation. She surely knew what she was doing, she'd made love to the camera enough times.

> *Happy birthday, Mr. President*
> *Happy birthday to you.*
>
> *Thanks, Mr. President,*
> *For all the things you've done,*
> *The battles that you've won,*
> *The way you deal with US Steel,*
> *And our problems by the ton,*
> *We thank you so much…*
>
> *Everybody! Happy birthday!*

After this brazen performance, the President announced to the world: 'I can now retire from politics after having *Happy Birthday* sung to me in such a sweet, wholesome way.' It was a premeditated marker; the dress was her weapon of choice. Designer Jean Louis was known as provocative. He had created the black satin dress worn by Rita Hayworth in *Gilda* [1946] which was daring in its day. He made the black bathing suit that Deborah Kerr wears rolling in the Hawaiian surf with Burt Lancaster in *From Here to Eternity* [1953] which had audiences' eyebrows leaping. But these creations were not the ones that made history. The Jean Louis dress that Marilyn wore that evening sold in November 2016, for $4.8 million.

It *was* titillating. Dorothy Kilgallen, who was present that evening, described Marilyn's performance 'as making love to the

President in the direct view of forty million Americans.' One of America's great golden-era newspaper snoops, Dorothy Kilgallen also noted that Marilyn and Bobby Kennedy danced five times together at a post-gala party held at the penthouse of Arthur Krim, a long-serving Hollywood studio boss and a Democratic Party moneyman. Miss Kilgallen also noted that Ethel Kennedy watched, unamused. One of the Washington White House press corps said he was strong-armed into not writing about Bobby Kennedy and Marilyn dancing together.

There is a photograph [one from a reel of pictures destroyed by the Secret Service who raided the offices of *Time* magazine to seize the negatives] of Marilyn standing, arms by her side, her lips pursed, in that Jean Louis gown, with President Kennedy talking to her with his head leaning forward to her. It's the habit that Shirley Anne Field recalled he had – a clever, passive stance, not standing with his head back like a snake poised to strike. To Marilyn's right is Bobby Kennedy. It seems a tense moment but that is a presumption. Guests at the party say the threesome spoke for fifteen to twenty minutes. There are no released files to corroborate how the evening ended, but the consensus is that Marilyn left with President Kennedy and went to his suite at the Carlyle Hotel. [The Carlyle Hotel was then connected to Arthur Krim's apartment building via basement corridors and the Kennedy suite was serviced by a private elevator.] Whatever was said that night or, more importantly, whatever Marilyn asked or even pleaded for, it was not enough. She'd lost this game of chance – a game with stricter parameters than the Hollywood gamble of hope or a broken promise. As far as anyone alive knows, she never saw President Kennedy again. On May 24, only about 100 hours after she breathily sang to him on stage, she was back in California. Peter Lawford telephoned her from Hyannis Port. He had a message from the President. It was brutal and clear: she would never see and must never try to contact the President again. It was a cruel letdown. Especially as the day before life had seemed so good, so positive.

She plunged back into her role in *Something's Got To Give*. As easily as she lost her ermine wrap on stage in front of the President, she slipped out of her swimsuit in a scene for her movie. The nude scene, a Hollywood first for a major screen star, was captured by still photographers who made more money – $150,000 – from the images than Marilyn was being paid for the picture. A body stocking was made for her, but she took it off and swam around in flesh-coloured bikini bottoms. The explicit images boosted her profile globally. She appeared on 70 magazine covers, relegating Elizabeth Taylor, photographed floating about a bath in a nude bodysuit in *Cleopatra*, to runner-up in this particular battle.

Marilyn was dismayed by President Kennedy's treatment of her. When she called the White House, her 'access' was declined. It had been, she was told by the switchboard, 'cut off.' What Peter Lawford had told her ['Look, Marilyn, you've just been another of Jack's fucks'] was her nightmare of abandonment come true. It couldn't be. She wrote letters to the President and the Attorney General. She telephoned the Department of Justice but couldn't reach Bobby Kennedy. All this was fed back to the brothers through Pat Newcomb whose job it had always been to 'look after' Marilyn. On the last weekend of May, after she had been unceremoniously dumped for political expediency, Marilyn was knocked out for 48 hours with sedatives which kept her off the telephone. Remarkably, helped by more stimulating medication supplied by Dr. Hyman Engelberg [he claimed it was B-12 vitamins not amphetamines] she made it to work on the morning of Monday May 28. She had a poor day but picked up on Tuesday and Whitey Snyder said [in his interview with the author] that he felt she was doing good work. 'I'd seen her on all the pictures and her heart was in this one. She was glowing and her skin was great. I know it's looking back but I think she was trying to prove just what she could do; that's what drove her on, her pride in being a serious actress. It was a struggle though, a struggle for her. She took everything to heart, you could see her physically changed by her being frightened or delighted in something. She'd lost weight, lost what appeared to be puppy fat, as though she'd been eating too many cakes, not the bloat women can get. And, although outwardly she looked terrific, especially on film, it was clear to me and Marjorie [he and his wife Marjorie Lecher – a talented Hollywood wardrobe mistress for stars like Katharine Hepburn, Doris Day, Susan Hayward, Raquel Welch – had often sat up until the early hours with Marilyn sipping a drink Whitey Snyder made involving cranberry juice and over-servings of gin] that she was troubled. Her terror was what I remember most.'

The director George Cukor, known for his sense of self-importance, was unhelpful no matter what his star delivered. He had a hissy fit on June 1, 1962, Marilyn's 36th birthday, when her co-stars and the crew wanted to make a fuss of her with a $7 birthday cake, a cartoon of a naked Marilyn holding a towel, which read 'Happy Birthday (Suit)' and champagne. Eerily, most involved would recall the moments that day more as a wake than a celebration.

Marilyn left the party that night and – unknowingly – the studio for the last time. With her co-star, Wally Cox, she went on to a muscular dystrophy fundraiser at Dodger Stadium where she met up with Joe DiMaggio. He would be one of the first to hear and be appalled by how she had been treated by the nation's most powerful men. Sinatra was another. She had been snubbed by the Kennedys. So had Frank and, once again, she found his shoulder to cry on. By then Sinatra and DiMaggio were on poor terms.

Peter Lawford, another Sinatra outcast, and the man who delivered the goodbye message from President Kennedy, was nevertheless still kept close by Marilyn. He, of course, was her last lifeline to the President and more crucially to Bobby Kennedy to whom she had become most closely attached. Some of those around her during 1962 said she was 'mesmerised' by Bobby. One of America's foremost newspaper columnists Earl Wilson, in his landmark biography *Sinatra* [W.H. Allen, 1976], admitted he had kept the secret of Jack and Bobby's 'sharing of Marilyn Monroe and other girls'. When he made the truth known in his book, he was sat on by the Kennedy family but nothing official was ever done against him. Still, the family and the authorities, including the LAPD – who had the evidence in their files – refuted any serious association between Bobby Kennedy and Marilyn.

There are records of telephone calls made by Marilyn to Bobby Kennedy when he was in Washington and at the St. Francis Hotel, San Francisco. And, never seen until now, extracts from Marilyn's diary read and noted by Mike Rothmiller confirm in Marilyn's own words the truth of the matter:

'Bobby is gentle. He listens to me. He's nicer than John.

'Bobby said he loves me and wants to marry me. I love him. John hasn't called. Bobby called. He's coming to California. He wants to see me.'

Mike Rothmiller reported on what he read in her diary: 'The entries weren't dated, but they indicated when Robert Kennedy and Marilyn first had sex. Robert Kennedy was in Los Angeles and briefly stayed with the Lawfords. She had dinner with Peter and Robert. Then Peter left for the evening. It was then she and Robert had sex for the first time. The entry read: 'Bobby and I made love at Peter's. He wants to see me again. This is our secret.' The Marilyn/Kennedy arrangement was *very* crowded.

Some of her immediate anger was deflected when 20th Century Fox played rough. George Cukor called for her dismissal when she failed to appear for work on Monday June 4. Four days later, Marilyn was fired. Whitey Snyder said that, at first, she didn't truly believe it. Fire Marilyn Monroe? Never. But dismissed she was. And there was a $1 million lawsuit against her by 20th Century Fox and lots and lots of lawyers earning a great deal by billing by the hour. There was scuttlebutt put out by the studio along the lines that Marilyn wasn't just being a diva, but her actions were those of someone who was mentally disturbed. The inference was that she was mad, like her mother. There was talk of her replacement in the movie and, with some irony, Kim Novak was named as a possibility. *Life* magazine took the opportunity for a big splash, as most publications did, and placed Marilyn, on set and wearing a towelling robe, with the headline 'The Skinny Dip You'll Never See'.

What the public did see and read was her interview [published on August 3, 1962] which reflected on her personal and professional dismissals and included remarks which were resonant of wit and amused reasoning – not those of a deranged person. On display was her core intelligence, the smarts she'd learned on the Hollywood treadmill and her resolution not to be anybody's casual playmate any longer:

> 'I never quite understood it, this sex symbol. I always thought symbols were those things you clash together. That's the trouble, a sex symbol becomes a thing. I just hate to be a thing. But if I'm going to be a symbol of something, I'd rather have it sex than some other things they've got symbols of. These girls who try to be me, I guess the studios put them up to it, or they get the ideas themselves. But gee, they haven't got it. You can make a lot of gags about it, like they haven't got the foreground or else they haven't the background. But I mean the middle, where you live. ... I now live in my work and in a few relationships with the few people I can really count on. Fame will go by, and so long, I've had you, fame. If it goes by, I've always known it was fickle. So, at least it's something I experienced, but that's not where I live.'

Her box office appeal was not easily dismissed and, in a most unlikely scenario, a Hollywood miracle happened and Daryl Zanuck rode to her rescue. Zanuck was ambivalent about Marilyn but worshipped the bottom line and her pictures made money. As part of re-taking control of Fox he pledged in a phone call with Marilyn that *Something's Got To Give* would be completed with her as the star. Marilyn was re-hired by the studio a couple of weeks after being kicked off the picture. Her fee soared to $500,000 with an additional $500,000 if the film was completed on schedule, her script suggestions would be taken up and Cukor was replaced with Jean Negulesco who she'd worked with on *How to Marry a Millionaire*. New contracts were being drawn up at 20th Century Fox.

The 20th Century Fox Studios were often visited by Bobby Kennedy that year for talks with Jerry Wald about a film based on his book about Jimmy Hoffa and the Teamsters Union, *The Enemy Within*. [Wald worked with Marilyn as producer of *Let's Make Love*, 1960, and had a run of popular successes including *Peyton Place*, 1957, but died suddenly on July 13, 1962, and Bobby Kennedy's movie was never made]. Captain James Hamilton booked Bobby Kennedy into the impersonal Beverly Hilton, a few moments' drive east along Santa Monica Boulevard, if he overnighted. He registered anonymously, but OCID files didn't state if it was as Mr. Hamilton or Mr. Rodgers.

There was more fanfare over Bobby Kennedy's California visit on June 26, 1962, when he was guest of honour at a dinner hosted by Peter and Pat Lawford at their beach house. Marilyn Monroe arrived to meet 'her General'. She had prepared to look her best. Agnes Flanagan billed her $70 for 'hairstyling, Dinner Party, Peter Lawfords [sic]'. Whitey Snyder's bill was: $100 for 'Personal make-up to attend dinner at Peter Lawfords home honouring Robert Kennedy. Call 7.30 p.m.[sic]'.

Bobby Kennedy had become more and more indiscreet with his visits to Marilyn. The Lawford beach house was seen as a safe haven, guarded as it always was by the OCID, but the Lawfords had neighbours and help, valet parkers and deliveries. Bobby's affections for Marilyn had already become quite apparent at his brother's Madison Square Garden birthday party though. At the after-party at Arthur Krim's were the elite of America's power brokers including Vice President Lyndon Johnson and the Kennedys' one-time Presidential rival, Adlai Stevenson.

Stevenson wrote in a letter about the evening saying: 'Marilyn Monroe was wearing skin and beads. I didn't see the beads! My encounters with her, however, were only after breaking through the strong defences established by Robert Kennedy, who was dodging around her like a moth around a flame.'

Arthur Schlesinger, Stevenson's one-time speechwriter and a special assistant to President Kennedy, the third man in the birthday party picture [taken by White House photographer Cecil Stoughton] of Marilyn with the Kennedy brothers, said: 'She was most agreeable to him [Bobby] and pleasant to me but then she receded into her own glittering mist. Robert Kennedy in some way got through the glittering mist as few did.'

Somewhere in that mist, Marilyn had decided Bobby Kennedy was meant for her. She'd been rejected by one Kennedy but felt she was secure with another. Their regular liaisons, including a Fourth of July celebration together at the Lawford's beach house fanned, for her, that absurdity.

Two days after that July 4, 1962, holiday Bobby Kennedy, as Attorney General, attended a test in the Nevada desert of the H-bomb, the first try-out of a thermonuclear weapon in continental America. The Sedan nuclear test device had an explosive power of 104 kilotons, the equivalent of eight Hiroshima bombs. This was at the height of the Cold War. J. Edgar Hoover was listening in on Bobby Kennedy's calls, as was Jesus Angleton at the CIA and Chief Parker and Captain James Hamilton at LAPD. Could the KGB have also been listening in on the calls? Of all these organisations, only the LAPD were pledged to protect the Kennedy brothers.

Bobby Kennedy also had his personal and close CIA agents, chief among them was William Harvey. The US tensions with Cuba became more and more threatening to world peace and there would be just 104 days from Bobby Kennedy and Marilyn's Fourth of July weekend to the Cuban Missile Crisis. William Harvey took charge of facilitating the Kennedys' obsession with crushing Castro in February 1962, along with responsibility for covert action, sabotage and subversion against Cuba. He called it Task Force W. CIA files, released later, disclose that he established an undercover operative – a man named Charles Ford. Part of the document reads: 'Cited files disclose that circa 1962–1963, Charles D. Ford was issued official alias documentation under the name "Charles D. Fiscalini".' Another part of the document gives a slightly different version of the undercover pseudonym: 'Reference request indicated that Charles Ford was an agency officer who was utilising the name "Rocky Fiscalini".' The documents further revealed that: 'Charles D. Ford has been an agency staff employee since 1952. A memorandum contained in his files, dated 30 March 1962, further indicates that Mr. Ford was then assigned to "Task Force W", and was to travel to New York on 31 March, 1962 to meet with an unidentified attorney who had contacted Robert Kennedy, the Attorney General, concerning assistance for Cuban prisoners ... these documents have been sanitised in accordance with established procedures.'

Charles Ford aka Charles Fiscalini was Bobby Kennedy's own operational CIA officer; his assignment was to act as a go-between with the Mafia while using the pseudonym, 'Rocky Fiscalini'. What Ford/Fiscalini exactly did for Bobby Kennedy is not filed. Task Force W Executive Officer Samuel Halpern told author Seymour Hersh for his book, *Dark Heart of Camelot*, that Charles Ford/Fiscalini saw Bobby Kennedy frequently in his office and regularly talked to him on the phone. Halpern was quoted: 'Charlie was a good officer, and Bobby was his case officer. He was Bobby's man.'

And Marilyn was Bobby's Girl. Or she most certainly thought she was. Yet their romance was not rosy. Fred Otash's wiretaps captured angry conversations between the two – usually because Bobby Kennedy could not fulfil an arrangement he made to see her. Marilyn thought she was more important than government business. And, at times, it appears Bobby Kennedy thought the same.

It was not a question of *if* but *when* it would all collapse into tragedy.

# XI: Torch Song

*'I've Got You Under My Skin,'*
— Frank Sinatra version, 1963, Cole Porter, 1946.

Bobby Kennedy was being pressured from many around him to resolve the issue of Marilyn Monroe. His was rotten behaviour, however it was viewed. It was also political suicide if it became widely known, or if he divorced his wife Ethel and abandoned her and his seven [they would go on to have eleven in total] children for a Hollywood blonde. It is remarkable how much expertise was deployed in subterfuge and how clever it was. So many people were afraid to breach the sanctity of the Kennedy myth. The tracks were blurred and the truth concealed just enough for there always to be 'reasonable doubt'. It has taken decades to reveal the truth about the attempts to assassinate Castro, the misogynistic debauchery of the Kennedys, so skilfully camouflaged by Colgate grins and a collegiate hidden society of enablers, and the murder of Marilyn Monroe.

Her demise had antecedents at the Cal Neva Lodge and Casino up in the hills of Lake Tahoe, Nevada. The Kennedys had longtime connections there going back to Joe Kennedy's visits with his mistress. Cal Neva was where he met his Mafia connections. If he'd been able, maybe he'd have found a different solution to the Marilyn problem but on December 19, 1961, at the age of 73, he'd suffered a life-threatening stroke. He survived, but lost all power of speech and was left paralysed on his right side. He couldn't pull the strings any more.

Meanwhile, events were gathering round his sons like mushroom clouds, those terrifying emblems of the atomic times. In the summer of 1962 people worldwide, the *Dr. Strangelove* generation, were terrified of the possibilities. Many were acutely aware of the nuclear threat, they'd done their homework: a decade earlier 'Ivy Mike', an apartment block of an atom bomb, detonated in the Pacific, at Eniwetok Atoll, at half a second before 7.15 a.m. on November 1,1952. The blast punched out the equivalent of 10.4 megatons of TNT, a power equal to 693 times more than the 'Little Boy' atom bomb dropped on Hiroshima from the Boeing B-29 Superfortress bomber *Enola Gay*. The fireball produced by this horror was nearly four miles wide. The malevolent cloud rose in its magnificent mayhem to a height of 25 miles into the sky and then, in neat numbers, spread 100 miles, taking 100 million tons of radioactive material into the atmosphere. In July 1962, Bobby Kennedy witnessed the first nuclear test on continental American soil. Now, America and Russia were pointing such devices at each other.

It puts the problem of Marilyn Monroe into perspective and reflects the pressure of the circumstances. Yet, strangely, it was the emotional time bombs which were to explode and race events to a conclusion and Marilyn's life to an end.

For Marilyn, Cal Neva was where the dam burst and where, despite being with a crowd of friends, she found herself isolated. She was, by 1962, a threat to many people, to their political well-being and wealth. The perils could not have been more acute for the men she was involved with, America was on the brink of nuclear war. It involved a cast of familiar names but not all in familiar roles. Yet, almost all of them could not have anticipated what was going to happen. Providence is descriptive of what follows but possibly is too saintly a word for the events.

From the moment it opened in July 1926, with 116,000 square feet of gambling space split between California and Nevada sitting smack across the stateline road, the Cal Neva had been a hot spot. It's been an ongoing Damon Runyon show, a real-life *Guys and Dolls*, on the shores of Lake Tahoe. In the early days they said even the cigarette girls talked out of the side of their mouth. It was a world where dames were dames and men were whomever they said they were. The silent film star Clara Bow lost a fortune at the tables in 1930 and refused to pay saying she thought the $100 chips she was flamboyantly playing with were valued at 50 cents. A thirteen-year-old Judy Garland performed there in 1935. It was always a suspicious place.

There were reports that Joe Kennedy always had shares in the business and later Scott Lankford would write in his book, *Tahoe Beneath The Surface*, [Heyday Books, 2010] that he had an 'endless series of extramarital affairs with wealthy divorcees and Tahoe's notoriously ubiquitous prostitutes' there. Arson burned the place down in 1937, but it was instantly rebuilt with insurance money into the property Sinatra and his cronies bought into in 1960.

Sinatra created the Celebrity Room Theatre and installed a helicopter pad on the roof. There was a maze of tunnels beneath the lodge which had been used to conceal and move illegal liquor during the prohibition years. Sinatra upgraded them so that VIP mobsters or high-profile guests could move out of sight of the crowds on the gambling floor. The FBI monitored all this, convinced that Joe Kennedy was financially involved and using funds supplied by Jimmy Hoffa's Teamsters Union.

Sam Giancana was banned from Nevada casinos but continued to stay at the Cal Neva lodge. Informants' reports, unconfirmed by files, said that Sam Giancana used specialist girls being trafficked through Hollywood and Las Vegas by Skinny D'Amato as honeytraps for the Kennedys [including Teddy], who 'had sex with prostitutes' – sometimes two or more at a time – 'in bathtubs, hallways, closets, on floors, almost everywhere but the bed.' What Sam Giancana wanted on the Kennedys was a negotiable commodity in the form of verified scandalous behaviour. He didn't want to destroy them, he wanted influence in the White House. Early on, he'd sensed a weak link in Frank Sinatra whom he believed was star-struck by JFK. He asked Johnny Rosselli to bring in 'a watcher' at the Cal Neva. They agreed on a hitman turned casino operator called Lewis McWillie for the assignment.

McWillie had worked in Cuba with Johnny Rosselli when mobster Meyer Lansky had first cut into the island's economy in the 1930s. Before Castro's revolution ended the gambling bonanza of the 1950s, Lansky was empire building. The Mob had links to the moorish Hotel Nacional which was owned by the Cuban Government. When Club Parisien, a casino complex with cabaret room and bar-restaurant, was created within the walls of the Nacional it was sublet to Lansky. Mafia boss, Santo Trafficante provided the entertainment through his International Amusements Corporation (IAC) and on opening night Eartha Kitt, at her feline prime as a sex kitten, was the star. The IAC fed talent to the casinos, the much-favoured Nat King Cole and Ella Fitzgerald, the premier names of jazz and cool, just as it did to the Hollywood studios. Every which way, the boys were earning. It was exquisite daiquiri diplomacy. They had casinos attached to the Capri, the Sevilla-Biltmore, the Commodoro and the Deauville. And it was all mentored by Lansky's lieutenant Dino Cellini and his team who kept these ocean-front money machines in round-the-clock working order. They also ran the gambling at the Tropicana, which was a Busby Berkeley style cabaret brought to life, in the jungle on the outskirts of Havana. Here the showgirls were startlingly beautiful and the best dancers with endless legs and smiles. The high kicks invited vertigo. On offer was an escape into fantasy, a world where, for a price, all desires could be provided for. Lewis McWillie ran the gambling and rightfully thought himself 'a key man' for the Mob in Havana. McWillie regularly flew up to Miami. He was visited by his friend Jack Ruby who owned a nightclub in Dallas and US official records show they both spent a short time in prison following Castro's coup. The connections breed. FBI files describe McWillie as a killer, and a very good one. On Rosselli's instructions the always-stylish, silver-haired gentleman became a blackjack dealer at Cal Neva where he could monitor the Mob's investment. And Sinatra's behaviour.

A short time later, there was a curious incident. Back in Chicago the FBI's agents heard, via a wiretap, one of Giancana's hoods, Chuckie English, claiming that if Bobby Kennedy wanted to know anything about Sam Giancana 'he should ask Sinatra'. When Bobby Kennedy was told about it, he instructed Hoover to 'prioritise' surveillance on the entertainer and the Cal Neva. Bobby Kennedy was not going to compromise himself now by following in his father's footsteps.

The FBI already had a file on the prostitution ring that Skinny D'Amato was operating from the front desk of the hotel. Women were being flown everywhere, including to Cal Neva to provide room service. While their binoculars were focused on the casino in the woods there was a shooting at the hotel. Full details have never been made public, but a man suffered a bullet wound but did not die. Shortly afterwards, on June 30, 1962, Deputy Sheriff Richard Anderson arrived at the Cal Neva to collect his new wife who was a waitress there. She had dated Sinatra before her marriage. Anderson noticed the way Sinatra stared at his wife and heard the suggestive remarks he made to her. A big man, Deputy Anderson warned the singer to stay away from her. Sinatra backed down – but he felt angry and humiliated by 'the big dumb cop'. Another evening when Anderson again arrived to pick up his wife, he stopped by the kitchen to talk with some of the staff. Sinatra came in, saw Anderson and ran up to him screaming, 'What the fuck are you doing here?' Anderson began to explain that he was waiting for his wife when suddenly, while the cop was still mid-sentence, Sinatra grabbed him and tried to throw him out. There was pushing and shoving and finally Anderson socked Sinatra hard in the face – a bruising punch which damaged his features as well as his ego.

Several weeks later, on July 17, 1962, Anderson and his wife were driving down Highway 28, not far from the Cal Neva, when they were driven off the road by a late model maroon convertible with California plates and a silver-haired man at the wheel. Anderson lost control of his car, skidded off the road, smashed into a tree and was killed instantly. His wife was thrown from the car and suffered severe broken bones and fractures.

The Cal Neva was Sinatra's lifetime albatross. And, arguably, what happened at his casino contributed to the death of Marilyn Monroe. For if things had gone differently there on her last weekend on earth, maybe Bobby Kennedy wouldn't have found himself in a corner with, to him, just one solution.

Aboard Sinatra's private plane [named *Christina* after his daughter], Marilyn flew to the casino, where jazz genius Buddy Greco was the current star attraction, with Peter and Pat Lawford on the last weekend of July 1962. Sinatra told her he wanted to discuss a film project, but she remained reluctant to go until Pat Lawford explained that Bobby Kennedy would be there after concluding his meetings in Los Angeles.

That evening, according to witnesses and the files, there was a dinner attended by Sam Giancana, Peter and Pat Lawford, Sinatra and Monroe. Giancana was on the Nevada blacklist but he didn't care. He was a Cal Neva regular – well, he owned most of the place. San Francisco's legendary, good-natured and kind newspaper columnist Herb Caen wrote in 1979: 'I saw Sinatra at the Cal Neva when Sam Giancana was there. In fact, I met Giancana through Frank. He was a typical hood, didn't say much. He wore a hat at the lake, and sat in his little bungalow, receiving people.' The ominous spook-for-hire, Joe Shimon was present that evening – and watching. Skinny D'Amato [later heard on tape] said: 'There was more to what happened than anyone has told. It would have been the big fall for Bobby Kennedy, wouldn't it?'

What happened next was vile, no matter what version of the story you accept. It is clear that something bad happened to Marilyn Monroe. There is plenty of circumstantial evidence but also testimony. Gambler and fixer Jimmy 'Blue Eyes' Alo told Dino Cellini, an associate of Meyer Lansky, that what went on that weekend was degrading, debauched and 'as bad as Havana'. Cellini, who had grown up with Dean Martin, said Alo told him that Sinatra tried to keep Marilyn sedated but she was drinking, and the combination produced a disorientated and obstreperous personality. Peter Lawford, discretion being the dominant part of his character, kept distant from Sinatra. Lawford had only been asked for the weekend because of the belief that he could 'control' Marilyn. Sinatra made it clear that he still hated him but was restraining himself as needs must.

Monroe got very, very drunk and told anyone listening at the table that the Kennedys simply used her as 'a piece of ass'. She made it clear she didn't ever again want to be pawed by anything but applause. Gone was the sexual sweetness, the easy swivel of her neck, the vivaciousness she had on screen, the pull of her shoulders and drop of her bottom beneath that long waist as she tottered along the train as Sugar in *Some Like It Hot*. The reality was awful. The exploitation much worse.

She was taken to her cabin and later, in her doped and drugged state, she was joined there by Giancana and Sinatra and some of Skinny D'Amato's girls. It was a free for all with Monroe as the central player. Photographs were taken of the men and women sexually playing with Monroe. The film was developed overnight by Hollywood photographer Billy Woodfield. The prints were not good.

In one image, Sam Giancana is atop Marilyn who is lying on her front. It is not clear what is going on, but it became an accepted story among the Mafia veterans from the Cuba gambling era that Giancana had forcibly anally raped Marilyn – so-called 'Sicilian sex' – as retribution for her affair with Bobby Kennedy. Whatever the truth of that, government wiretaps recorded Johnny Rosselli saying to Giancana: 'You sure get your rocks off fucking the same broad as the brothers, don't you…?'

We now have Marilyn's own confused recollection of her ordeal. Mike Rothmiller read and noted down Marilyn's thoughts from her diary kept in the OCID files. 'Noted in the diary were several entries regarding the weekend,' he says. 'The Cal Neva weekend was also documented by other agencies and a report detailing that weekend was placed in OCID's secret files.' From Marilyn's diary he noted the following:

'Frank invited me to the lodge (Cal Neva Lodge at Lake Tahoe). He said it will be fun. He said never to mention Sam at the lodge. He's mafia. [sic]'

'It appears the following entries were made after she returned home,' Rothmiller continues. 'Before and after the entered items were scribbled out and not legible.' Then more entries he noted from the diary:

'Frank, Peter and others were there.

'Frank said I can't keep my fucking mouth shut. He told me to get out. I don't know why he's treating me this way.'

This entry immediately followed the above.

'What happened to me. I was drunk. I don't remember. Did I have sex. [sic]'

'Intelligence files regarding her weekend at the lodge clearly stated she was drunk and forced to depart early,' reports Mike Rothmiller adding: 'Sinatra said she was embarrassing him, so she had to go. Also, in attendance was Paul 'Skinny' D'Amato of the Chicago Outfit. Skinny kept an eye on Sam Giancana's interest in the lodge and was a part-time FBI informant. It must be noted that the CIA had requested Sam Giancana and his Mob associates assassinate Cuba's Fidel Castro. Robert Kennedy and President John Kennedy both knew and approved of the assassination plot.'

Presumably, the sedatives being supplied to Marilyn over the weekend had amnesiac effects. Either that or she'd blacked out the full horror of events. All her life she had a trick of putting aside events and people she did not want to recall. She often said: 'I have the most wonderful memory for forgetting things.'

In the blur of the following morning, Peter Lawford, still not entirely sober himself, was instructed to tell Marilyn that Bobby

Kennedy, just named 'Father of the Year' by a national magazine, had remained in Los Angeles – and there was to be no contact with him or any of his family ever again. It was logical but not to Marilyn. [Her phone records which survived show she repeatedly called the Department of Justice and also telephoned Hickory Hill, the family home in McLean, Virginia to try and contact Bobby.]

Until his death in January 2017, Buddy Greco was the last notable survivor from that weekend at Cal Neva. He was also the most open, for he was there as the talent and for no other reason. Greco, a singer with Benny Goodman's Band, made his breakthrough solo recording, *The Lady is a Tramp*, in 1961. He later settled in England, where he spoke of what he saw that weekend. Around the hotel were Dean Martin, Sammy Davis Jr., Juliet Prowse who was involved with Sinatra, and the hairdresser-playboy Jay Sebring who would later die in the Charles Manson killings. Buddy Greco was sitting out by the lake with Sinatra when Marilyn made her entrance: 'That day we were just sitting around reading the paper when suddenly a limousine pulled up and this gorgeous woman stepped out. It was Marilyn. I had no idea she was coming. I had first met Marilyn when I was performing with Benny Goodman. She came to the clubs where I was working. I adored her from afar. She was very intelligent but also like one of the guys; she drank a lot, smoked a lot and partied a lot. She loved attention.

'When she arrived that Saturday, you'd never believe that she had a care in the world. I was sitting with Frank outside Frank's bungalow, when a limousine pulls up and this gorgeous woman in dark glasses steps out. She's dressed all in green – everything green: coat, skirt and scarf. Before I realised who it was, I thought: "My god, what a beautiful woman. No taste in clothes, but what a beautiful woman."

'We'd said hello a few times but were never properly introduced. When Frank introduced us, I said: "You won't remember me, but I was the piano player when you auditioned for the Benny Goodman band in 1948."

'She got emotional at that and hugged me. She had such warmth – and I was moved. It was an unrepeatable moment, a time that would never happen again. It was magical.'

Things became less magical as the day wore on. Buddy Greco had completed his first performance that evening and had joined the Sinatra table in the lounge. He continued: 'Suddenly the room went silent and very still. It was surreal. As if somebody had turned the sound off. I looked at Frank. I could immediately tell he was furious. His eyes were like blue ice cubes. He was looking at the doorway where Marilyn stood, swaying ever so slightly.

'She was still in the same green outfit she'd worn all day. But the woman I'd met that afternoon – smart, funny, intelligent, fragile – had gone. Now she looked drunk and... well, defiant. She was clearly angry and I think I heard her say, "Who the fuck are they all staring at?" It was clear Sinatra was worried. She was in a state where she could have said anything. Sinatra motioned to his bodyguard – Coochie – to get her out of there. Coochie, a big guy, escorted her out. Actually, he picked her up and carried her out. It wasn't the star we were used to seeing. She was on my mind. I was worried about her. I went outside to find out whether she was okay. I knew that she had taken accidental overdoses in the past. I found her by the pool. There was nobody around. It was late and the pool was deserted. Maybe it was the moon, but she had a ghostly pallor. It still didn't occur to me that she might be a woman not long for this world.

'She was distressed, out of it, but that was all. Maybe her friends were used to seeing her like that, but it worried me. Anyway, we talked. I walked her back to her bungalow in the complex reserved for the guests of Frank and Giancana where we all stayed.'

Greco then went off to perform his second show of the evening. 'I thought that the next morning I could put her with Pat Lawford who was her companion, and make sure she got back to LA safely.

'But the next day when I called, she had already left. That was the last time I saw her. After she had created that problem, Frank certainly wanted her out of there. He could be quite firm with her.' Asked whether he thought that Marilyn had been brought to the Cal Neva to be warned off the Kennedys the entertainer said: 'It's a possible scenario.'

The London film critic Tim Robey had an intriguing reaction to a photograph of the initial arrival of Marilyn Monroe at the Cal Neva. His perception is acute: 'The world hardly wants for books about Marilyn Monroe and Frank Sinatra, and yet there are still mysteries to be cleared up, particularly during the brief period of their lives when they knew each other intimately. There's a photograph – not so much of the two of them, but one in which they both separately appear – taken at the Cal Neva lodge in Lake Tahoe, five days before Monroe died. In the foreground, she poses with the singer and pianist Buddy Greco, smiling, maybe a little drunk. In the background, Sinatra slouches in a pool chair, a newspaper on his lap.

'He's gazing at them with an extraordinary, faintly chilling sidelong expression. It's hard to tell if he's jealous, concerned, wary or a mixture of all three. But there is something strange going on in that picture, and it's something no biography has adequately explained yet.'

Of course, circumstances were far stranger than what was captured in that image. On Sunday July 29, 1962, Marilyn, with Peter Lawford, was taken to Tahoe Valley Airport and put on Sinatra's plane for a flight back to Los Angeles. Santa Monica Airport closed in the late evening and they were directed to Los Angeles International as their flight arrived in the early hours of the Monday morning. OCID detectives at LAX noted her arrival, as they recorded all VIP arrivals. There's never been an explanation for this journey in the middle of the night.

Marilyn, in dark glasses, her hair hidden beneath a scarf, had appeared more drugged than drunk, spaced out, as she was discreetly moved out of Cal Neva and back home. A limousine took her from LAX to Cursum Perficio, and Sinatra's pilot Don Lieto gave Peter Lawford a ride back to his beach house.

Lawford knew his home was bugged. He'd paid Fred Otash to do it. Lawford asked his ride to stop before he reached his home: he wanted to make an urgent call and he used a roadside pay phone on Ocean Avenue to do it. The filed telephone records show he called the White House and spoke for almost twenty minutes shortly after 7.30 a.m. Washington time while the mist was thinning over the Pacific coast at 4.30 a.m. The triangle was the constant: Marilyn–Lawford–Kennedys. Most of the stories of Marilyn being a basket case at and in the days following the Cal Neva weekend all emanate from the Kennedys' friends, aides and family, like Peter Lawford and his wife Pat, still disenchanted with her husband and whom Joe Shimon said was involved, or at least having sex, with Frank Sinatra. Marilyn was surrounded by people keen to share information about her. Pat Newcomb was close to Bobby Kennedy. Housekeeper/nurse Eunice Murray was reporting back to Dr. Greenson and the FBI. And Dr. Greenson was getting face to face information direct from Marilyn about her feelings and intentions, almost every day. After Marilyn's death he submitted a bill to her estate [dated July 15, 1963] which he copied to the law offices of his brother-in-law. He prefaced: 'The following is an itemised account explaining the bill for professional services which I sent to the estate of Marilyn Monroe for the sum of $1,400. I shall list below the date and place where the psychiatric interviews took place.' And he did. Other than Saturdays in July and Marilyn's weekend that month at Cal Neva he saw her *every* day – eight times at his home, four times at his office and at Marilyn's home. At the bottom of the bill, he writes: 'Explanation: All office visits lasted a minimum of one and a half hours. All visits to the home were approximately two hours in duration. On those days on which it is stated that the patient was seen both at the office and at her home, it means there were two separate visits on that particular day. I had arranged with Miss Monroe that her fee would be $50 an hour. However, since she needed a great deal of extra time and since I did not want her to think I gave her extra time or made extra visits for monetary reasons, I decided that I would charge her $50 for every day that I saw her professionally. The sum of $1,400 therefore represents the fact that I saw her professionally on 28 days from July 1 through August 4, 1962.' That last date, of course, was the last day of her life.

It didn't appear that Marilyn intended it that way. Dr. Hyman Engelberg had paid a home visit on August 3 and given her a B-12 injection [he said it was one of many regular $10 injections] to boost her for that weekend for which she had plans. Much gathering of reports about her mood has been done over the years and many talked of her being buoyant about being back on good terms with Fox. She had removed her nemesis George Cukor as her director for *Something's Got To Give* and was planning new projects including a film with the British director J. Lee Thompson [*The Guns of Navarone*, 1961].

Wiretaps revealed conflicting views, depending on who Marilyn was speaking to. Some said she had emotionally dismissed the Kennedys from her life, but others said she was simmering with rage at what she saw as their disrespect of her. She was angry, truly angry, at being used. A lot of information that emerged after the event was contradictory or were clearly mundane mis-recollections rather than part of the truth of the elaborate cover-up.

Outwardly, Marilyn's lost weekend at Cal Neva seemed to be forgotten. On Monday July 30, after she returned from Lake Tahoe, she saw Dr. Greenson at his office and Dr. Engelberg paid her a home visit, no injection charged for. There is a record of an eight-minute call to the Justice Department and the hypothesis is she spoke to Bobby Kennedy, but it could have been a dismissive but chatty girl on the switchboard.

On Tuesday July 31, she discussed plans to attend the opening night of Irving Berlin's final Broadway show, *Mr. President*, on October 2, 1962. It had been announced that President Kennedy and the First Lady would be in the audience. Marilyn ordered an elaborate new 'look-at-what-you're-missing' designer dress for the occasion. On the first day of August, she talked with Gene Kelly [he had a cameo in *Let's Make Love*] about her appearing with him in a musical which would be part of the new two-picture deal she had negotiated with 20th Century Fox. She was also discussing a stage project involving Frank Sinatra – a Broadway musical version of Betty Smith's *A Tree Grows in Brooklyn* and the brainchild of composer Jule Styne who'd created *Gentlemen Prefer Blondes*. She arranged to meet Jule Styne in New York the following week to talk more about the show. She had also made a date to meet Gene Kelly in Beverly Hills on Sunday, August 5.

On August 1, 1962, the columnist Dorothy Kilgallen is recorded telephoning the Justice Department and asking if Bobby Kennedy will confirm his affair with Marilyn Monroe. She and Florabel Muir of the *New York Daily News* were two of the most determined of the contemporary investigative journalists who simply didn't accept what they were told. [Kilgallen applied the same pressure about the assassination of President Kennedy and was writing a tell-all book about it when she was found dead on November 8, 1965, in her Manhattan apartment from 'a drug and drink overdose'. There was no investigation into her death despite a clearly staged crime scene and her friends' suspicions that she had been murdered because of what she knew and was about to publish.]

On Thursday, August 2, Marilyn went furniture shopping with Eunice Murray who also drove her in her open-top Cadillac over to Montana Avenue to a garden centre to look at shrubs and plants to buy for Cursum Perficio. She had psychiatric sessions with Dr. Greenson at his office every day that week and that Thursday was only different in that he also attended her at her home. That evening she went to a party out at the beach hosted by Peter and Pat Lawford which was recorded by the OCID detectives monitoring the property. It was a very movieland evening and among the guests were Warren Beatty and his *Splendor in the Grass* [1961] co-star and girlfriend Natalie Wood, who had left her husband Robert

'R.J.' Wagner for him. They were the moment's 'golden couple'. [Decades later there was confusion following an October 2016 *Vanity Fair* article in which Beatty talked about the party at the Lawfords. He said in his interview that the day after he was called and told of Marilyn's death. This brought some doubt about his reminiscence, but Beatty only got his days telescoped. He was logged by OCID as being at the *Thursday* night party. *Vanity Fair*'s Sam Kashner recounted what Beatty told him of the evening with Marilyn: 'Peter Lawford had invited him out to his house for a night of tacos and poker, and Monroe was there. "I hadn't seen anything that beautiful," Beatty recalls. She invited him to take a walk along the beach, which he did. "It was more soulful than romantic." Back in the house, he played the piano. Marilyn sat on the edge of the piano in something so clingy that Beatty could tell she wasn't wearing underwear. "How old are you?" she asked. "Twenty-five," he answered. "And how old are you?" he asked cheekily. "Three. Six," she said, as if not wanting to bring the two numbers together. By then, the tacos had arrived, and no one really played poker that night.'] Marilyn left the party not long after 9 p.m. and met Whitey Snyder and his wife Marjorie back at her home. Marjorie recalled [to the author] that all through that last week of her life Marilyn was upbeat. 'She could be very funny, funny in an amusing way. Of course, she could be a pain in the you-know-where too but we loved her. She talked mostly about going back to work at Fox and we were happy too, for it meant we were going back to work as well. Marilyn was looking good in the picture and she said that she was happy – not champagne happy – that night. Her eyes had a sparkle and she had that determined look when she pushed her chin out. We went off feeling good about things.'

On Friday, August 3, Marilyn's love life was the lead item in Dorothy Kilgallen's column in the *New York Journal-American*. She wrote that Marilyn was the 'talk of the town again *and* ... she's cooking in the sex-appeal department too; she's proved vastly alluring to a handsome gentleman who is a bigger name than Joe DiMaggio in his heyday ... don't write Marilyn off as finished.'

That day Bobby Kennedy and his family were to check into the St. Francis Hotel on Powell Street in San Francisco, but that reservation had been changed and the Kennedys were staying with their friends at Gilroy. Marilyn tried in vain to contact Bobby Kennedy at the hotel. She wanted to have a civilised conversation about their situation. She was hugely frustrated at not getting all her anger out and was bloody-minded at Dr. Greenson's office session that day. At some point that day her 'minders' decided that Pat Newcomb would stay overnight with her to prevent her 'mouthing off'. Newcomb, who had kept in close touch with Bobby Kennedy, had also been given the job of finding Marilyn's notes and diaries, anything at all linking her intimately with the President and the Attorney General.

That evening Pat Newcomb enlisted Peter Lawford and they went to La Scala, a restaurant on Canon Drive in Beverly Hills a fifteen-minute drive from Marilyn's home. Afterwards, Pat Newcomb, because of her supposed bronchitis, would stay over with Marilyn and get some sun by the pool of Cursum Perficio the next day. Peter Lawford dropped them off in his Lincoln Continental and then drove himself home to Palisades Beach Road. Until Mike Rothmiller decided to release, for this book, the information he'd gathered over the years from interviews [including the interview with Lawford] and his study of the OCID files, the events of the next 36 hours have been – as intended by Captain James Hamilton and his co-conspirators – a confusion of time, events and encounters in order to perpetuate the great lie: that Bobby Kennedy wasn't in Los Angeles that weekend. Using all the power and wealth at their disposal the determined men mounted a cover-up which led to decades of whisper and innuendo, a smörgåsbord of theories always with a seasoning of the truth which left the suspicions a little less bitter. From the moment Rothmiller began studying the OCID files, and most certainly after he had read her diary and talked to cops involved, Mike Rothmiller had not one doubt that Marilyn had been murdered.

An extract from his [unedited] notes from her diary reveal for the first time the exact state of play that evening from her perspective, and indicate Marilyn was the unwitting architect of her own denouement. Mike Rothmiller wrote: 'Reading the final entries, it was apparent she was angry with John and Robert Kennedy for using her as a sex toy and tossing her aside. She noted her many unanswered calls to the President and Attorney General which added to her mounting frustration. The [diary] entry read "They are not calling back. Bob and John used me. They used me."

'According to OCID and other intelligence records, Peter Lawford took her calls and acted as an intermediary relaying the final few days of messages between Marilyn, Robert and President Kennedy. And Lawford was requested by the Kennedys, specifically Robert, to stop her from going public.'

But Marilyn wasn't having any of it. She had Hollywood on her side once again, a movie waiting and new projects to explore. Mike Rothmiller's notes continue: 'Her entry read: "I told Peter they're ignoring me. I'm not going to stand for that. I'm going to tell everyone about us."' From the diary entries and OCID intelligence documents, there's no question Marilyn threatened and planned to call a news conference within days to publicly expose her relationship with the President, Robert Kennedy and reveal national security items revealed to her [by them]. The final diary entries indicate that Peter Lawford had asked her to stay home because Robert Kennedy and Lawford were coming to her residence the next day.

'Peter said Robert will come tomorrow. I don't know if he will.'

# PART FOUR

## A Star Is Dead

*'Presidents and Senators don't have people killed,'*
— **Diane Keaton as Kay to Al Pacino**
**as Michael Corleone, who replies:**

*'Oh. Who's being naive, Kay?*
— **The Godfather, 1972.**

# XII: Public Eye

*'The solution, once revealed, must seem to have been inevitable.'*
— Raymond Chandler, *Raymond Chandler Speaking*, 1962.

The story surrounding Marilyn Monroe's death verges on the mythical. It is almost always unworldly in tone. The vagaries about the circumstances are as whimsical as the cast of characters placed centre stage over the years. We know that Bobby Kennedy was in Los Angeles on August 4, 1962, although he and all around him swore he was not. LAPD Chief Daryl Gates, who was working in Chief Parker's office on that day, states emphatically in his book [*Chief,* Bantam, 1992] that the Attorney General was in Los Angeles and giving his opinion: 'Frankly, I never bought into the idea that she killed herself because he dumped her.'

In 1975, *Oui* magazine published an article, written by Anthony Scaduto that called on details from *The Life and Curious Death of Marilyn Monroe* [Pinnacle Books, 1975] written by Robert F. Slatzer, a longtime friend who claimed to have been married to Marilyn for a short time. It called into question the official narrative of Marilyn's death and caused enough of a stir for the LAPD to re-examine the investigation. The LAPD chief at the time was Ed Davis and he put Daryl Gates in charge of the new investigation into Marilyn's death. Gates writes in his biography: 'I turned it over to the Organized Crime Intelligence Division [OCID].' The very people who had led the cover-up in the first place.

Mike Rothmiller later discovered that the 1975 re-investigation and subsequent others were lacklustre showpiece inquiries, a way for the LAPD to be seen as going through the motions. The 1975 inquiry was handled by Rothmiller's one-time colleague and Gates' favoured OCID detective, Neil Spotts. As with the initial investigation, the pattern was repeated: present a story with a beginning, a *muddle* and a convincing ending. It was the one constant.

On August 6, 1962, the *Los Angeles Times* printed an early version of the suicide narrative pushed by Captain James Hamilton:

'Marilyn Monroe, a troubled beauty who failed to find happiness as Hollywood's brightest star, was discovered dead in her Brentwood home of an apparent overdose of sleeping pills Sunday.

The blonde, 36-year-old actress was nude, lying face down on her bed and clutching a telephone receiver in her hand when a psychiatrist broke into her room at 3.30 a.m.

She had been dead an estimated six to eight hours.

About 5.15 p.m. Saturday she had called the psychiatrist, Dr. Ralph Greenson, and was told to go for a ride when she complained she could not sleep, police reported.

Her body was taken to the County Morgue, where Coroner Theodore J. Curphey said after an autopsy that he could give a "presumptive opinion" that death was due to an overdose of some drug.

He said a special "suicide team" would be asked to investigate Miss Monroe's last days to determine if she took her own life.

Further medical tests as to the nature of the suspected killer drug will be completed in 48 hours, he said.

An empty bottle found among several medicines beside her bed had contained 50 Nembutal capsules. The prescription was issued only two or three days ago and the capsules were to be taken in doses of one a night, said Dr. Hyman Engelberg.

It was learned that medical authorities believed Miss Monroe had been in a depressed mood recently. She was unkempt and in need of a manicure and pedicure, indicating listlessness and a lack of interest in maintaining her usually glamorous appearance, the authorities added.

The coroner's office listed the death on its records as possible suicide while the police report said death was possibly accidental.

No suicide note was found.

Dr. Robert Litman, a psychiatrist serving on the suicide team, said notes are left by less than 40 per cent of those who take their own lives. Miss Monroe's body was discovered after her housekeeper and companion, Mrs. Eunice Murray, awoke about 3 a.m. and saw a light still burning in the actress's room.

Mrs. Murray found the bedroom door locked. She was unable to arouse Miss Monroe by shouts and rapping on the door, and immediately telephoned Dr. Greenson.

Dr. Greenson took a poker from the fireplace, smashed in a window and climbed into the room.

He told Det. Sgt. R. E. Byron that Miss Monroe was under a sheet and champagne-coloured blanket which were tucked up around her shoulders.

Dr. Greenson took the telephone receiver from her hand and told Mrs. Murray, "She appears to be dead."

He called Dr. Engelberg, who had prescribed the sleeping pills for the actress, who pronounced her dead on his arrival at the house a short time later. Dr. Engelberg called police at 4.20 a.m. and two officers arrived in five minutes, followed by Sgt. Byron at 5 a.m.

Byron said he learned that Miss Monroe had called Dr. Greenson Saturday night and talked with him for about an hour. He quoted the psychiatrist as saying: "I was under the impression she was going to take a ride... to the beach or something like that."

Byron said he went through the rambling Spanish style home at 12305 5th Helena Drive and found "nothing unusual or amiss."

He reported there were between 12 to 15 medicine bottles on Miss Monroe's bedside stand, some with prescription labels.

Miss Monroe only recently bought the $75,000 house and it was only partially furnished.

By dawn reporters and photographers were milling around its lawns and swimming pool, silent in the morning quiet as officials closed out the life of one of filmland's most glamorous stars.

Miss Monroe's body was wrapped in a pale blue blanket and strapped to a stretcher as it was removed from the home.

Seals were placed on entrances to the home with the notice:

"Any person breaking into or entering these premises will be prosecuted to the fullest extent of the law."

A special guard was hired to watch the home.

Miss Monroe's body was loaded into the back of a station wagon and transported to the Westwood Village Mortuary, just yards away from the grave sites of her grandmother and one of her guardians in early life.

The body later was transferred to the County Morgue where the nation's No. 1 glamour girl became coroner's case No. 81128 and the body was placed in crypt 33.

Funeral services are tentatively scheduled for Wednesday afternoon at Westwood Village Mortuary chapel.

Her mother, Mrs. Gladys Baker Eley, 59, is a patient in the Rockhaven Sanitarium in Verdugo City.

News of Miss Monroe's tragic death quickly circulated to much of the world. Even Moscow Radio made mention of it.

Friends of the actress were stunned, unbelieving and saddened.

Joe DiMaggio, baseball hero and the actress's second husband, flew here from San Francisco as soon as he heard. His face was lined and he appeared deeply saddened when he alighted from a United Air Lines plane.

DiMaggio checked into a Santa Monica hotel, where he declined to talk with reporters or pose for pictures.

He and Miss Monroe had been seeing each other recently since her third attempt at marriage, with playwright Arthur Miller, collapsed in 1961.

In Woodbury, Conn., Miller replied "I don't, really" when asked if he had any comment.

Her first husband was Jim Dougherty, now a Los Angeles policeman. His only comment was, "I'm sorry."

One of the first friends to arrive at the home Sunday morning was Pat Newcomb, a close friend of the actress and her press agent.

Miss Newcomb, nearly hysterical with grief, sobbed: "When your best friend kills herself, how do you feel? What do you do?"

She said she spent Saturday evening with Miss Monroe, had a quiet dinner and left the home about 7 p.m.

"This must have been an accident," she said. "Marilyn was in perfect physical condition and was feeling great.

"We had made plans for today. We were going to the movies this afternoon."

Milton Rudin, Miss Monroe's attorney, also went to the house and told reporters he had talked with the star Saturday.

"She appeared to be happy," he said. "She wanted to see me in my office Monday."

Miss Monroe was hopeful she could settle her difficulties with 20th Century-Fox Studios which earlier this summer fired her from the movie, "Something's Got to Give."

The studio claimed she refused to report for work costing it $2 million because of delays. It sued her for a half million dollars.

Despite this, Rudin said Miss Monroe hoped to work out a settlement with the studio and get the picture back in production.

Miss Monroe claimed throughout the dispute with 20th Century-Fox that she was ill and unable to report for work.

"She wanted to finish everything she started," said Rudin.

Some believed Miss Monroe was depressed because her career was supposedly on the skids after two straight movie flops in *Let's Make Love* and *The Misfits* – her last two movies.

But friends were nearly unanimous in believing her death was accidental.

They said two motion picture executives were bidding for her services at the time of her death. One of them was reportedly J. Lee Thompson, director of the film *The Guns of Navarone*, who planned to meet with her Tuesday.

Producer Sam Spiegel also wanted her to star in a picture for him, it was reported.

Miss Monroe had received an offer of $5,500 a week to star in a night club appearance in Las Vegas recently, but she turned it down.

Further evidence that her career was on the upswing was indicated by a typewritten message on a table in her home. It was from a representative of Anita Loos, creator of *Gentlemen Prefer Blondes*, and said:

"Dear Miss Monroe: On behalf of Anita Loos, now in Europe, we would like to know if you would be interested in the star role new musical based on French play *Gogo*. Book by Anita Loos, lyrics by Gladys Shelley and enchanting music by Claude Leville. Can send you script and music if you express interest. (signed) Natalia Danesi Murray."

An associate of Miss Monroe said her 23 pictures since 1950 when she had a bit role in the *Asphalt Jungle* have grossed $200 million.

"Does that sound like she was depressed about her career?" he asked.

By mid-morning Sunday the crowds of reporters, photographers and friends cleared away from the officially sealed home where the tormented actress had spent her last hours.

Miss Newcomb took the housekeeper home and carried with her Miss Monroe's small white dog "Maf". All that was left behind for the eye of the curious were the dog's two stuffed toys, a tiger and lamb, lying in the rear yard.'

There is no mention of Peter Lawford or, indeed, any condolence message from President Kennedy whom she had sung so sweetly for only weeks earlier. Lawford was smuggled away, out of the city and flown to Hyannis Port. He was never interviewed by the police or the coroner's office at that time. Detective Sergeant R.E. Byron, who is mentioned in the *Los Angeles Times* report, is the signatory [R.E. Byron # 2730, W. LA Detectives] on a file note about the Marilyn investigation: 'An attempt was made to contact Mr. Lawford, but officers were informed by his secretary that Mr. Lawford had taken an airplane at 1p.m., 8 August 1962. It is unknown at the time the exact destination, however his secretary stated that she did expect to hear from him and she would request that he contact this department at his earliest convenience. [sic]'

There was never any police interview or follow-up until October 16, 1975, when Lawford was questioned in Los Angeles by the team taking a fresh look at the case following the *Oui* magazine article. Lawford told the story he had learned and memorised, rehearsed and performed to near perfection until his meeting with Mike Rothmiller when he finally revealed the truth. His story is detailed in the LAPD report of the 1975 inquiry:

'Mr. Lawford stated that most of what has been written by various authors, such as Slatzer, Scaduto, [Norman] Mailer and others regarding the last days in Marilyn Monroe's life is "pure fantasy." He states that Miss Monroe was a regular weekend guest at his beachfront home in Santa Monica.

'On August 4, 1962, Mr. Lawford telephoned Marilyn Monroe at approximately 5 p.m. to ask her if she was coming to his house that weekend. She sounded despondent over her loss of contract with 20th Century Fox Studios and some other personal matters − presumably the romance with Robert Kennedy. Lawford tried to convince her to forget about her problems and join him and his wife Pat for dinner that evening. She replied she would consider joining them. At approximately 7.30 or 8 p.m. Lawford telephoned her a second time to ascertain why she hadn't as yet arrived at his home ... Lawford stated Miss Monroe was still very despondent and her manner of speech was slurred. She stated she was tired and would not be coming. Her voice became less and less audible and Lawford began to yell at her to revive her [he described it as a verbal slap in the face]. Then she stated: "Say goodbye to Pat, say goodbye to Jack [JFK] and say goodbye to yourself, because you're a nice guy." When the phone went dead, Lawford, assuming she had hung up, tried several times to redial her home number and received a busy signal each time.

'Lawford never told Milton Ebbins [his agent and a dinner guest] he was going to Marilyn's house. Ebbins recommended against it ("You know how agents are?") and suggested that he [Ebbins] would call her doctor or lawyer. Eventually Ebbins was able to reach her attorney.

'Lawford stated he often talked to Marilyn on the phone when she was under the effects of downers and her voice this evening sounded about the same. For some reason, however, he had a gut feeling that something was wrong. He states that he still blames himself for not going to her home. Approximately three weeks prior to this event, on a weekend, Lawford states Marilyn was a guest of the Lawfords' at the Cal Neva Lodge in Lake Tahoe where Frank Sinatra was headlining. When Lawford awoke one morning his wife told him Marilyn had overdosed the evening prior. She had been discovered when she fell out of bed and was unable to be revived without professional medical assistance.

'Regarding Robert F. Kennedy, Lawford is adamant that the Attorney General was not in the Los Angeles area on August 4 or 5. He states that whenever RFK came to town he would come to the Lawfords' home and swim in the pool.

'Lawford states he has no knowledge of RFK's stay in San Francisco as alluded to in the *Oui* article.'

The truth is that both Lawford and the LAPD inner circle knew, even if the Los Angeles taxpayers didn't, that Robert Kennedy was there on the day. The investigators knew the verdict before they heard the case. The LAPD said their reopening of the inquiry of Marilyn's death was hampered because the initial reports were destroyed in 1973, as was legally allowed after ten years. But they wanted to be seen as doing a definitive investigation so, out of the blue, some copies of the files were suddenly found in the garage of Thad Brown, the deputy chief of the detective bureau at the time of Marilyn's death, who had himself died in 1972. There were more than 700 pages in the Marilyn files but only nineteen were said to be matters 'for the public record'. Thad Brown had copies of the 'sensitive' OCID files at his home to prevent them being made public by court order or revealed in any legal actions. They were part of the OCID files read by Mike Rothmiller.

From the moment Marilyn died, a chilling conspiracy began to concoct a fictional version of the events, echoing the words of Churchill: 'History is written by victors.' Orchestrated by Captain James Hamilton, the LAPD conspirators worked to disguise the truth. Their version of Marilyn's last day makes mention of the drug Nembutal, portrays her mood as argumentative, difficult and suggests she was losing self-control. Although it was presented in chronological order with events witnessed by outsiders – delivery boys and others – for veracity, it contradicts itself because that's what it was intended to do: confuse.

**8.00 a.m.** Eunice Murray arrives at Cursum Perficio, 12305 Fifth Helena Drive.

**9.00 a.m.** Marilyn gets up, has juice and tells Mrs. Murray that Pat Newcomb has stayed over.

**10.00 a.m.** Larry Schiller [the photographer] calls to the house to discuss Marilyn's racy photos from the set of *Something's Got To Give* appearing in *Playboy* magazine.

**10.30 a.m. – 12.00 p.m.** A bedside table is delivered, and Marilyn writes a cheque for it. Marilyn's citrus trees from the Montana Avenue garden centre arrive.

**12.00 p.m.** Pat Newcomb gets up and is about to leave when Eunice Murray offers her breakfast. Newcomb decides to stay on and spends the afternoon with Marilyn. The two argued over the fact Newcomb had slept so late.

**1.00 p.m. – 2.00 p.m.** Murray claimed Marilyn asked her if they had any oxygen in the house.

**2.00 p.m. – 4.00 p.m.** Henry D'Antonio and his wife arrive with Eunice Murray's car. [D'Antonio, a mechanic, had repaired Mrs. Murray's car that morning.] Mrs. Murray brings them in to the kitchen and tells them Marilyn is resting in her room.

**4.30 p.m. – 5.00 p.m.** Dr. Greenson arrives. Greenson sees Marilyn in her room.

**6.00 p.m.** Greenson comes into the living room, where Newcomb and Murray are chatting, and asks Newcomb to leave. Newcomb gets up and leaves without saying another word.

**7.00 p.m.** Greenson leaves to attend a dinner party with his wife.

**7.30 p.m.** Joe DiMaggio Jr. [Joe DiMaggio's son] calls and tells Marilyn he has ended his engagement with his fiancée. Marilyn is happy with this news and sounds upbeat on the phone.

**8.00 p.m.** Marilyn calls Greenson to inform him about the call from Joe Jr. It is suggested that at this point Marilyn and Greenson had an argument, possibly about his need to get off the phone. Marilyn asks him 'Where is my Nembutal?' This would be the first time that Greenson realised Marilyn had any Nembutal, as he understood his colleague Dr. Hyman Engelberg was not prescribing it to her any more. Greenson has to go and the call ends. Following that call, Marilyn returns to her room.

**8.00 p.m. – 9.00 p.m.** Marilyn had agreed to attend a dinner party on the basis that she would go home early as she said Sunday was to be a busy day for her, and Peter Lawford telephoned to check if she was coming. Marilyn, sounding 'weird, fuzzy and sleepy' according to Peter Lawford [after events] says she is tired and won't be going. He claimed it wasn't unusual to hear Marilyn like this and thought she was either drunk or about to sleep after taking pills. What Marilyn says next worries Lawford and he quotes her saying: 'Say goodbye to Pat, say goodbye to the President, and say goodbye to yourself because you're a nice guy.' Marilyn's voice trails off and Lawford said he presumed she had fallen asleep.

**9.00 p.m. – 10.00 p.m.** According to the autopsy report Marilyn has swallowed 42 or so barbiturate tablets, enough to kill several people. Dr. Hyman Engelberg, who was helping Marilyn keep off Nembutal by putting her on chloral hydrate, had, in this scenario, prescribed Nembutal for her on August 3.

[That prescription for 25 Phenergan 25mg strength capsules was dated August 3, 1962, and filled by the Vicente Pharmacy, 12025 San Vicente Boulevard. The number 20857 was given to the Phenergan prescription and 20858 was assigned to the Nembutal prescription. Dr. Engelberg said that he had prescribed a refill of Nembutal and there should have been 50 capsules at the time of the refill. The prescription was for 25 capsules and was not a refill as it was given a new order number. The only thing clear from the doctors' stories is there were a lethal number of pills available should Marilyn want to ingest them.]

**9.30 p.m. to 10.00 p.m.** Milton Rudin calls the house to ask if Marilyn is OK. Eunice Murray, unaware Rudin has received a call from a worried Lawford, thought nothing of it and told Rudin that Marilyn was in bed.

**12.00 a.m. to 3.00 a.m.** Eunice Murray wakes up feeling something is wrong and sees Marilyn dead in her bed.

**3.15 a.m.** Dr. Greenson arrives at Marilyn's house.

**3.30 a.m.** Dr. Hyman Engelberg arrives.

**4.25 a.m.** The police are called by Dr. Hyman Engelberg: Marilyn Monroe is pronounced dead.

**4.28 a.m.** West Los Angeles Police Division are informed of a death at 12305 Fifth Helena Drive.

There is no mention of Bobby Kennedy or Peter Lawford being at the house during that time period and no official confirmation of Bobby Kennedy being in town at that time until Chief Daryl Gates' book in 1992. And that was not a formal confirmation, simply, the then retired Gates revealing what he had known for many years. During all the decades of searching around by private and media investigators there was a piece of paper that would have told so much, and it was sitting in the OCID files. It was a deposition from Bobby Kennedy that he was in Los Angeles on August 4, 1962 and was at Marilyn's home. Captain James Hamilton kept that paperwork secured.

The timeline, or variations of it, were developed from the moment Marilyn died and with each day more tapestry was hung and the picture was constantly being retouched. Her demise was packaged as the tragic end of a sex symbol who had reached the end of the line. The public couldn't get enough of the gossip and innuendo which was being dripped out. It was said that upon her death 'she was thin', her hair 'ruined' by bleach and that she wouldn't leave the house without her make-up man and hairdresser to prepare her. [The definition of her being 'unkempt' was very Hollywood: she needed a manicure.] She was 'flagrantly promiscuous' and there had been an abortion. '*Of course, she killed herself.*' The headlines kept coming.

Yet, the week before her death, she was the cover star of *Life* and *Paris Match* who reported on the triumph of her return to Fox and the set of *Something's Got To Give*. Not signs that she was suicidal due to a failing career. The truth, arguably, is that she was probably somewhere in-between, unhappy but hopeful or vice versa.

It's not clear when she died. It was not 4.25 a.m. on Sunday, August 5, 1962, which is the official time recorded. And it was not due to a massive overdose of 47 Nembutal capsules which was the Los Angeles coroner's verdict. There was no trace of drugs in her stomach, or evidence of her having taken the tablets orally. Forensic evidence went missing shortly after she died. All the prime witnesses contradicted each other, and some changed their versions of events. Her doctors made the ludicrous claim that they needed permission from 20th Century Fox to send her body to the morgue. Subsequently, many rent-a-quote characters appeared and were dismissed while others, although suspect, were given the benefit of doubt. Taken against the events as presented in this book they show how brilliant the cover-up was. They created false trails and ensured that there was finger-pointing here, there, everywhere. There were men who knew the truth – what Mike Rothmiller knew when he interviewed Lawford and Fred Otash – either first-hand or second-hand through wiretaps, and when you understand that, the enormity and brazen scale of it becomes clear.

The contradictions in the accounts of that day are many. Pat Newcomb said she resolved her argument with Marilyn and went shopping and when she returned Marilyn was happy and upbeat. By contrast, Dr. Greenson said that when he arrived for his daily visit, his patient was in 'a highly emotional' condition. Peter Lawford said when he called at 7.30 p.m., Marilyn was 'out of it'. Joe DiMaggio Jr. said that she was in a very good mood at the news he was breaking off an engagement she disapproved of when *he* phoned her at 7.30 p.m. Eunice Murray woke up and claimed she saw a light under Marilyn's door. Concerned that something terrible had happened, she called Greenson at 3.30 a.m. They peered into Monroe's bedroom window and saw her naked body, she said. Dr. Greenson says he broke into the room via the window with a poker, before calling Dr. Engelberg, but the window had been mended by the time the police arrived. Others insist it was broken – but from the *inside* with telling particles of glass scattered around outside the window. There were debates over whether Marilyn's door was locked or unlocked. The details, like a rash of clues in a credulity-stretching mystery novel, add up to not very much. The truth, as always, was in the details which had been covered up.

Eunice Murray admitted during a BBC interview in 1985 that Bobby Kennedy had visited Marilyn that day. Even more telling was her revelation of the premeditated arrival of an ambulance while Marilyn was still alive. Neighbours who had seen and reported an ambulance parked in front of Marilyn's home had been told they were mistaken, too upset by events to recollect what actually happened and when. The same neighbours also reported a helicopter hovering overhead, raised voices and the sound of breaking glass and these were noted in an LAPD report. The reports omitted any mention of an ambulance sitting outside 12305 Fifth Helena Drive.

The instinctive Florabel Muir didn't believe for a moment that Marilyn had killed herself and said so in her *New York Daily News* column:

"'Strange pressures are being put on Los Angeles police investigating the death of Marilyn Monroe,' sources close to the probers said last night.

'Police investigators have refused to make public the records of phone calls made from Miss Monroe's home last Saturday evening, hours before she took an overdose of sleeping pills. The police have impounded the phone company's taped record of outgoing calls. Normally in suicide probes here, the record of such phone calls would have been made available to the public within a few days.

'The purported pressures are mysterious. They apparently are coming from persons who had been closely in touch with Marilyn the last few weeks.

'No one knows exactly how many people had access to the house the night Monroe's body was found. Papers were destroyed, telephone records seized. Were they searching for that little black book?'

Police chief Thad Brown had leaked the story that Marilyn's telephone logs had been confiscated from the General Telephone Company by the LAPD to Florabel Muir and was reprimanded for that by Chief Parker.

Hairdresser Sydney Guilaroff reported that, late Saturday afternoon, an upset Marilyn had telephoned him twice and said that Bobby Kennedy had been at her house with Peter Lawford and he was threatening her. This echoes what Peter Lawford told Mike Rothmiller in the park in 1982. It is testimony never revealed until now and it makes so much clear about the day Mike Rothmiller believes Marilyn Monroe was killed by Bobby Kennedy, the Attorney General of the United States and the younger brother of the President. From Peter Lawford's testimony, we now know how fear can coerce people to collaborate. The stark contrast of Lawford's words to the official line are staggering and they rewrite history.

# XIII: The Truth

*'The secret of a great success for which you are at a lost to account is a crime that has never been found out, because it was properly executed.'*
— Honoré de Balzac, *Le Père Goriot*, 1835.

Mike Rothmiller says he still feels overwhelmed when recalling his interview-interrogation of Peter Lawford. Rarely a day goes by when Rothmiller doesn't, for a moment, see Lawford's face and feel the burden he carried. Here for the first time is what Lawford told Mike Rothmiller – the truth about what happened to Marilyn Monroe:

What I already knew – and what Chief Daryl Gates, former LAPD Chief's Tom Reddin and William Parker, the FBI and CIA, and former Los Angeles Mayor Sam Yorty already knew – was confirmed by Peter Lawford. Robert Kennedy secretly came to southern California the day Marilyn died.

The days leading up to Marilyn's death were filled with emotional telephone calls from her to Peter Lawford, President Kennedy, Attorney General Robert Kennedy, and others. As the days passed without Jack or Bobby returning her calls, Marilyn transformed from a woman pleading with her lover to a scorned woman on the path to revenge. She was rapidly moving toward a showdown with the most powerful men in the world. If she wasn't immediately brought under control, the Presidency was in danger. This was the conclusion reached in top secret documents and, at the time, by Peter Lawford and more importantly, by President John F. Kennedy and his brother Robert.

On August 5, 1962, Robert Kennedy covertly travelled from the San Francisco area to southern California via a private aircraft. Lawford picked him up at the airport and drove to his beach house in Santa Monica where RFK and Marilyn exchanged telephone calls before Lawford drove Robert Kennedy to her residence for the first visit of that day.

Between calls with Marilyn, Robert Kennedy telephoned President Kennedy providing updates on the situation. Robert Kennedy also made several, presumably guarded, telephone calls after requesting that Lawford leave the room.

Although OCID documents indicated that Lawford and Kennedy secretly visited Marilyn's home twice that day, Lawford vacillated on the number of visits. He was firm that they visited during the evening [when she died] but seemed to be confused regarding the earlier visit. However, he could not be sure that they did not visit twice. When I informed him that the files had recorded two visits that day, he nodded in agreement.

Keeping Lawford on point was challenging during our time together. He'd start to answer a question then drift off into an unrelated field. I'd quickly stop him. 'Peter. That's interesting, but it has nothing to do with my question.' He'd look at me and say, 'Oh. Sorry.' And I'd state the question again.

What occurred during their evening visit was the heart of the interrogation and my primary focus. I didn't know how long he would continue to talk, so it was imperative I forced the conversation to that evening.

'What happened when you and Robert arrived at her home that night?'

He didn't turn to me or acknowledge my question. He just stared straight ahead in silence. When he answered, he started to retell the story of the earlier visit, not the evening visit.

'Ah, an old woman answered the door. I think she was the housekeeper. I gave her some money and told her to leave.'

'Did she leave?'

He nodded.

'That meant only you, Robert and Marilyn were in the house.'

He nodded again.

I believed Lawford was confusing some details of their earlier visit with the final evening visit since intelligence documents indicated that the housekeeper was present during the first visit and was ordered to leave. Fortunately, I had the benefit of having viewed the intelligence documents and having spoken to Fred Otash so I was apprised of that information. When Lawford seemed confused, I was able to fill in the blanks. 'That's right,' he would reply.

'Wasn't the housekeeper there during your first visit and not the second?'

He turned to me and thought before he answered. 'Yeah.'

I had him back on track. He started to speak openly without my prodding or interruptions. As he spoke, it was apparent he was reliving that night, and it was painful. I have witnessed people under interrogation lapse into this state where the images, sounds, smells, and pain of the horrific event resurface. He was a man unburdening himself of a terrible nightmare he'd kept secret for years. Now, he could tell his story and relieve that incessant pressure and guilt.

When they arrived for the evening visit, Marilyn answered the door. Peter Lawford thought she was slightly under the influence of alcohol or drugs, but she was not intoxicated. Almost immediately, the situation became heated as they moved into the living room where Marilyn accused Robert Kennedy and his brother of treating her as a whore and added that she had had enough of them. Robert said something to the effect of 'What do you want?' That question pushed Marilyn into a tirade. She stepped toward Robert and yelled:

'What do I want?! What do I want?! I don't want to be treated like a fucking whore and ignored!'

'What do you want?' Robert asked again. With his voice raised he shook his hand in her face.

Marilyn slapped his hand away, and Kennedy slammed her to the floor near the sofa. He leaned over her, screaming profanities and grabbing her flailing arms by the wrists. She struggled free of his grip and slapped him, enraging Kennedy to a point where Lawford believed Kennedy was about to strike her. Peter grabbed Kennedy from behind and pulled him away. Lawford recalled few of the details of the rest of the argument but remembered it was heated and involved a physical altercation.

He helped Marilyn to her feet and sat her on the sofa while Bobby stormed out of the room and began searching the house – through cabinets and drawers – while Lawford stayed with Marilyn to try and restrain and calm her. He wasn't sure exactly what Bobby was trying to find, but he already understood that Kennedy wanted her diary and other items linking the Kennedys to her.

Marilyn stood, pushed Lawford away and stormed into her bedroom where Bobby was rummaging through the dresser. She screamed at him to get out and jerked him away from the dresser. Kennedy angrily spun around and violently pushed Marilyn, causing her to fall onto the bed and tumble to the floor. Instantly, Kennedy leaned over her, grabbed her wrists, and pulled her onto the bed. She was now crying. Kennedy held her down on the bed and repeatedly yelled: 'Where is it?' He said he had to have it and they'd pay her [Lawford understood this to mean they'd pay for her silence]. Again, Lawford interceded by pulling Kennedy away. Lawford didn't remember the exact words but recalled Kennedy leaning over her and screaming something to the effect of 'You'd better shut your mouth.'

Marilyn was hysterical and crying when Kennedy stormed out of the bedroom. Lawford was stunned by Kennedy's actions and at a loss to explain his violent outburst and the apparent threat. He didn't know what he should do. He helped Marilyn into a seated position on the bed and did his best to console her. He hugged her for several minutes before she pushed him away, stood up, and went in search of Robert. Peter quickly followed her into the living room, grabbed her, and convinced her to sit with him on the sofa. Reluctantly, she complied. He glanced around the room looking for Robert but didn't see him. He heard a noise in the kitchen and begged Marilyn to remain seated while he spoke with Robert.

At this point in our conversation, Lawford paused, dropped his head, and covered his face with his hands. He was silent for several moments, and I was worried he had decided to stop talking. I placed my hand on his shoulder and gently squeezed, attempting to console him. 'What is it?' I asked softly. He remained silent for a few seconds more and then said: 'Nothing.' He rubbed his face, raised his head, and looked straight ahead before taking a deep breath.

'Are you OK?'

He nodded, yes.

'Ah, I left her on the sofa and went into the kitchen. Bobby was by the sink. He had a glass of water and was stirring it.'

'Why was he stirring a glass of water? Did he put something in it?'

'I asked him [Bobby], "What are you doing?"'

'Did he tell you?'

216

Peter shook his head, implying no.

'What do you think he was doing?'

He gazed forward, then looked at me. His expression had changed. He suddenly looked like a man on the verge of crying. He took several moments before – in a near whisper – he said, 'He put something in it.'

'What was it?' I asked.

'I don't know.'

'Was the water coloured or clear?'

'Clear.'

'Then what happened?'

He took another long pause.

'I pointed to the glass and asked what was in it.'

'What did he say?' I asked.

He told me that Kennedy had snapped, 'Nothing!' Lawford watched as Kennedy placed the spoon into a drawer and picked up the glass. They remained in the kitchen for a few moments as Lawford repeatedly asked Kennedy why he was doing this [meaning the outrage and violent attack on Monroe]. He didn't receive an answer. He told Kennedy they had to leave because the neighbours might have heard the yelling and could have called the police. Bobby didn't respond.

Marilyn could be heard weeping in the living room. Lawford, clearly pained, recalled that he followed Kennedy as he took the glass and walked to the living room where Marilyn was seated on the sofa, cradling her head in her hands and crying. They stood in front of her, and Kennedy extended the glass to her.

'Drink this, you'll feel better,' Kennedy said to Marilyn. She looked up and refused at first, but, with Lawford's coaxing, she took a drink and immediately remarked on the unpleasant taste. Lawford indicated that at the time he thought it contained a sedative which would calm her and defuse the situation.

'Finish it,' Kennedy told her. 'Hurry up.' She glanced up at him, and then looked to Lawford, who said: 'It's OK.' Lawford motioned to the glass. 'It's OK; finish it.'

With that, she finished the drink.

To the best of his recollection, Lawford and Kennedy then left Marilyn on the sofa and proceeded to search the other rooms before returning to the living room. His time frame was sketchy, but he remembers that when they returned to the living room, Marilyn hadn't moved from the sofa. She was leaning back with her head tilted backward. She appeared to be sleeping. Kennedy approached and shook her shoulder until a groggy and obviously drugged Marilyn stirred.

Her voice was a whisper, slurred and completely unintelligible. Kennedy shook her again and said something to her that Lawford could not clearly hear. Marilyn mumbled a couple more unintelligible words and appeared to pass out. Kennedy again shook her shoulder and said her name, but she didn't respond.

Lawford realised she was unresponsive and didn't appear to be breathing, he asked Kennedy, 'What did you give her?' Kennedy momentarily stared at her then turned to Lawford but didn't answer. He moved to continue his search of the house and Lawford followed him.

'What items did he take from her house?' I asked.

'I don't know.'

It was then they heard a knock at the front door. Lawford feared it was the police. He and Kennedy quickly moved to the living room. He glanced at Marilyn, who was in the same position and clearly unconscious. 'Her complexion was now waxen.' Lawford moved to Marilyn and gently shook her by the shoulder: 'Marilyn. Marilyn!' He touched her face and concluded she wasn't breathing.

He turned to Kennedy standing nearby and said, 'She's not breathing! We need to call an ambulance.'

'What did Bobby do?' I asked.

'Bobby grabbed my arm and said, "Leave her." He pulled me toward the front door.' With Kennedy standing behind him, Lawford cautiously opened the door and was confronted by two men; startled, he immediately thought a neighbour - having heard the banging and shouting — had called the police. But the men were not in uniform, so he assumed they were detectives or CIA agents. For a moment he thought his life and the world of the Kennedy Camelot was crashing to an end.

It happened so quickly but Lawford didn't recall speaking to the men before Kennedy grabbed his arm and promptly guided him out the door. As they passed the men, Kennedy only glanced at them and continued. No words were spoken.

As Kennedy hurriedly led Lawford to their car, Lawford asked, 'Who are they?'

Kennedy only responded, 'We must leave.'

'But Marilyn!' Lawford looked back and saw the men enter Marilyn's home and close the door.

'Let's go!' Bobby insisted. He and Bobby entered his car and Lawford drove away. Bobby told him to take him to the airport. Lawford recalled it was eerily quiet during the drive and neither of them spoke.

I let Lawford rest for a few moments before asking my next question.

'Did you recognise the men?'

Lawford thought for a moment, 'One's a cop. I've seen him with John and Bobby before. I don't know the other.'

'Was the cop named Hamilton?'

He raised his hands from his lap in frustration. 'I don't know.' It was apparent this interview was taking an emotional toll on him. I felt sorry for the man and decided I had to end it with my final questions.

'Peter, I must know. Why did they do this? Why was she killed?'

He sat in silence as a tear ran down his cheek. 'I don't know. I don't know.'

'I understand.' I tried to console him and rubbed his shoulder.

'When you left Marilyn, did you believe she was dead?'

He began to cry and nodded, yes. Then, in almost a whisper, he said, 'They didn't need to do this.' I believed Lawford. I saw his pain. 'Did you know why there was a delay in calling the police after you left her?'

He shrugged, shook his head and softly said, 'I'm not sure.' He paused and added, 'I heard it was to give him enough time to fly to San Francisco.'

'Who told you that?'

'I don't remember.'

'Was the delay to establish his alibi?' He simply nodded. Yes.

As Lawford ended his story, it was even more apparent that telling it had taken a heavy toll. He was emotionally and physically drained. His trembling hands wiped away the tears trickling down his cheeks. He coughed several times and did his best to clear his throat. During my years of interviewing victims and interrogating suspects, I had only seen this type of response a few times. It was clear he had been carrying the burden of guilt for many years and, in all likelihood, this guilt had destroyed his career and, sadly, him as a human being. But now he appeared comforted and serene having released the horrible burden he'd been forced to carry.

Surprisingly, I also felt emotionally drained. Nothing I had learned *should* have surprised me, but it did. My detective experience and my gut now convinced me that Lawford had no prior knowledge of what was going to occur and played no role in Marilyn's death, beyond driving Robert Kennedy to her home, away from the crime scene and then remaining silent for all these years. Witnessing his unmistakable anguish at that moment drove that point home. For the emotions of both of us, I had to end this.

I turned to him, reassuringly placed my hand on his thigh and asked my final question.

'Do you think John and Bobby wanted her dead?'

He stared straight ahead and whispered: 'Yes.'

# XIV: The Big Sleep

*'The poison came in liquid*
*She was naked all the time*
*And no one could explain it,*
*It's the same sad echo coming down,'*
— Tom Petty, *Echo*, 1999.

On Sunday August 5, 1962, the world awoke to headlines and broadcast news announcing the death of Marilyn Monroe. Immediately, it was declared a suicide and straightaway millions wondered why she would take her own life? Sergeant Jack Clemmons, the first LAPD detective to arrive in an official capacity at Cursum Perficio never thought she ended her own life. He believed her bedroom and everything around it had been created to show 'she was alive enough to kill herself'.

His initial conclusion over what he found at Marilyn's home brought him a lifetime of badgering and death threats – often from his own colleagues. Officer Clemmons hadn't yet met Mike Rothmiller, but he contacted him in 1992 after Rothmiller's book *LA Secret Police: Inside the Elite LAPD Spy Network* was published with its passing mention of Marilyn Monroe's death. Clemmons was ashamed of some of the interviews he'd been forced to give by his superiors and provided revelatory new information to Rothmiller during many subsequent meetings.

Clemmons had started work at midnight on August 4, 1962, as a watch commander of the West Los Angeles Police Division headquartered not far away south of San Vicente and down and over Wilshire Boulevard near MGM studios. He took a telephone call at 4.28 a.m. from Dr. Hyman Engelberg who told him: 'Marilyn Monroe is dead. She committed suicide.'

Normally, for a supposed suicide, he would have sent a patrol car with a two-man unit. But... Marilyn Monroe? Dead? He drove over there himself. When he arrived at 12305 Fifth Helena Drive it was some hours after Bobby Kennedy and Peter Lawford had left the scene [as earlier noted they were stopped with Dr. Greenson in the front seat of the Lincoln Continental at 12.10 a.m. by Beverly Hills officer Lynn Franklin.] Mike Rothmiller made extensive notes from his sessions with Jack Clemmons. Here are his findings:

We had several lunch meetings and many telephone conversations. Just weeks before Jack Clemmons' unexpected death in April 1998, I had arranged for him to be the guest speaker at the Orange County Sisters in Crime [a crime writers' organisation] to talk about Marilyn Monroe's death. This is his story which we discussed, studied, ratified and investigated over more than six years.

Jack was the first LAPD officer to arrive at Monroe's home and view her body. Within minutes of his arrival, he suspected and quickly determined that the people at her home were not telling the truth and that the death scene had been staged. Her body had been posed on the bed, legs stretched out perfectly straight, unlike the contorted bodies of most victims who have overdosed on sleeping tablets.

Within just a few days, he sensed an LAPD cover-up was underway but didn't know why or who was behind it. Over the following months, he was harassed by his superiors, and his statements and reports regarding Monroe were falsified. He strenuously objected to the changes in his reports but was ordered to shut up and never speak about Monroe's death again. This bothered Jack greatly, that's why he told me his story and asked that I, in some fashion, tell his story to the world.

Jack appeared on *The Geraldo Show* and other programmes where he recounted the basic story he told me many times. However, he never disclosed the specific details which follow. These were told to me in confidence and only after we had built up a rapport over several face-to-face meetings. I assured him I'd never disclose the information without his permission or would do so only after his death.

As with all unsolved homicides, cops withhold certain key details that only the killer would know. That's why Jack never disclosed the information below. He hoped that someday, it would prove or disprove a person's knowledge of the killing.

On arrival at the scene in 1962, he noted that the people in Monroe's home appeared extremely nervous – not upset as you might expect people to be about the sudden death of a loved one. When Jack made eye contact with them, they either looked down or quickly looked away – except for Dr. Greenson who was confrontational. This is very unusual behaviour at the scene of a death. Within minutes of Jack arriving and confirming her death, he rapidly uncovered evidence which indicated it was not a suicide. And the people in her home grew more nervous and less cooperative as he asked questions.

Jack recalled: 'Monroe had some livor mortis on her back which indicated the body had been moved after death and placed on the bed face down. At first, the doctors said they hadn't moved her or rolled her over. Then they changed their story and said they *did* roll her over on the bed to see if they could save her. If the doctors rolled her over to check for life, that meant she was face down when she died. And, if they rolled her on her back to check her vital signs, why did they bother to roll her face down again?'

Livor mortis or lividity is the gravitational pooling of blood in the dependent parts of the body, both externally in the skin capillaries and venules but also in the internal organs. Its onset is variable but is usually most evident about two hours after death. The significance of this in Marilyn's case is not the cause of death but that her body must have been manhandled and positioned this way and that, to cause the extent of livor mortis Jack Clemmons saw and the bruising on Marilyn's body. A casework on livor mortis gives an understanding of what livor mortis can tell crime scene investigators:

'A body is found in a field lying on her back with the legs and arms flexed at the elbows and knees. The decedent was noted to have left-side livor. The rigor was present throughout the body and the livor was fixed on the left torso. A gunshot wound was noted on the left of the scalp. These findings indicate the body has been moved. Rigor assumes the position of gravity and upward flexion of the extremities is not consistent with the death occurring at that site. Fixed lividity on one side of the body is also inconsistent with the body being on her back at the time of death, confirming the body was moved. The body was in the position for a period of at least six to eight hours or longer prior to being placed into the field where it was found.'

Jack squeezed her neck and shoulders and noticed rigor mortis had set in and she was cold to the touch. Meaning she had been dead for some hours. He was disdainful of the doctors. Jack didn't believe them since she had a great deal of lividity on her face and they certainly would have seen it and known she had been dead for some time. Simply touching her body or checking for a carotid pulse would have told the doctors she was dead, negating any need to roll her onto her back.

Not long after the empty pill bottles next to her body were pointed out to him, Jack heard a toilet in another part of the house flush twice. He moved in that direction and saw Dr. Greenson exit the bathroom. Greenson seemed startled when he noticed Jack staring at him and made an off the cuff remark that he had to use the restroom. That was a strange statement since it was obvious Greenson had used the bathroom, and no explanation was required.

Jack was suspicious of Greenson, and after the doctor walked away, Jack entered the bathroom and noted some residual of pills in the toilet (a couple of pills were only partially broken down and resting at the bottom of the bowl) and the water was a light pinkish colour. He asked Greenson if he dumped pills in the toilet and the doctor denied it. Jack told him not to use the toilet again and left the area. A few moments later he heard the toilet flush again. He walked back and noticed Greenson had again flushed the toilet. Jack confronted him by saying: 'I told you not to use that bathroom.' Greenson played stupid and replied, 'Oh, I thought you meant the other one.' Jack immediately entered the bathroom and noticed the pill residual was gone and the pinkish water was now clear.

Dr. Greenson and Dr. Engelberg told Jack Clemmons that their delay in alerting the police of Marilyn's death was because they were busy telephoning 20th Century Fox and her 'business associates'. Four hours of business phone calls as Marilyn lay dead? Eunice Murray was doing the laundry when Sergeant Clemmons arrived which literally pointed to a clean-up.

When he had arrived at Monroe's home, he had seen an unmarked LAPD car parked down the street with two men inside. He thought they were responding to a radio call about the incident, but they never came inside while he was there. When he left Monroe's home, they were still parked down the street. Jack could not confirm they were LAPD since he didn't speak with them. But he later learned they were LAPD intelligence.

During one of our talks Jack asked, 'What was LAPD intelligence doing there before I arrived and why didn't they enter the house when I was there?' It was obvious to him (and me) that LAPD intelligence were aware of Monroe's death long before the police were called.

The following week, two detectives came to his station unannounced. They had a completed sergeant's log (every patrol sergeant completes one per shift), a completed 15.7 continuation sheet (this is a generic form used to write long reports) already completed about the death and a series of photographs of Marilyn's body in bed and of the interior of the house. He was told to simply sign the reports. Jack read the reports but said he didn't write them and that they were not correct. He refused to sign them. One of the plain-clothes detectives identified himself by badge and ID card. It was Captain James Hamilton from OCID. Hamilton again ordered him to sign the reports. Jack still refused. Jack later learned that, by direction of Chief Parker, his signature was forged on the reports and others related to that night. He complained to his captain, who said to ignore it – these were orders coming from the chief's office, and he was not to discuss it with anyone.

Jack said the story in the false 15.7 report left out many details and changed others. He vividly remembered the series of photographs they asked him to initial on the back. In particular, there were two images, one with Monroe's body in bed holding a telephone and another where she was not holding the telephone. He was told to initial the back of all the photographs. This is not the standard LAPD procedure. The cop never initials photographs if he didn't take the picture. It's the photographer whose ID and the DR (Division of Records) number which appears on the images, and that's for later court testimony if needed. Jack initialled some of the images but refused to initial the two staged 'telephone' images. He believes the photographs with and without the telephone in her hand were part of the staging and they'd later only release the photo which aided the cover-up. The two diametrically opposed telephone photos present overwhelming evidence that the death scene was staged. Something Jack knew from his own eyes, not the photographs. When he entered Monroe's bedroom, and checked her body for any signs of life, she was not holding a telephone.

Within weeks of Marilyn's death, Jack was receiving death threats at home to scare him into keeping his mouth shut. These continued even after he left the department after a falling out with Chief Parker over Monroe's death and an unrelated political brochure. One threat was particularly frightening and cemented in his mind the idea that LAPD was conducting a cover-up. When he was still a cop, he received a call on the LAPD Gamewell System telling him to keep quiet and not say anything about Monroe's death. The Gamewell system was a series of telephones mounted on a pipe with a metal lock box containing a telephone. In most patrol divisions there were about 20 of them located throughout the division, generally on the corner of a major street. They were strictly for the use of police. Only cops had the skeleton key to open the box and the telephones only connected to police divisions – no outside calls could be made or received. So, when he received that call, he knew it had to come from a cop – no one else could have made the call or understood the dial codes.

To the day Jack died, he believed entirely that Marilyn was murdered on the orders of the Kennedys. He also believed LAPD Chief William Parker and LAPD intelligence Captain Hamilton conducted the cover-up and that Hamilton was directly involved in her death.

When Marilyn's body was found she was naked which is unusual for someone who has taken their own life. Also, she usually slept wearing a supportive bra to keep her famous 'tits tilted up' shape. There was no glass of water in her room. How did she swallow enough pills to kill herself? When this was questioned, an LAPD crime scene photograph was produced from the files showing a drinking glass near her bed.

The furtive clean-up operation began and was almost complete before Sergeant Jack Clemmons walked in the door of Cursum Perficio and stepped into the scene of Marilyn's murder. Her body was, of course, not dressed or on the couch where Peter Lawford and Bobby Kennedy had left her. As we learned from Lawford's confession to Mike Rothmiller, she went from comatose to apparently lifeless in a matter of minutes.

Evidence dictates that the substance used to kill her was not traceable and did not figure in the analysis of her chemical make-up at the time of her death. More importantly, standard Los Angeles County Coroner's toxicology testing at the time was primitive [compared to today] and would not detect an engineered poisonous substance created by scientists. From released CIA records, it's been established the agency had a wide variety of poisons in their arsenal to carry out assassinations and would not hesitate to use them. Whether Bobby Kennedy was supplied with the substance through his CIA contacts is not known.

Circumstantial appreciation suggests it could have come from William Harvey, the agent who researched viable poisons to kill Castro, via Bobby Kennedy's personal CIA man Charles Ford. The CIA had in their armoury in 1962 some 'good stuff' [according to their chemist Dr. Nathan Gordon, speaking in 1975] which comprised of shellfish toxin. A small dose was lethal, and it killed by blocking the transmission of nervous system impulses.

One of the shellfish toxins developed, refined and stored by the CIA, the US Army's Chemical Corps at Fort. Detrick, Maryland and the US Army's laboratory at Edgewood, Maryland was Saxitoxin. This poison is perhaps the deadliest known to mankind. Just one to four milligrams of Saxitoxin will kill an average sized person from respiratory failure within minutes – one milligram is equal to 0.0002 of a teaspoon. The same measure of sugar wouldn't sweeten a cup of tea, and in dry form, it would be smaller than a grain of sugar. It is instantly absorbed through the gastro-intestinal tract and passed in the urine.

During World War Two the British authorities had a poison, code name 'I', that they intended to use to kill Hitler. It was also tasteless and odourless so, when added to a variety of drinks and food, did not advertise its presence. Whether William Harvey got details of this from Peter Wright of MI6 when he talked to him about undetectable poisons is not known.

The CIA began to develop poisons as part of the top secret 'Project Naomi'. In charge of the project was Dr. Sidney Gottlieb, director of the CIA's Technical Services. Gottlieb and his staff secretly tested many of their non-fatal drugs such as LSD on unsuspecting CIA employees and civilians.

The CIA 'killer popper' was regarded as so quick-acting and painless that, not long after its development, it was supplied to Francis Gary Powers, the U-2 spy pilot, for his flight over the Soviet Union in 1960; the fatal toxin was in a tiny needle concealed in a silver dollar. The idea was to provide Powers with 'an option' if he was shot down, which he was. He went for a different option.

Marilyn didn't have a choice. She gulped the tasteless and odourless toxin. Robert Kennedy would have had no need to titrate a dose correctly as it was already measured.

The CIA at the time of Marilyn's death was at its least transparent, a powerful, paranoid and shadowy organisation, where even the bureau chiefs had bodyguards, sometimes as protection from their own agents. Anything was possible and cloaked in the mystique of national security. Operatives were authorised by the White House to work in secret. Talk of assassination was shunned and publicly abhorred in the offices of power in Washington; that was the business of those at woodland-surrounded CIA headquarters in Langley, Virginia. President Kennedy, like Eisenhower before him, did not want to know the details of operations by the CIA's Deputy Directorate for Plans (DDP), he only commanded that they were effective and secret. Kennedy and other presidents, before and after, always sought plausible deniability of such operations.

The toxin supplied to Francis Gary Powers was also employed to attempt the murder of Abdul Karim Kassem, an army brigadier and nationalist who overthrew the Iraqi monarchy in 1958 in the violent 14 July Revolution. Once in power, Abdul Karim Kassem antagonised Washington by restoring relations with Moscow. He had to go. Theoretically, only a President can approve the assassination of a foreign leader. Kassem's murder was never officially 'sanctioned' yet in April 1960, an attempt was made to incapacitate Kassem with a poisoned handkerchief created, like Powers' deadly silver dollar, by the DDP's Technical Services Division. Kassem escaped, the handkerchief never reached him. [He survived until the Ramadan Revolution of February 1963 when the brutal dictator was executed by firing squad in Baghdad, a death that was shown live on television.]

In 1961, the CIA sent poison to its secret African outpost to kill the Congo Premier Patrice Lumumba. CIA operatives were not able to poison the Premier but were able to incite a military coup which ended with Lumumba's execution. Declassified documents prove the CIA, and the Kennedy administration, were not opposed to assassinating world leaders via poison. In 1970, President Richard Nixon ordered the stockpile of CIA toxins destroyed. This included a variety of shellfish toxins, strychnine, cyanide pills, cobra venom and other 'exotic compounds' such as 'BZ' a chemical that attacks the central nervous system. However, in 1975, Senator Frank

Church discovered the CIA had spent three million dollars in order to maintain a secret cache of the poisons and sophisticated weaponry which could kill a person without leaving a trace at the CIA's top secret South Laboratory near the Department of State and just minutes from the White House and the Department of Justice. Later, CIA Directors Richard Helms and William Colby denied knowledge of the secret poison stockpile made in direct violation of presidential order, as did the CIA man storing the poisons – he claimed he never heard the order to destroy the poisons.

By the time of Marilyn's death, the CIA's activities including illegal domestic spying, secret and loosely controlled experiments with drugs, illicit connections to the underworld, and plots to kill various foreign leaders were well underway. Marilyn, if anything, should have been a cameo in such matters. Still, her death was covered up for the truth would have been more hugely damning to the Kennedy Administration. In August 1962, America was still in its icy nuclear chess game with the Soviet Union and in the embryonic stage of the Cuban Missile Crisis. [On August 10, 1962, a meeting was held in the office of US Secretary of State Dean Rusk to debate Operation Mongoose where a Kennedy plan to eradicate Castro was mentioned. On August 13, Bobby Kennedy's CIA contact, William Harvey, received an official note from Edward Lansdale, the Kennedy brothers' personal appointee in all things anti-Castro, to prepare procedure plans against Castro 'including liquidation of foreign leaders'.]

There is nothing to absolutely dictate exactly which toxin was used to end Marilyn's life, but it was readily on hand and was effective. Dr. Thomas Noguchi, known as the 'coroner to the stars' carried out the autopsy on Marilyn. His skills as a forensic pathologist have never been questioned. But he admitted [in an interview with Douglas Thompson] that he endured great political pressure during his autopsy of Marilyn Monroe. It seemed like a set-up, for a start. While Bobby Kennedy went to church in Gilroy on Sunday August 4, 1962, Dr. Noguchi drove into work at the Los Angeles County Coroner's Office. As a deputy medical examiner, he often worked seven days a week – there's always much sudden death in Los Angeles. There was a message waiting for him from chief medical examiner, Dr. Theodore Curphey where he instructed Dr. Noguchi to perform the autopsy on Marilyn Monroe. At first, he didn't believe it could be the film star but must be someone with the same name. There was glory in celebrity and if there was any glory going, he was certain Theodore Curphey would have taken the job himself. He presumed the name was a coincidence, and that he had been requested because there was a scientific challenge in the case, and he had expertise in clinical and anatomical pathology.

Dr. Noguchi, with wary and always blinking grey eyes – from years of working under bright lights in autopsy rooms – has been quizzed hundreds of times about the cause of Marilyn's death and the only thing he can be definitive about is that there is room for discussion. He won't call it doubt; he'd rather think that nothing has been proven.

Before the autopsy, he studied the reports then available on the case: the dead woman was 5 feet 4 inches tall and weighed 115 pounds. She had been pronounced dead by Dr. Engelberg. The report told him that many bottles of pills had been found on a bedside table including an empty one of the sleeping pill Nembutal and a half-full container of another sleeping pill, chloral hydrate, the 'knockout drops' used in 'Mickey Finns' which rendered a person unconscious.

In the autopsy room, heavy with the aroma of formaldehyde and beneath the cruel, glaring lights, Noguchi lifted up the sheet that had been placed over the naked body and realised the name was no coincidence. He's been asked many times about this moment and he always replies quoting Italian poet, Petrarch: 'It's folly to shrink in fear, if this is dying. For death looked lovely in her lovely face.' He recalled: 'I felt pressure, but I resolved not to be distracted by who she was.'

Everyone else was. In the autopsy room observing his work at table one was Los Angeles County Deputy District Attorney John Milner. With a hand–held magnifying glass, Noguchi examined Marilyn's whole body looking for injection marks and signs of violence. He said a coroner's first instinct is to look for clues of murder. There were no needle marks but there was a fresh bruise on her left hip. He marked this evidence on the diagram which accompanied his report but said it always remained unexplained. The possible significance of the bruising was ignored by subsequent investigative inquiries. He thought it 'was a possible clue to indicate violence'.

In Marilyn's stomach there was no visual evidence of any pills and none of the yellow dye with which the Nembutal capsules were coated which might have been expected. Along with samples of blood, the internal organs were sent off for toxicology tests. The tests on the blood showed 8.0 mg per cent of chloral hydrate, while the liver tests revealed 13.0 mg per cent of pentobarbital [Nembutal]. Both of these were well above a fatal dose.

Dr. Noguchi certainly did not test for saxitoxin or a CIA derivative. He had no reason to. At the time, he probably didn't know of its existence and would not have had the technology to detect it in her body. It is a possibility that Robert Kennedy gave her a high dose of choral hydrate or Nembutal in the glass of water. Since she may have ingested the drug or others earlier, the additional amount was enough to push her over the threshold into death.

Dr. Noguchi, in a 2009 interview, admitted he made an error having the toxicology tests only on the blood and the liver and not on the other internal organs. He should, he said then, have insisted that all the organs were examined. 'I didn't follow through as I should have.'

Later that Sunday, Dr. Thomas Curphey, announced that Marilyn's death was a 'probable' suicide. Dr. Noguchi did not question his conclusion. Yet, he was concerned enough to request the toxicology lab to examine the internal organs he'd sent over. He was told that the organs had already been disposed of as the case had been marked as closed. 'I think that was a great shame,' Noguchi said. Although he will not point fingers and says that, although the vanishing of crucial evidence was disappointing 'it was not suspicious.'

Dr. Noguchi [who reached the age of 94 in 2021 and who inspired the long-running medical-detective television series, *Quincy*], has been given a difficult time from critics since Marilyn's death with his report called at the most polite, 'a sham'. But why did Dr. Theodore Curphey assign him, a junior doctor, the task of cutting open the most famous woman in the world? 'That is something I still don't understand. I have thought about it a lot over the years. Maybe he thought that I would do a good job.' In 1967, the poetry-loving Dr. Noguchi was appointed Chief Medical Examiner of Los Angeles County, a position he held until 1982.

The evidence – medical samples, photographs, slides of the organs that were examined, and the examination form showing bruises on the body – disappeared shortly after Marilyn's death. The liver, kidney and stomach and its contents, which could have proven definitively that she did or did not kill herself vanished overnight. Pills and puzzles.

In his only slip during questioning, Dr. Ralph Greenson – when asked what had truly happened that night – in a recorded and voice verified outburst brought on by agitation or tiredness and probably a mix of both barked: 'Ask Robert Kennedy.' His other deviation from the script was to acknowledge that Marilyn was involved with suitors at 'the highest level of government'. Other than that – nothing.

With the autopsy complete, arrangements for Marilyn's funeral moved quickly, and Dr. Greenson and his family were present when it was held on Wednesday August 8, 1962, at Westwood Village Memorial Park Cemetery in Los Angeles, only a few minutes' drive from Marilyn's home in Brentwood. As always, Marilyn stopped the traffic. The Memorial Park is where Sepulveda Boulevard meets Wilshire Boulevard [Los Angeles commuters will swear it is longest stop light in the world] next to the intersection of Wilshire and Westwood Boulevards. Into this confusion of traffic, as if into a brick wall, drove the funeral cortège before finally entering the cemetery.

Joe DiMaggio took charge of the funeral arrangements and, in doing so, excluded Marilyn's high-profile Hollywood connections. ['If it wasn't for her so-called friends, Marilyn would still be alive today.'] The Kennedys, if they had tried to attend, would not have been welcome. Peter Lawford and his wife Pat were blatantly banned. DiMaggio couldn't do anything about the OCID detectives and LAPD who needed to be there to control the curious crowds and the weeping fans, but he hired his own Pinkerton agents to police the real police as well as the crowd.

The guest list, in terms of who was and who wasn't invited, is as curious as the fans were that day to see their screen goddess laid to rest. On the list were her half-sister Berniece Miracle, Joe DiMaggio and Joe DiMaggio Jr., acting coaches Lee and Paula Strasberg, Dr. Ralph Greenson and his family, Whitey Snyder, Inez and Pat Melson, hairdressers Sydney Guilaroff and Agnes Flanagan, friends Anne and Mary Karger, Pat Newcomb, Eunice Murray, Marilyn's chauffeur Rudy Kautzky, chambermaid Florence Thomas, lawyers Aaron Frosch and Mickey Rudin, her secretary May Reis, Ralph Roberts and Erwin and Anne Goddard from Marilyn's foster mother, Grace Goddard's, family.

Still tearful many years later and talking at his home way north of Seattle in the Pacific Northwest overlooking the waters of Puget Sound, Whitey Snyder, who was a pallbearer on the day, explained how he had ensured that Marilyn looked like Marilyn for those who saw her in her coffin. 'She'd always been afraid of death – or rather what happened after. When she was about 27, we were making *Gentlemen Prefer Blondes* [1953], and she said to me: "Whitey, promise you won't let anyone touch my face." Something like that. It was morbid I guess, but I said: "OK, honey, bring me the body when it's still warm, and I'll be interested."' [Whitey Snyder showed Douglas Thompson the gold money clip which Marilyn gave him. It's inscribed: 'While I'm still warm, Marilyn.'] And Whitey made good on his promise. At Westwood Memorial Park on the eve of the funeral, he and his wife went to look after Marilyn Monroe's appearance for the last time but didn't find the Marilyn they remembered. Her face and breasts had dropped. He sighed: 'Marilyn without a bust – she'd have freaked.' With pieces of cushions and plastic bags, they re-created the famous figure, and Whitey Snyder revived her face with his cosmetics skill. Mourners, unaware of his work, and who viewed her open casket, told him how beautiful she looked.

In death, Marilyn was dressed in the mint green Pucci dress that she had worn at her press conference in Mexico and was holding a bouquet of small pink roses. They all said, of course, that she looked ethereal as Tchaikovsky's Sixth Symphony and a recording of Judy Garland singing *Over the Rainbow* wished her farewell. DiMaggio was devastated. He kissed Marilyn's forehead: 'I love you, I love you, I love you.'

Following the ceremony, Marilyn was interred at crypt No. 24 in the Walk of Memory [her crypt is the most attended in Westwood and the fourth most visited grave in the world]. When they were married, Marilyn had asked DiMaggio to put flowers on her grave every week like William Powell, the original screen 'Thin Man', had done for his lover Jean Harlow. He agreed and arranged for long-stemmed red roses to be placed in a vase attached to the crypt; it was a gesture which endured until 1982.

Her other former husband, Arthur Miller, sent flowers that day, a bouquet from himself and one from his children. Miller wasn't able to attend; his wife at the time, Inge Morath, was almost nine months pregnant with their first child. For the rest of his life Miller suffered the fury of Marilyn fans who felt he had shown cold-hearted disregard for the woman he married in 1956 and divorced in 1961, just nineteen months before her death.

In 2018, a different story emerged. When the University of Texas at Austin acquired a private archive of Miller's work papers, part of a handwritten essay dated on the day of Marilyn's funeral was discovered and revealed Miller's true reasons for not attending. He accuses a selection of the mourners of 'killing' his former wife. He writes:

'Instead of jetting [from New York] to the funeral to get my picture taken I decided to stay home and let the public mourners finish the mockery. Not that everyone there will be false, but enough. Most of them there destroyed her, ladies and gentlemen. She was destroyed by many things, and some of those things are you. And some of those things are destroying you. Destroying you now. Now, as you stand there, weeping and gawking, glad that it is not you going into the earth, glad that it is this lovely girl who you, at last, killed.'

Professor Christopher Bigsby, Professor of American Studies at the University of East Anglia and a close friend of the playwright, and author of an admired biography of him [*Arthur Miller*, Weidenfeld & Nicolson, 2009], was asked by *The Independent* newspaper for his thoughts after the essay was discovered. He told the British newspaper on January 11, 2018: 'He did think that Hollywood had in some sense destroyed her. If this was happening now [in the #MeToo era], it would be major news, because it was the casting couch. That kind of sexual abuse – which is now hitting the news – was commonplace then, and Marilyn Monroe was a victim of it. She was bruised, treated with profound disrespect, and passed around as a kind of product when she was in Hollywood.'

Bigsby says that Miller reworked the essay over the years and was aware that Marilyn was trapped in Hollywood: 'The irony was that it was a world [one that she'd fought so hard to be a part of] she could not leave. The world of film was where she came into her own, where she existed, because she was *somebody* – even if that somebody was an artifice constructed for her by Hollywood. She felt that when she was being 'Marilyn', people gave her respect and attention, which maybe she erroneously thought was love – something she thought she had never received when she was growing up. It was inconceivable that Marilyn could have walked away just like that. He [Miller] was completely bowled over by her. It was certainly a love affair. One of his love letters to her was an almost adolescent outpouring of love; both of them went into this marriage believing something about [the character of] the other person which turned out not to be true, but they were scarcely a unique couple in that respect.'

Miller wrote fondly of Marilyn: 'She relied on the most ordinary layer of the audience, the working people, the guys in the bars, the housewives in the trailers bedevilled by unpaid bills, the high school kids mystified by explanations they could not understand, the ignorant and – as she saw them – tricked and manipulated masses. She wanted them to feel they'd got their money's worth when they saw a picture of hers.'

In 2002, Miller showed Bigsby into the garage of the house where he had lived with Marilyn. Miller pointed to the wall and something hanging on it: 'Her bicycle. It's been hanging up in here for 40 years.' For Arthur Miller, and for millions since, Marilyn was undying.

She certainly was for Peter Lawford who destroyed himself in coming to terms with his betrayal of her. Lawford was enraptured by the Kennedys – seduced by John and rather terrified of Bobby and his black moods – and finally isolated by them. He and Pat divorced in 1966. He had no friends, no emotional or financial support. In 1976, he signed to write his autobiography for $60,000. The following year he was offered $100,000 on top of that by the *National Enquirer* for the serialisation of his story. In 1977, reporters from the magazine, Malcolm Boyes and Haydon Cameron, spent two weeks with Lawford in Palm Springs, California. Malcolm Boyes went on to become a successful television producer and speaking at his home in Sonoma, California in May 2018 said: 'Peter was as good as gold with us. He told us wonderful stories about The Rat Pack and lots of salacious material about all the women he had slept with during and after his marriage to Pat Kennedy Lawford. It was fascinating material, but the one thing we wanted was for him to talk about Marilyn Monroe and the Kennedys – their relationships, the truth about how she died. We went around the subject, circled it, and around it again. He told the same story time and time again.

'The story never wavered, never changed in any detail. It was as if he had been given the story, a script of the story, and he had learned it, emblazoned it in his head so his tongue could offer no other version.

'When he wouldn't talk about the death of Marilyn, the owner of the *Enquirer*, Generosa Pope, pulled the plug on the story and Peter's hundred grand. I kept in touch with Peter for the next few years, close enough for him to be borrowing money from me to pay his rent.'

Boyes published some extracts from the interview in 1982 which included Lawford saying: 'I blame myself for the fact that she [Marilyn] is dead.' Boyes, speaking in 2018, said, 'Although he said that, and burst into tears many times while doing so, he stuck to the script: he talked to Marilyn on the telephone, she seemed fine, later he worried about her and told his agent, Milt Ebbins he was going to her home and the regular spiel – as in it was all a tragic mishap.

'Peter never lost the focus of what he was saying even with a bath full of booze in him. Toward the end, he seemed more haunted, but I'd moved on and when we talked it was about how he was, incidental stuff, and always, finally, about money. And [it was] strange about his need of money. He wouldn't tell the truth about Marilyn's death for money, but it always seemed to me he wanted to unburden himself of something. Of his guilt? He badly wanted to get rid of it so it wouldn't be on his tombstone.'

Peter Lawford was abandoned by the Kennedy family and he always pondered how, in a little more than a decade, his clever, witty friend Marilyn could go from being a voluptuous if vulnerable girl into a woman the Kennedys came to see as Lady Macbeth and believed to be just as dangerous?

In the years after the break with the Kennedys, Peter Lawford was lost in Hollywood. He spent his days abusing his liver and his conscience. Elizabeth Taylor, who'd held a teenage fancy for Lawford, stepped in, now as a motherly figure, to help him in 1984. She'd been pleased by her treatment for drink and painkiller addiction at the Betty Ford Center in the California desert and convinced Lawford to check in too. At the time he said: 'I really think Elizabeth saved my life by persuading me to check into the Betty Ford. Her entering there made a lot of people wake up to the fact that they had a problem, myself included. There is a joke going around town at the moment that you're nothing unless you've been to Betty Ford. But, seriously, it is terrific that people like myself who do have a problem are facing it.' Taylor also got him a $2,000 fee for two days' work on her television film *Malice in Wonderland* [1985] in which she played Hollywood gossip columnist Louella Parsons opposite Jane Alexander as rival Hedda Hopper. For the all but down-and-out Lawford, it was a kindness. In late 1984, a few months after his stint in the Betty Ford, where he was able to receive visitors, he was primed to make his appearance in *Malice in Wonderland*. It didn't happen though: his fourth wife, Patricia Lawford Stewart, found him smoking marijuana and drinking vodka. Spaced out, he was taken to Cedars–Sinai Medical Center in West Hollywood where he was given a blood transfusion and vitamin shots. After treatment, he turned up for work on December 14, 1984, but collapsed on the film set. Lawford returned to Cedars–Sinai, now dying from liver and kidney problems.

By then, many of the media who dealt with him had accepted his 'official' version of events involving Marilyn's death. Then, when he was so very seriously ill and in such a frail state, he was interviewed by the *Los Angeles Times* and asked about Marilyn and the Kennedys. For what must have seemed most of his life, even if his own choreography was adrift, Lawford had kept straight to the party line. However, at this fragile moment and ever so publicly, he diverted from the script addressing the decades of rumour, gossip and blatant accusations: 'Even if those things were true, I wouldn't talk about them.'

With Detective Mike Rothmiller pressing him, the distraught Lawford had realised he couldn't get away with simply offering the much-rehearsed narrative dictated by Captain Hamilton. And he couldn't stay silent. Eighteen months after he confessed the truth to Mike Rothmiller, Peter Lawford died. At age 61, he slipped into a coma on December 19, and died on Christmas Eve at Cedars-Sinai from a heart attack brought on by renal and liver failure. He drank himself to death, drowned in booze and melancholy.

# XV: The Rashomon Effect

*'Doubt is an unpleasant condition, but certainty is an absurd one.'*
—Voltaire, 1768.

Akira Kurosawa's 1950 film *Rashomon*, in which a murder is detailed by four witnesses in four contradictory ways, gave name to the Rashomon Effect: a situation where an event is remembered or interpreted by multiple witnesses in very different and sometimes contradictory ways. Failing memory or self-interest influences what a person perceives. Getting a series of events exactly correct is difficult enough with prime witnesses, but the Rashomon Effect can be even more evident with the accounts of those on the outskirts of events. Many have intruded to theorise on Marilyn's death – as we do now – time has warped the story, constant repetition has mangled it and the facts have mixed with hearsay. Yet, with Peter Lawford's statement to Mike Rothmiller, we have a first-hand spotlight on events. And with the revelations from Fred Otash, who planted listening devices next or close to so many of the important players, we have key evidence. These revelations correct a great number of previously believed theories about Marilyn's death.

There is another person who sent ripples back and forward through the Marilyn story both before and after her death and that was Robert Slatzer. In 1952, he was working for an Ohio newspaper and used his press pass to get onto the set of *Niagara* where he met Marilyn and had some close-up photographs taken with her [the 'selfies' of the day]. He was a smart operator and got his pictures quickly developed then returned the next day to ask Marilyn to sign them. They are the only images of the two of them together. He used the pictures when Marilyn was first dating Joe DiMaggio to imply he was the baseball hero's rival for her love and, in May 1957, was paid by Hollywood's *Confidential* magazine for saying he had had an affair with Marilyn. After Marilyn's death, Slatzer tried to sell a short article he had written about how Marilyn's death was a conspiracy to journalist Will Fowler who rejected the article but told Slatzer: 'Too bad you weren't married to Monroe. That would *really* make a great book.'

*Zip-a-dee-doo-dah, zip-a-dee-ay* – as quick as you could sing that, Slatzer recalled that he and Marilyn *had* married in October 1952, in Tijuana, Mexico. The snag was that the marriage had been annulled, on the orders of Daryl Zanuck [who we will recall had no interest in Marilyn until she was huge box office]. Slatzer wrote a book [*The Life And Curious Death Of Marilyn Monroe*, W.H. Allen, 1974] in which he detailed their romance and conversations. He also promoted the theory that John and Bobby Kennedy were involved in her death. It was all but impossible to verify anything Slatzer, who died in 2005, claimed happened so his writing was and is more distraction from the truth.

Slatzer's versions of events helped perpetuate the misdirection and deliberate confusion set-up by Captain James Hamilton in the first instance. Others turned up, like Jeanne Carmen [aka Saba Dareaux] who surfaced in 1985 to say she had been Marilyn's roommate and best friend. She said she had had a 'dangerously close' relationship with Marilyn and the Kennedys and that after Marilyn's death she had been warned off by Johnny Rosselli. Fearing for her life, she fled to Arizona where she led a quiet family life. She died in 2007.

The strident anti-Communist and FBI agent, Frank Capell, was convinced Marilyn was a follower of Moscow and said so in his book [*The Strange Death of Marilyn Monroe,* Herald of Freedom, 1964] but he considered everyone but his friend Walter Winchell, America's most famous newspaper columnist, as a leftist. Capell was the first to ever say in print that Bobby Kennedy was involved in Marilyn's death:

'There are person-to-person telephone calls, living witnesses, tape recordings and certain writing to attest to the closeness of their friendship. Did the trouble begin when Marilyn realised that her VIP had no intention of getting a divorce and marrying her? Did she insist he fulfil his promise to her or face her making public their relationship? Neither of these alternatives would appeal to Mr. VIP.

'Since Marilyn could destroy him either by talking or with written evidence, did he decide to take drastic action?

'Book publishers and newspaper owners have been reluctant to print this story although it is known to many. That failure has not been due to fear of libel since many deal with that problem almost daily. What they do not like to admit is fear of anti-trust suits, Internal Revenue examinations and other forms of official harassment.

The mention of Mr. VIP seems to put fear in the hearts of too many people. With his personal Gestapo, he does not hesitate to persecute those who incur his displeasure. General Walker has tasted this treatment as has Jimmy Hoffa. [General Edwin Walker was committed to a mental asylum for a 90-day evaluation on the orders of Attorney General Bobby Kennedy following the 1962 riots at the University of Mississippi].

'The circumstances surrounding the death of Marilyn Monroe are extremely suspicious, and the events following her death are also suspicious. They reek of intrigue, pay-offs and official disinterest in trying to find the truth. Have things gotten so bad in the United States that a possible murder will go uninvestigated because pressure is brought to bear or someone important may be involved? Is everyone really equal before the law or have some people gotten so powerful, they are above the law?'

He suggested nearly six decades ago that all the stories about phone calls, dinner arrangements and Marilyn's mood that day were the confections of a cover-up, but he could not have known what a brilliant one it was. Capell, like so many of those who did not accept the official LAPD version of Marilyn's death, found himself discredited one moment and smeared the next. Yet, being a Red-baiter and anti-Kennedy did not negate everything he had to offer; nevertheless, it tainted it.

The world was different in 1962, and Los Angeles was more different than anywhere else. In New York, they said they turned the United States on its side and all the nuts rolled into California. It's often seemed that way. What provides so much insight into the times and the mystery of Marilyn Monroe are the secret recordings made of the main players. It is extraordinary that so much was heard on tape through the expertise of Fred Otash and his operatives, and equally amazing that the condemning material was suppressed for so long.

Mike Rothmiller was a seasoned detective with OCID when he interrogated Fred Otash. His interview provides an intensely fascinating portrait of the place and time, the culture and the fears, and the risks that many took. It reveals the ethics and morals of all levels of society, highlighted through the prism of Hollywood and Washington, from the privileged and rich to the criminal, and the poor mugs in between. It reveals much of what was happening in the shadows during the last days of Marilyn Monroe's life. This is Mike Rothmiller's account of his meeting with Fred Otash:

We met at Nate & Al's Deli restaurant, Beverly Drive, Beverly Hills. Fred Otash's secret OCID dossier was exceedingly impressive and would have been ideal for a movie script – more so than anything Hollywood could conjure up on their best day. Fred's notoriety in Hollywood drew the attention of noted writer, James Ellroy of *LA Confidential* fame. Ellroy said he met with Otash several times and found him to be pretentious and a 'bullshitter'. However, Ellroy wrote extensively about him in his book *Shakedown*, and Otash influenced the star role in his 2021 novel, *Widespread Panic*. Ellroy's take on him was not without merit. Fred did have the gift to weave a fascinating yarn to impress a potential client who didn't know better. However, my take on Fred was very different because I had access to decades of intelligence Ellroy never knew existed and would never have had access to. Fred's intelligence dossier was massive but neither Fred nor Ellroy had any idea what information OCID had accumulated over the decades. Because of my access to the file OCID held on Fred, I was in the unique position to call him out if he attempted to bullshit me.

I initially contacted Fred by telephone thinking that this would be a softer and less scary approach than an Organized Crime and Intelligence Detective knocking on the door unannounced. In policing there are, of course, times when a no warning interview is essential for an investigation. However, knowing Fred's background, I thought that a few preliminary telephone calls to break the ice and establish a foundation was most likely the best approach. It was a gamble and it worked.

Weeks later, he agreed to an in-person meeting. After easing into an isolated restaurant booth at Nate & Al's, he momentarily stared at me before cautiously scanning the other patrons. It was apparent he was attempting to determine if I was alone. I had done the same inquisitive scan of the place when I entered. Determining if a person is alone is a prudent first step undertaken by all intelligence operatives. You never want to be surprised.

After a few silent moments, he turned back to size me up and said, 'Let's see your ID.' I removed my police identification card and badge from my pocket along with an official business card and handed them across the table. He carefully examined my credentials, nodded and returned them.

'Satisfied?' I asked.

'Yeah.' I didn't blame him for being overly cautious; I would have done the same.

During the meeting, we went over our initial telephone conversations, and I gradually led the discussion to his time as a private detective to the stars. I wanted to test his memory, open the door to talking about Monroe and determine if he planned to bullshit me. He started to spin a story about a particular Hollywood intrigue in which he claimed he was heavily involved. It was damned interesting, but I knew it was not entirely correct. I weighed my options: go along with the story or call him out. Calling him out was risky and could shut down the entire interview. However, it wasn't a matter of wanting the truth, I *needed* to hear the truth, so I made another gamble.

I stared eye-to-eye with him and shook my head, 'Fred, that's interesting, but I read the intel reports on that, and you were barely mentioned. How can that be if you claim you played an integral role?' My stare turned into a broad smile. I'd caught him, and he knew it.

He thought for a moment, 'Well, maybe I was thinking of something else and not that one.' He grinned, but he now knew I would not accept his stories at face value. More importantly, he now understood – without me saying it – that OCID had been keeping tabs on him for years.

Pointing out his embellishment was a significant step in moving him along the path of becoming a semi-trustworthy informant. I say semi because an intel detective never places complete trust in an informant's information, even if the information comes from an FBI agent. If the information is serious, it still has to be verified through other means. But now, Fred knew I would do my homework and call his bluff.

What he didn't know is that I needed him as an informant more than he needed me. Frankly speaking, he didn't need me. But I could not reveal that salient point. He was a former LAPD cop and understood what information we cops wanted. He also understood how LAPD intelligence worked and, without question, he realised that with our immense power, we could destroy any person who crossed us. That fear is what motivated people like Fred and other Hollywood notables to become forced 'friends' of the LAPD, especially the OCID. He had the potential to be an astounding and entertaining informant but only if I could build a trusting relationship and induce him to speak relatively freely.

As OCID intelligence detectives, my colleagues and I sought out the most corrupt, despicable, and ruthless individuals within the criminal underworld as well as their most trusted co-conspirators who could be cultivated as informants. Why? Because criminals know what other criminals are doing. Like honest businessmen bragging about their latest sale or acquisition, criminals can't stop themselves and they tend to brag about their most recent caper. As in the business world, in the criminal underground, status among peers matters.

A good intelligence detective will know how to apply the proper amount of real or imaginary pressure to informants. They want to ensure that their sources see the risks of becoming hostile and the benefits of being a friendly informant. Imagined pressure works exceptionally well with active criminals since they have so much to lose. If they believe the detective knows about other crimes they've committed and could drop the hammer on them at will, this can encourage them to be more cooperative. Likewise, if informants were confident that the cops would protect them, they were usually willing to disclose a significant amount of information concerning their criminal competitors. If you seek inside information regarding the Mafia, you target Mafia members as potential whistleblowers. Information regarding political corruption? Well, you leaned on just about any politician or traditional mobster. And when I wanted information regarding crimes and scandals in Hollywood, Fred was the inside person.

Back in 1955, Fred was in the LAPD and butted heads with LAPD Chief William Parker and other high-ranking officers. The chief believed he was selling confidential police information to the media, the scandal sheets and others. He was partially correct. Fred and several high-ranking LAPD commanders *were* selling sensitive police information and receiving envelopes stuffed with cash from illegal business operations and LA's Mafia. Parker knew that the problem was widespread, but Fred was the lowest ranking cop, so he was a clear choice to be sacrificed in the name of cleansing the LAPD of corruption while other, higher ranking leakers remained untouched.

Fred resigned to become a private detective. And would eventually provide services to the stars, the Mafia, Jimmy Hoffa, the CIA, the FBI, high-powered politicians and, of course, the OCID. Fred was a man with elastic ethics and, in most instances, didn't see the benefit in obeying the subtler points of the law. Especially when he was working for the CIA. Laws were meant for honest people and those who got caught, and he was rarely either of those. Fred was a man willing to do just about anything for the right price. Would he have killed for the right amount? I can't say. But in recent years, even some LA cops have carried out contract murders.

Fred was not a complicated man. One week he worked for you and next week he'd be hired to spy on you. If he hadn't become a private detective after leaving the force, he could have made a successful ethically-challenged politician. Fred remained faithful to only two motivators: money and self-preservation. And OCID and its intelligence allies could, and did, supply both.

Otash had a long working relationship with the OCID but, over the decade before I joined, as the older OCID detectives retired and were replaced by us young guns, he fell off OCID's radar. To my surprise, when I arrived, nobody was speaking with him.

The reason why Otash had slipped from the department's attention was straightforward but challenging for a newly minted intelligence detective to understand. As it turned out, the recent captains and lieutenants of OCID had spent the majority of their careers in administrative positions. They had no experience in intelligence or undercover work. They therefore lacked basic knowledge of informant development, and they did not understand the value informants brought to all intelligence operatives.

As a result, for years, the pogues [slang for incompetent LAPD managers] never authorised anyone to use Fred as an informant. The reasoning behind this was bizarre at best. In part it was because they despised Otash — he was an ex-LAPD cop and they hated all cops who quit, for any reason. In their minds, quitting equated to abandoning them and it was viewed as a personal insult. There were, however, detectives who were considerably more intelligent and unquestionably more streetwise than the pogues running the department. As a result, a few OCID detectives continued to secretly use Otash as an informant while never revealing that their sensitive information was obtained from him. The pogues were never the wiser and were constantly astounded by the intelligence produced.

During our initial telephone conversations, I posed several control questions regarding his past activities, tales about movie stars and his work for the old gossip magazine *Confidential*. These were softball questions designed to steadily lower his guard and test his credibility and memory regarding past events. I found he only deviated slightly from the truth. I designed our initial phone conversations to build a feeling of trust and rapport and I saved the hardball questions for our face-to-face meeting when the extra pressure of facing a cop is at its most persuasive.

When we met at Nate & Al's restaurant, it was blatantly clear he was nervous about being contacted by an OCID man once more, but he still attempted to project a self-confident 'who the fuck are you?' attitude. My first objective (as with all first face-to-face meetings with potential informants) was to alleviate what would surely be his immediate concern — that he was currently the subject of an investigation. I knew far more about his past and present activities than he could have imagined but he wasn't my primary interest.

During our lunch, I intentionally mentioned a few details I knew about his recent questionable activities, which demonstrated that I had done my homework and had some power over him. Without saying it outright we both understood that, if I so desired, I could cause him a great deal of grief. Fred had played this game a thousand times before and understood the genuine consequences of not cooperating. He faced a difficult choice. Either work with this young detective or run the risk of the OCID's retribution. Out of fear or curiosity, he chose wisely and stayed to talk.

Fred Otash and his cohorts had installed and maintained the wiretaps and bugs in Marilyn Monroe's home located at 12305 Fifth Helena Drive, Brentwood and Peter Lawford's beach house at 625 Palisades Beach Road, Santa Monica. This I already knew from the OCID files. Equally known within OCID was the fact that he was initially paid by Teamsters' president Jimmy Hoffa to carry out these services, who later told Fred he was doing it as a favour for Richard Nixon.

As soon as the Monroe and Lawford eavesdropping operation was underway, OCID learned of it, as did the CIA and FBI. Soon, Otash was receiving payments for the operation from the three agencies who all desperately wanted the information garnered. It appears that Fred was very selective with the information he provided to the people paying him. Sometimes, he offered up the same information to all and was paid by all. Sometimes, a selected detail would go to one intelligence agency while he'd provide just a snippet to another. Probably because the LAPD was the ultimate hometown muscle, it appears he provided a majority of his information to OCID. However, knowing Fred, I do not doubt for a moment that he also withheld some too. After all, that was his business, and he still loathed many within the LAPD. But Fred was not stupid. He understood the rules of survival in southern California; when pushed, play ball with OCID; poking the LAPD tiger with a sharp stick never ends well.

At that lunch meeting, I eventually asked Fred to explain how he wiretapped and bugged Marilyn Monroe and Peter Lawford's homes. I specifically didn't ask him *if* he had wiretapped and bugged their homes. I posed a decisive, forceful question, leaving no doubt I knew of his involvement, and he knew it would not be wise to lie to me.

It was apparent this line of questioning touched a raw nerve. Fred nervously stirred on the vinyl covered seat, looking from side to side as his breathing quickened. He was experiencing anger, fear and a great deal of anxiety. His body language alone told me he knew significant details which he didn't want to discuss. But he understood, we were too far along for him to play dumb. At that moment, it had become painfully clear to Fred that I had walked him down a path, and he had fallen into the trap. He understood I possessed enough information regarding his current activities to cause him unbearable grief. He already knew that the OCID was exceedingly competent at leaking damaging information to the press and, more consequentially to the country's various Mafia families who would not be pleased to hear that he had been an informant. Until that moment, it's possible that Fred thought I was an eager new detective that he could regale with fascinating stories of the old Los Angeles mobsters and movie stars. Well, that day, our relationship changed.

Taking a napkin from the table, he wiped the sweat from his brow and, after several uncomfortable moments, he said, 'You know what happened.'

'I do. But I want to hear it from you,' I said.

Again, there were several uneasy moments as he anxiously stirred in the booth and looked around the restaurant for unwanted ears. It was clear to me he was weighing his only two options, both were unpleasant, but he needed to make a choice and make it now. Tell this cop what he wants to know or get up and leave and face the consequences. The decision was his alone.

He turned back to me, placed his napkin over his mouth, leaned across the table and whispered, 'Are you recording this?'

'No.'

That seemed to relieve a portion of his stress. However, we both knew that recording conversations in a restaurant is nearly impossible. In most cases, the ambient noise overrides the recording. That's why I had chosen a busy restaurant; I wanted to ensure *he* couldn't record *me*. He again hesitated, and ever so slowly, he started to talk and disclose more and more detail. It was fascinating to witness as he painfully and slowly released drips of information, hoping I would say that it was enough. But I kept asking questions and, once he'd started, he was forced to continue.

His dialogue did not flow in chronological order. He nervously jumped from beginning to end then to the middle and back again. It was evident that discussing this subject gave him a genuine sense of fear. And for a person like Fred to experience fear so many years after the statutes of limitations had expired for most of his activities, it could only mean he feared disclosing details about crimes for which the laws had not expired, and those were extremely serious.

But there was another possibility; if Fred Otash had been involved in a conspiracy to kill Monroe and some of the co-conspirators were still alive and in powerful positions, they may seek to silence him… permanently. I already knew that there was a conspiracy to silence Marilyn Monroe and that it had been directed from the highest levels of government. It's possible that Otash was contemplating what the consequences of him breaking his silence would be.

The following is a summary of what he disclosed, combined with the information I read in the OCID secret files and information from other intelligence contacts and sources. My primary interest was Marilyn's death, so I kept my questions focused on the weeks before she died, the day of her death and what occurred immediately after her death.

A few days before her death, Marilyn had indeed placed a flurry of emotionally laced telephone calls to Peter Lawford, the White House, the United States Attorney General's Office, José Bolaños, several other friends, and her psychiatrist.

Lawford had telephoned Robert Kennedy to discuss Marilyn's demands that she be able to speak to the President and her threat to hold a press conference and disclose her affair with the President and her relationship with Robert Kennedy. In a secret transcript that I read of a conversation with José Bolaños, Marilyn told him what she planned to disclose at the press conference which would include top-secret information President Kennedy told her, apparently during pillow talk. The information went well beyond their sexual relationship and would have stunned the world. Bolaños was shocked by the information and begged her not to do it since he believed her life would be in danger if she did.

Otash claimed he didn't recall the names of the friends Marilyn telephoned during her last days. But when I mentioned Bolaños, he said, 'Oh yeah. That's right. I remember him.' He did recall that she complained bitterly to several people she called regarding the Kennedys' apparent dismissal of her. She told some friends of her plan to expose the truth at a press conference. Without exception, all warned her not to do it and not to threaten the Kennedys since they were too powerful and something terrible could happen to her.

Telephone transcripts showed Monroe received a call from Lawford informing her that Robert Kennedy had agreed to fly to Los Angeles and meet with her privately.

He begged Marilyn not to call a press conference. She didn't believe Lawford, but after a heated discussion, she relented on the condition that Bobby came quickly to see her.

Possibly for the first time in his life, Fred Otash said he was stymied. He could have quickly sold this information to scandal sheets and others for a massive sum of money. But, unlike Marilyn, he understood the very real danger he'd face if it became public knowledge. There would be inquiries and, eventually, accusing fingers would point at him. The intelligence communities, Hoffa, and his Mafia associates would not allow their involvement to become known. The only method to prevent disclosure would be eliminating Fred. What Marilyn knew and was threatening to reveal was a clear breach of national security and would have irrevocably destroyed the Kennedy presidency and legacy. It's been argued that the cover-up was maintained because so many of those who knew the terrible truth had a great allegiance to the Kennedys – an admiration for and a fellowship with them. But many who have come forward over the years to offer clues and tiny parts of the jigsaw, have said it was fear of revenge by the Kennedys which kept them quiet.

The confirmation that Marilyn not only knew details about issues of national security but was threatening to reveal them was startling. And Otash had more. He had listened to telephone calls between President Kennedy in the White House and Bobby Kennedy in Los Angeles – the very place he had always denied being on that August day – in the hours before the death of Marilyn Monroe. In the OCID files, I had seen covertly taken photographs of Bobby Kennedy and Peter Lawford in Los Angeles dated the day Marilyn Monroe died. And I understood that I had to convince Otash to tell me what he knew.

The day before Marilyn died, Fred, Marilyn, Peter Lawford, OCID and others knew Robert Kennedy would secretly arrive in Los Angeles the following day aboard a privately chartered aircraft. At that meeting at Nate & Al's Deli, Otash told me that he thought Robert Kennedy arrived at Santa Monica airport, but it was, in fact, Los Angeles airport where he landed at midday. He was quietly picked up by Peter Lawford and taken to Lawford's residence. Fred could not answer many of my questions regarding what happened between Lawford and Kennedy after that because he claimed that the audio was extremely poor at times as they moved from room to room in Lawford's home. Only a few rooms in the house were bugged. Fred also didn't recall a great deal from their first visit that afternoon to Monroe's home but remembered a great deal from the evening visit and the conversations he was able to hear at Lawford's home that day.

Fred remembered Lawford and Kennedy discussing what it was that Marilyn wanted to prevent her from going public. Robert Kennedy said his family would pay any amount, but Lawford said she wasn't after money and that no matter what she agreed to today, she might change her mind tomorrow. Considering her alcohol and drug abuse, and her less than stable mental state, she posed a significant security risk. Lawford said what she wanted most was to not be ignored by the Kennedys. After an hour or so, Robert Kennedy placed a telephone call to the President and updated him on events. Otash didn't recall the details but said the President asked Robert to call him back after he met with Marilyn.

Peter Lawford then placed a call to Marilyn and turned the telephone over to Robert Kennedy who told her that he and

Peter would be coming to her home later and she should not mention his planned visit to anyone. Otash thought Marilyn was slurring her words on the other end of the phone. She agreed to keep the scheduled visit secret for the moment.

Fred paused here in his narrative. 'You know they went to her house twice?'

'When?' I asked. I already knew this from the files, but I saw this as another test of his credibility. I found it interesting that this fact was something he found so salient.

'Once in the afternoon and then again that night.' He was truthful, and that made me confident he was being honest in his overall statements.

That evening, the second of the visits that day, Lawford drove Robert Kennedy to Marilyn's house. From the bugs he planted in her home, Otash said he heard the conversation between Marilyn and Robert Kennedy become heated almost immediately. Kennedy asked Marilyn how much money she wanted to keep her relationships with himself and his brother a secret. Otash said that the question infuriated Marilyn. She began screaming at Robert, and the two engaged in a bitter argument. Fred couldn't understand what was said, but confirmed that the exchange required Lawford to intervene and calm both sides.

Kennedy left the room, allowing Lawford to speak with Marilyn and decompress the situation. When Kennedy came back, the argument resumed. He said Kennedy was furious and kept asking Marilyn for something. Otash assumed Kennedy was after her diary. For several minutes, Fred could hear the sounds of a person moving from room to room and rummaging through various items. This ended with Kennedy in a rage screaming: 'Give it to me!' This was followed by sounds of what seemed like a physical struggle. Marilyn was screaming and he heard Lawford yelling to stop several times. Otash then said he heard Marilyn crying, and he distinctly recalled Kennedy yelling at her to shut up. The two men spoke in inaudible whispers as Marilyn wept. Lawford then informed Marilyn that he and Robert had to leave and he [Lawford] would call her later. Marilyn didn't respond.

Otash indicated that, moments after Kennedy and Lawford exited the house, he heard what sounded like several people moving quickly through and rummaging around the house. He assumed it was Kennedy and Lawford returning, but he couldn't be sure. He thought he heard Marilyn say something akin to 'Who are you?' but again, he wasn't sure. This was followed by sounds of another struggle interlaced with muffled screams and men's voices telling someone to shut up. He estimated that after roughly twenty minutes, he no longer heard Marilyn's voice or the sounds of a struggle. He said the subsequent sounds seemed to be people searching the house and the words 'Take this,' 'Take that,' and 'Did you find it?' Otash surmised these men might have administered a drug to Marilyn to subdue her, and they were probably searching for her diary and other items related to her affairs with the President and his brother. [Two OCID detectives, Archie Case and James Ahern, half of the Kennedys' guard supplied by the LAPD, were identified at the house by neighbours' testimony of that day and they could have been the officers spotted by Sergeant Jack Clemmons in the unmarked car.]

According to intelligence documents and Fred's own confession to me, well before the LAPD was officially notified, he was contacted by Peter Lawford informing him that Marilyn was dead. Lawford asked him to rush to her house and remove any items linking her to the President or Robert Kennedy.

Near the end of our gruelling interview, I still had significant questions regarding what Fred knew about LAPD's involvement. He had already disclosed extremely sensitive information, so I believed he would continue. Staring at him across the table, it was easy to see Fred was more than anxious to leave. He glanced to the side, down at the table, at me and around the room. I extended my hand across the table, and shook his hand.

'Thank you. You've been upfront with me and what you told me will not be shared. No one will know,' I said.

He looked at me, nodded and replied, 'OK' then he started to slide out of the booth.

'Wait a minute. I have a few more questions that just came to mind.' Truthfully, I had planned these questions earlier and had waited until the most opportune moment to pose them. He stopped, thought for a moment, and said, 'What?'

'Who were your contacts at LAPD intelligence?'

From his expression, I knew the question had caught him off guard. I was working for LAPD Intelligence – so surely, I would already know that. He settled back into the booth and folded his arms across his chest. With a look of bewilderment, he said, 'Why are you asking that? You know who I dealt with.'

'Yes, I do, but as before, I need to hear it from you.'

He was silent. Our eyes were locked on each other. I knew what he was thinking, 'What the fuck is he after? Why is he asking me that?'

After a few uneasy moments, he said, 'Hamilton.'

'You mean Captain James Hamilton?'

'Yeah.'

'After Hamilton left, who was your contact?' From his body language, it was clear he did not want to answer that question. It appeared to make him even more nervous. In a firm voice, I pressed him. 'After Hamilton, who was your contact?'

He again stared at me for several moments and, in a whisper, said: 'Just a few times. It was Gates.'

'You mean when Gates was the Captain of OCID?'

He nodded affirmatively. I was shocked. Daryl Gates was the current Chief of Police. But it made complete sense since in 1975 Gates directed OCID to reinvestigate Monroe's death and that investigation was a sham.

For me, his acknowledgment of Hamilton and Gates as his prime LAPD contacts completed the circle of conspiracy around Monroe's death. The Kennedys' involvement and ultimately the cover-up all made sense. Hamilton, a close friend of both the Kennedy brothers, was the captain of LAPD intelligence at the time of Monroe's death. He had personally handled the cover-up.

'Just one more question.' I took a drink of water. 'I assume the electronic gear you used was quite sophisticated. Was it?'

'Yeah, the best.'

'I thought so. I couldn't see you using anything but the best.' I paused as he nodded in agreement. 'So, tell me, who provided you with that stuff?'

Again, he paused, naturally wondering where I was going. 'Some of it I got myself and some came from the Feds.'

'Which government agency and who?'

'Some from LAPD and some from… you know…' He paused.

'I don't know. Who?' I asked. Beads of sweat began forming on his brow and it was overwhelmingly clear he didn't want to name the government agency or agencies. Of course, I already knew the answer. His OCID dossier indicated that his sophisticated electronic eavesdropping equipment had come from the FBI and CIA. While he was thinking, I decided not to press him any further as I wanted to finish the interview with a potentially less stressful question.

'The night she died, what did you do when you were at her house?'

'Well, Peter asked me to grab anything related to the Kennedys and get it out of there.'

'Yeah, but what else did you do?'

He rubbed his chin, thinking. 'The first thing I did was pull the mics [microphones] and other shit I planted. I didn't want that shit found.'

'Because that stuff could have led back to you?'

'Maybe. I just didn't know, so I wanted it out of there.'

'Was anyone else in the house?'

He rubbed his face and paused before he nodded.

'How many others and who? I asked.

'Just a few other people.'

'Did you know them?'

'One guy.'

'Who was that?'

'Ah, Hamilton.'

'Captain Hamilton?'

Again, he nodded affirmatively.

It was now apparent that Fred was becoming irritable and mentally fatigued by this demanding round of questions – the response of most people when pressed by police to divulge potentially incriminating information. All experienced interrogators understand that when you have a person talking, you don't break it off to continue another day. Ending the moment allows them time to reconsider or, worse, hire an attorney. When that occurs, they'll never speak with you again.

Fred looked at me, attempting to anticipate my next question.

'This is my final question,' I smiled. 'I promise.' He nodded. 'At any time after Monroe's death, did Peter ask you to do anything for him or anyone else?'

He thought for a moment, rested his elbows on the table and covered his face with his hands. 'Yeah, he did. He asked me to check his phones and house for bugs and take them out.'

'Wasn't that a bit strange since you installed bugs for him in his house.'

'No. He was worried that somebody else could have installed others, and he wanted all of them out.'

'OK,' I paused for a moment. 'Did you conduct an electronic sweep of his house and did you find anything?'

'I checked his place and pulled my stuff. I didn't find anything else.'

'Did he say why he was worried or who he thought may have planted the bugs?'

'He didn't say, but my gut tells me he thought it was the CIA.'

'OK,' I said. I had pressed him enough. I never believed in rattling an informant to the core if not required. In this case, he had answered my questions and I wanted to retain him as an informant. I concluded it was best to end the interview now.

The answers Otash had given me were staggering. He had affirmed much of what I had concluded from the scores of top-secret intelligence documents I reviewed. There was a conspiracy to eliminate Marilyn Monroe, and it had come from the highest levels of government. The cover-up was as premeditated as the death of Marilyn. But how? How was it possible?'

# XVI: Blue Shield

*'To Protect and to Serve.'*
— Motto of the Los Angeles Police Department, since 1963.

The government of the day and the LAPD were acting as one. The Kennedys were bonded with Chief Parker and Captain

James Hamilton and through them with Daryl Gates. [In his autobiography, *Chief*, Gates says of Bobby Kennedy: 'He and Pierre Salinger (the future White House press spokesman and then legal counsel to Bobby Kennedy's Senate committee) spent many hours with LAPD Intelligence in the days when his brother was Senator Jack Kennedy, and he was bombarding the Teamsters Union over the corrupt use of their pension funds. I talked to him on the phone many times']. What is revelatory and instructive is something not mentioned in *Chief*. For much of his career at the LAPD, Chief Daryl Gates worked 'off the books' for the CIA running domestic intelligence operations for the agency. Mike Rothmiller revealed:

'I knew of at least three other OCID detectives who served as CIA assets, not officers. A CIA Officer is a full-time employee of the agency. The CIA does not directly employ assets; they have civilian jobs as cover but carry out missions or supply intelligence to their CIA handler. The CIA will never identify its assets.

'Additionally, at the time, LAPD's Public Disorder Intelligence Division (PDID) was also busy gathering intelligence for Chief Daryl Gates. That division kept files on elected officials considered hostile to the LAPD and infiltrated any organisation they deemed liberal including churches, schools, the PTA, colleges and human rights organisations.

'PDID also housed a cadre of detectives working for the CIA. That Daryl Gates served as a CIA asset for many years was confirmed to me by Neil Spotts and a few other high-ranking LAPD staff officers. And in the early 1990s, Ted Gunderson, the former special agent in charge of the Los Angeles FBI office, also confirmed it to me. In 1977 Gunderson was interviewed to become director of the FBI. Instead, the position was given to William Webster.

'After Gates retired, he refused to answer any questions regarding his years of affiliation with the CIA, and the CIA will not answer questions regarding Gates. Some secrets cannot be kept, and Gates' ties to the CIA was one some people from OCID knew. CIA ties to various police and sheriff's departments are not new. However, most people don't understand why the relationship is incredibly close, secretive and necessary. The CIA is prohibited from gathering intelligence on US citizens within the boundaries of the United States; while law enforcement is allowed to gather intelligence within the US on any individual.

'Cops assist the CIA for several reasons; most law enforcement officers consider themselves patriots, many are former military and believe they are helping America by helping the CIA. There are other reasons law enforcement assists. The CIA offers training, equipment and support to various law enforcement agencies, and they sweeten the deal with gratuities. The CIA has numerous safe houses in the US and worldwide. They rewarded the chiefs, sheriffs and high-ranking officers for their assistance by providing free use of their safe houses located in high-end resort settings, providing free use of vehicles and other valuable rewards. Few cops are willing to turn down the free use of a resort home in Hawaii, Miami, Italy or Santa Monica.'

The CIA's working relationship with LAPD's intelligence unit gave officers and agents carte blanche for their activities. It provided complete legal cover from the highest levels of the Federal Government. CIA cover was especially useful when OCID's two electronic experts planted bugs, placed bird dogs [tracking devices] on vehicles, conducted illegal wiretaps and general subterfuge.

In 1975, growing media pressure, following the *Oui* magazine exposé questioning Marilyn's death, forced LAPD Chief Davis to order a new investigation. It was directed by Daryl Gates and handled by OCID Detective Neil Spotts and was a whitewash. Mike Rothmiller recalled:

'In May 1978, when I became a member of OCID, and during the ensuing months, I asked several senior OCID detectives if the 1975 re-investigation was valid since I heard rumours it was not. Nearly everyone just grinned and admitted: "You know it wasn't." After being a trusted member of OCID for several years, I posed the same question to OCID commander, Captain Stuart Finck. Finck [died, aged 78, in October 2014, while living in retirement in Gettysburg, Pennsylvania] was one of Chief Gates' most trusted men and was always cautious when discussing the misdeeds of the Chief. He studied me for a moment, and said: "What do you think? You've been in OCID for some time."

'I was caught off guard by his question. I thought for a moment and said: "Well, I've heard it wasn't a real re-investigation. It was meant to reinforce LAPD's past story and appease the media." He stared at me for a moment and said, "Uh-huh" before turning and entering his office. Over the years, Finck performed many secretive and highly questionable, if not illegal, acts, on behalf of Chief Gates. He was not liked or trusted by the detectives of OCID. When he retired, no one from OCID turned up for his party. At that time, I was stunned by his truthful answer.'

Los Angeles District Attorney John Van de Kamp began a four-month reassessment of Marilyn's death upon the twentieth anniversary of her passing and delivered a 29-page report in December 1982. The sudden inquiry had been brought about by an accusation by private investigator Milo Speriglio who worked for Robert Slatzer, the now discredited man who claimed to have married Marilyn in Tijuana, Mexico. He suggested that Marilyn was murdered by 'a dissident faction' of the CIA or similar group because she knew of a plot against Fidel Castro. Speriglio produced a book [*Marilyn Monroe: Murder, Cover-Up*, Seville Publications, 1982] in which he alleged Marilyn was murdered by Jimmy Hoffa and Sam Giancana. His conclusions were formulated drawing on the work of Robert Slatzer and Anthony Scaduto, the writer who produced the 1975 *Oui* magazine article. He also relied on Lionel Grandison who was with the Coroner's Office when Dr. Noguchi performed his autopsy on Marilyn. Grandison, who was 22-years-old when Marilyn died, was a Los Angeles Deputy Coroner aide. His basic duty being picking up dead bodies and taking them to the Coroner's Office for autopsies. He made many suggestions in regards to doctored paperwork and the actual cause of death but his legitimacy suffered and his claims were later dismissed when he was found not reliable after being accused of stealing from corpses. In *Memoirs of a Deputy Coroner: The Case of Marilyn Monroe* [Bait-Cal, 2012] he charged that the city's Chief Medical Examiner, Dr. Theodore Curphey, ordered him to take part in a cover-up. In an interview when the book he wrote with his son, Lionel Grandison Jr., was published in 2012, he said: 'They just called it suicide and ordered me to forget all about it. She was connected to the President and his Attorney General brother. Marilyn knew too much and someone – the FBI, the CIA or the Mafia – killed her to shut her up. She did not commit suicide, she was murdered.' In a letter to Speriglio, Saltzer said Marilyn was taken by ambulance to a hospital in Santa Monica, where she died in the emergency room. Then, her body was taken to her home, left there and the police were notified. This, he claimed, was the start of an elaborate cover-up of Coroner's Case No: 81128.

Van de Kamp was not impressed by the evidence and said no further criminal investigation into the death was planned. He said the District Attorney's office decided on the review because there was, to his surprise, no District Attorney investigation in 1962, as would have been expected. His report said that a murder 'would have required a massive, in place conspiracy covering all the principals at the death scene, including the actual killer or killers; the chief medical examiner–coroner; the autopsy surgeon to whom the case was fortuitously assigned; and most all of the police officers assigned to the case as well as their superiors.'

A further re-investigation into the death in 1985 was, like the 1975 inquiry, directed by Daryl Gates, but this time in his capacity as chief of police. By then John Van De Kamp, who had found no need to pursue the 1982 inquiry, was the Attorney General of California. Again, it was found that there was no case to answer. A questioning television documentary was censored from a prime-time television network screening in America. Of course, OCID had an extensive dossier covering John Van De Kamp and, on Chief Gates' orders, Mike Rothmiller and other OCID detectives conducted ongoing intelligence operations of him.

The 1985 investigation followed publication of Anthony Summers' book [*Goddess: The Secret Lives of Marilyn Monroe*, Weidenfeld & Nicolson, 1985] which, to public surprise, suggested Bobby Kennedy *had* been in Los Angeles the day Marilyn died. The book surmised that Bobby Kennedy visited Marilyn to end their affair and that Peter Lawford destroyed a suicide note and other evidence, and delayed telling the police of her death so that Bobby Kennedy would have time to get out of Los Angeles to save embarrassment and, more importantly, accusations of complicity.

A similar proposition was put forward in the BBC documentary *The Last Days of Marilyn Monroe* first broadcast in 1985. In this programme Marilyn's housekeeper Eunice Murray's account finally puts Bobby Kennedy in Marilyn's home on the day she died. This fact had, as we know, been in the OCID files since 1962. The documentary did not even hint at Bobby Kennedy being present and directly involved at the time of Marilyn's death, but the suggestion he was even in Los Angeles that day was enough to freak Roone Arledge, the president of America's

ABC News, to not broadcast the show in the US. Although the BBC, Anthony Summers and some American newsmen, protested, Arledge maintained that the programme contained little substantive evidence, dismissing it as 'gossip column stuff'. Summers claimed the decision was a personal one and that Arledge – a friend of Bobby's widow, Ethel – was influenced by pressure from the Kennedys.

The fact that Bobby Kennedy was in Los Angeles on the day was news and was true. The difficulty was the perception of the sources which included Peter Lawford's third wife, actress Deborah Gould, whom he had married in 1976 having met her three weeks earlier. They had separated two months later and were divorced within the year. In 1985, Gould was paid an unknown amount for an interview in which she claimed Lawford had told her there had been a cover-up to get Bobby Kennedy out of town.

Marilyn's life and death have been the subject of a raft of publications, some were banal and contrived offerings, like those of Milo Speriglio and Robert Slatzer – and finding everyone from the Rat Pack to the Mafia responsible for her death. But amid all the hysterical theorising there was always a hint of the truth – that her death was no accident, not suicide and not misadventure, but murder. A murder of convenience.

With *The Last Days of Marilyn Monroe* [William Morrow Paperbacks, 2012, first edition, 1998], Donald Wolfe covers much of Marilyn's life and speculates the cause of her death being an injection of enough barbiturate 'to kill fifteen people' and that Sam Giancana and Dr. Ralph Greenson were involved. Wolfe attempted to quiz Mike Rothmiller after his book *LA Secret Police* was published, but he refused to reveal what he knew. Rothmiller recalled:

'It all added up to nothing. He was a friendly guy, but his book, as with all the others, presents lots of names, dates and times which give the reader the impression that since he knows all those minor details, he probably knows the big picture regarding the primary players. It's a nice technique to create an illusion of knowledge.

'He tried to get me to talk by saying he had interviewed Neil Spotts years earlier. When I spoke to Neil, he admitted he had and sold him a couple of images of Marilyn Monroe, but not pictures that gave evidence of her romantic entanglements. Wolfe paid Neil $1,000 cash for two pictures. A few years later, Wolfe sold copies of the photographs to a publication who paid him $10,000. Neil called Wolfe, livid that the photos were sold for substantially more than he received. Wolfe refused to give Neil any of the proceeds.

'Beyond Chief William Parker, Captain James Hamilton and later Chief Daryl Gates, if one man knew a great deal of the inside story and was deeply involved in continuing the Marilyn/Kennedy cover-up, it was Neil Spotts. During my time in OCID, Neil and his partners were known as 'The Quiet Team' because they worked covertly to gather embarrassing or incriminating intelligence on politicians and judges from across the country. Although they were listed on the OCID roster, they did not report to our captain. They only reported to Chief of Police Daryl Gates and did his bidding – legal or otherwise. The intelligence 'The Quiet Team' gathered would be used to intimidate politicians into conforming to LAPD wishes. Most would see this as blackmail – the LAPD viewed it as "acquiring and helping friends".

'Neil was an interesting fellow. Before joining the LAPD, he was recruited by the CIA. He claimed to have only served a short period with the CIA before joining the LAPD. However, one of Neil's longtime OCID partners confidentially told me that Neil was tasked by the CIA to join the LAPD. This would enable him to have the perfect cover and the ability to perform missions only a cop could carry out, with complete immunity. When I asked his partner how he knew that, he said: "Neil told me."

'Neil and his partner joined me a few times during my surveillance(s) of politicians. One politician we jointly surveilled by order of Chief Gates was Los Angeles County District Attorney John Van de Kamp who later became California's Attorney General. The chief wanted us to obtain photographic evidence Van de Kamp was gay. We were unable to provide any proof of that assertion. Later on, OCID also expended a great deal of time and effort gathering intelligence on then California Governor Jerry Brown for the same reason.

'The day after we surveilled John Van de Kamp's beach house near Laguna Beach, California, I sat next to Neil in OCID's office to discuss what we learned the prior day – which was nothing. Knowing that Neil headed LAPD's re-investigations into the assassination of Robert Kennedy in 1968, and the 1975 re-investigation into Marilyn Monroe's death, I asked a few questions relating to both.

'Neil never mentioned his investigations unless asked and, if he provided an answer, they were short and to the point. While discussing Marilyn Monroe, I asked about her and the Kennedys. Neil didn't say a word but unlocked his desk drawer. He removed a standard legal-size manila envelope and handed it to me.

'"Here," he said.

'"What's in it?" I asked, taking the envelope and opening it.

'"You'll see."

'Opening the envelope and looking in, I saw a series of photographs and removed them. A few were 8x10s but most were smaller standard size prints. They were all black and white. It was apparent these were surveillance photos.

'"Who are they?" I asked, pointing to the first image of two men talking.

'Neil leaned into me to determine what photo I was viewing and whispered: "Bob Kennedy and Lawford."

'I flipped through a few more and stopped when I saw a photo obviously taken through what looked like a window to a residence and immediately recognised the people. It was John Kennedy and Marilyn Monroe seated on a sofa. They were passionately kissing.

'"Where was this taken?" I asked.

'"Her house."

'"Who took it?"

'In a matter-of-fact voice, he said: "Some OCID guys back then."

'I'd estimate there were roughly fifteen to twenty surveillance photographs of Monroe in romantic engagements with either John Kennedy or Robert Kennedy. Neil said the photos were taken not just at her residence but also at Peter Lawford's residence, and a hotel in Beverly Hills. I was stunned by his willingness to allow me to view the photographs. Usually, Neil was extremely guarded. I can only surmise he was comfortable with me and had momentarily dropped his guard.

'"Are these the only photos of Monroe and the Kennedys together?" I asked.

'"No," he replied.'

The OCID detectives secreted away anything they believed would give them influence over the supposed power brokers and lawmakers. The sneak photographs, the evidence of incriminating hotel stays and illicit relationships – all these details could be useful in extortion and they were their currency of choice.

The OCID teams would even spy on each other. They might find out that a superior was having a clandestine love affair and would casually leave a photograph or a business card from the love motel of choice on the senior officer's desk as a message. Promotion rather than retribution was usually the result.

But it was a two-way street when it involved those who inhabited the White House. Marilyn's untimely death was, they all proclaimed, sad but, for the Kennedys, Frank Sinatra and Sam Giancana it was convenient. She knew too much, which worried the Kennedys, and for Sinatra and Giancana there were the horrifying details of her last weekend at the Cal Neva. By the time Marilyn drank Bobby Kennedy's concoction, attempts had been going on for some months to sanitise the Kennedys' Hollywood connections. It was most certainly not easy.

# XVII: Marilyn's Diary

*'Ask not what your country can do for you –*
*ask what you can do for your country',*
— President John F. Kennedy, January 1961.

Mike Rothmiller made his notes from Marilyn's diary on what paper he had on hand as he worked among the files in the OCID offices. When he ran out of suitable writing material, he grabbed what he could. Which is why some of his extracts from Marilyn's diary are on the back of an LAPD Training Bulletin [Module No. 590.451] emblazoned with the LAPD name and Daryl F. Gates, Chief of Police, on the letterhead of Volume X1, Issue 3. That Bulletin is dated February 1979.

The diary has been something of a Holy Grail for those trying to solve not so much Marilyn's death but the mystery of her life. When she was killed, she was a fabulously successful Hollywood actress and within hours the legend had begun. And, as we know from a movie, *The Man Who Shot Liberty Valance* [1962], released just weeks before she died, you always print the legend. Marilyn never grew old in front of the camera or in the public imagination. Memories of her became fascinating and valuable. Bounties starting, in the early days, at around $10,000 then reaching up to $150,000 and $200,000 were offered for her diary, sometimes called the Red Diary. Since then, inflation has added zeroes. The diary was regarded as vanished proof of her relationship with an American President and his brother, the nation's Attorney General. Implicit but unsaid was that it would be a health warning about the toxicity of sleeping with powerful men. But would it also provide a clue to her true personality forged by her traumatic childhood and the truth about her death?

Here Mike Rothmiller tells the full story of how he found the diary in the OCID files and reveals what he was able to copy from it:

How a copy of her diary found its way into the OCID top-secret files remains a mystery, at least to me. Someone from LAPD Intelligence would have had to obtain it and place it into the filing system, but the extraordinarily atypical aspect of the entry into the files is the fact that it wasn't attached to a completed detective's intelligence report which serves as a cover sheet. In my years as an OCID detective, I never saw a single file entry without a completed intelligence report attached. Additionally, critical items were missing from the intelligence report, such as the date of inclusion into OCID's archives. So how it was acquired, its origin, the date it was obtained, its significance and, most importantly, the detective(s) names who entered it into OCID's files were missing. The detective names would only be omitted to safeguard them and others. The absence of this information could not have been a simple error; it was intentional. Before a document was approved for inclusion into OCID's vast secret records system, it was reviewed and approved by a section lieutenant before going to OCID's captain for final review and approval. During the review process, these significant omissions would have been noticed and corrected. However, in this case, they were intentionally overlooked. Who authorised its inclusion into the files will never be known.

The significance of the missing detective(s) names is only apparent to other OCID detectives. When names are listed in the report, future detectives would know who to contact for additional details or clarification of a document. Whoever placed the diary on file didn't want to be questioned about how or why they came to acquire it.

The most likely person to have obtained the diary is Captain James Hamilton. He was the cop Peter Lawford recognised when he and Robert Kennedy were leaving Monroe's house the night she died. As the Commanding Officer of OCID, he could have entered the diary into OCID files with missing information. However, since he was the primary LAPD officer involved in directing the cover-up of Marilyn's death, I do not believe he was responsible. It is illogical for the man behind the cover-up to place items in LAPD's secret files which could incriminate him and Robert Kennedy in a murder – a crime for which there is no statute of limitations.

Finding a copy of the diary in OCID files would send any investigator's mind racing toward several startling possibilities. According to nearly all the authors and researchers and also Marilyn's friends, she faithfully made entries in her diary. It was always close at hand and, when she died, it mysteriously vanished and has never resurfaced. Until I came across it in the OCID files. Having perused it, the reason it was taken is clear. The question over who took it is more difficult to determine.

Based on OCID dossiers, my numerous conversations with Jack Clemmons and discussions with detectives who were members of OCID at the time of Marilyn's death, I have drawn some reasonable conclusions. Reinforcing my findings is the information I received from Peter Lawford and Fred Otash [I do not believe Otash took the diary]. I believe there are only four viable theories.

First, a member, or members, of OCID, or their asset(s), searched Marilyn's home during the time between her death and Jack Clemmons' arrival and removed the diary. Captain James Hamilton was, according to Lawford, at the property during this time.

The second possibility is that a copy of the diary was provided to OCID from another intelligence agency or a private source which either obtained the original or a copy.

The third scenario is that the diary was placed in OCID files sometime after Captain Hamilton retired from the LAPD. By whom and how it was acquired are the unknowns here.

A fourth possibility is that someone removed her diary earlier in the day of her death, but this is highly remote, and I'd place it at a near zero possibility. If that were the case, only Robert Kennedy or Peter Lawford could be suspected of removing the diary during their first visit that day.

Marilyn's missing diary has raised serious questions for those who insist she killed herself. If she elected to commit suicide, it is doubtful she would have disposed of her diary in advance. It also raises questions regarding the role LAPD and others may have played in her death.

Although Robert Kennedy and Peter Lawford [as Lawford confirmed] desperately attempted to find her diary and other items the night she died, all intelligence data indicates they were unsuccessful. If Kennedy *did* find her diary, he would have immediately destroyed it, and he would certainly never have provided a copy to OCID or anyone else.

The fact that it had ended up in the OCID files just reinforced the notion that information was power. Keep it and hide it in the files for when it might be needed or useful.

When I was with OCID, there were about 60 detectives in the division at any given time, in addition there were the office staff. We worked in teams of two and 99 per cent of our work was undercover. We had false IDs and we created false businesses. We never wore suits and placed out of state licence plates on our unmarked cars. Each team had their specialty: gambling, prostitution, various Mafia families and of course, political corruption at all levels. This included secretly gathering intelligence on all Presidents dating back to Harry Truman. I collected quite a bit of intelligence on President Reagan, and all teams gathered intelligence on the rich and famous.

Also, there were no borders on our jurisdiction. We quietly gathered information from throughout the United States and from any country we thought may provide it. My specialties were the Chicago Mafia known as 'The Outfit'. organised crime in Mexico and in Las Vegas and big-name entertainers. At the time, Vegas was the hub of organised crime and always provided a wealth of information. It was useful to learn which congressmen or senators visited Vegas to meet with mobsters or partake in the gifts offered by the sex workers the Mob supplied. The sex workers were both male and female, and most of the prominent and nationally known politicians had their favourite. One well known West Coast senator visited often. Everything was recorded in the files.

As a member of OCID, we were forbidden from making arrests by order of the chief of police. An arrest meant court and subpoenas and the chief did not want our questionable and, at times, illegal operations to become known. During my five years in the division, I only knew of one arrest, and I orchestrated that.

Before news of Marilyn's death was made public, Captain Hamilton, accompanied by an OCID detective, departed her residence and quietly arrived at the General Telephone headquarters in southern California where he demanded all of Marilyn's and Peter Lawford's telephone records. The records were quickly provided and promptly vanished forever. Some claim to have recovered Monroe's missing telephone records, but I find that very dubious. If they have produced telephone records, it is very probable they are forgeries made long after the fact.

In 1975, during the inquiry that followed the *Oui* magazine article, Chief Gates also claimed to have found Marilyn's telephone records. In later years, Hamilton admitted to others that he had indeed confiscated the telephone tapes and toll tabs, so this fact has never been in question. And, of course, Thad Brown had told Florabel Muir that he saw Marilyn's telephone records on Chief William Parker's desk. Chief Parker personally held the missing telephone records in his office safe which was locked whenever he wasn't present. According to intelligence documents, Parker had the original copies of Monroe's and Lawford's telephone records and its highly unlikely he would have provided copies to anyone outside of OCID, with the exception of the Kennedys. Remember, Chief Parker's gopher and driver at the time was the young police officer Daryl Gates.

Another high-ranking LAPD official who reviewed the telephone records in Chief Parker's office was Tom Reddin, then deputy police chief. In 1993, Reddin contacted me and said he was in Parker's office when Captain Hamilton gave the telephone records to Parker. He and Parker discussed the records, and Parker said he'd keep them in his private safe. Of course, when Reddin became chief and requested the files he was told there were none. OCID had no files on Monroe or the Kennedys. Reddin said he knew the OCID supervisor at the time was lying but could not prove it. He also knew that to attack OCID was dangerous, and that was not something the new chief wished to experience. The OCID made their own rules and ignored what they considered an inconvenient request no matter where or from whom it came.

The diary contained pages dated during 1962, but not all pages were dated. The nature of some entries – including details of her sexual relations with President John F. Kennedy and Robert Kennedy, and the information they disclosed to her during intimate moments – would have destroyed the President and the Attorney General, and set the country on a dangerous course. Considering the state of world affairs in 1962, one must ponder the most fundamental question; who was expendable and who had power? The President, the Attorney General or Marilyn? The answer is obvious.

To this day, I do not know if the copy of the diary I read was complete, a portion of the original or a compilation of several diaries. I believe it may have been a compilation because the information did not appear to be listed in a chronological order. Typically, a diary contains vast amounts of everyday activities only of interest to the author, and that kind of information rarely serves an intelligence purpose. Removing those pages and retaining only those that contained valuable information would not be unreasonable. Additionally, the pages appeared to have been torn from a small binder because the ragged edges were visible on the copies. I would describe the diary copy I read as an early photocopy. I did not count the pages, however I'd estimate there were roughly 50 to 70. The pages were printed on standard size copy paper with the faint outline of the smaller diary pages visible. All entries were handwritten and not typed. At times, the passages were in a rough cursive style; not refined, smooth or elegant. Most entries were printed in block letters and easy to read. In some of the entries her penmanship was sloppy, broken and confusing, if not impossible to read. Some words and sentences were scribbled over, making them illegible. Some passages weren't coherent. It's purely my speculation that the sloppy and incoherent entries were made during times of drug and/or alcohol intoxication.

Before reviewing the diary, I had never read any of Marilyn's writing. Like most people, I perceived her as a typical ditzy blonde actress of the period with limited worldly knowledge and of moderate intelligence. After reading the diary and various intelligence reports, my impression of Marilyn changed. She was indeed a glamorous woman, but she also seemed to be quite intelligent with a keen interest in and grasp of political and world affairs. For me, the idea of her as simply a dumb blonde was erased. Where she fell short and seemed clueless was in her love life. I'm not a psychiatrist, but from her actions, it appeared she was insecure and more than willing to allow men she perceived as powerful to use her for their self-gratification. And they did. According to details within both their respective OCID dossiers, the exception was Joe DiMaggio who appeared to have genuinely cared for her. It's clear President John Kennedy and Robert Kennedy viewed her like a shiny new toy, and when they no longer wished to play with it, they tossed it aside for another.

As I read the diary, I took notes of what I believed to be the most significant entries, the entries which were clear in their meaning or were interesting and useful for intelligence purposes. Most entries seemed to revolve around mundane issues and only mentioned first names which I did not bother noting since they were meaningless to me.

The following entry probably referred to Jack Lemmon. He and Tony Curtis starred with Marilyn in *Some Like It Hot*. The entry read: 'Jack called. He's so nice. We talked about our movie and Tony. We had lots of fun. I love them.' Another read: 'Joe called and asked how I'm doing? I will always love him. He always listened and cared.' This entry likely referred to her former husband baseball notable Joe DiMaggio. Another entry read, 'Talked with Joe Jr. He likes the Marines. Said his dad is OK and asked how I am.' Joe Jr. is, presumably, DiMaggio's son who was serving in the US Marine Corps at the time. She wrote of her psychiatrist's garden, 'I love Dr. Greenson's roses they are beautiful.' Another entry referred to her physician. 'I told Dr. Engelberg I can't sleep. He's sending me another medicine to help. I hope it does. I'm so tired and sick.'

Then the more eyebrow raising entries: 'John said Mr. Hoover believes I'm a Communist. He said don't worry about it. He's wrong. John can handle him.' There is ample evidence in both the FBI and the OCID files that Hoover believed Marilyn Monroe was a Communist and a danger to the country.

Then, in a telling entry, she wrote, 'The President said he'll give me his private telephone number and a name to use when I call the White House.' All presidents have a private telephone number they only provide to their family and close associates. In some cases, a code name is given to the person, which only the president knows. That provides safety and deniability if the call is intercepted.

'John hates the vice president. He doesn't want to talk with him. He's just a dumb cowboy.' It was Washington's worse kept secret that President Kennedy and Vice President Lyndon Johnson just about tolerated each other.

'I wanted to talk about his time in the war. He doesn't want to talk about it. He said that's in the past.' This passage is rather curious since Kennedy openly spoke of his World War Two navy experience to appeal to voters. Why he didn't wish to discuss it with Marilyn is unknown. It may be as simple as bad timing.

Marilyn's dossier also included covert photographs of secret rendezvous between her and President John Kennedy and later with Robert Kennedy – these were in addition to the photos held by OCID detective Neil Spotts. I don't recall the locations where the images were taken. A few of the, clearly covertly taken, pictures of Peter Lawford and Robert Kennedy were dated the day she died. The date is significant since it's yet more evidence that Robert Kennedy was in Los Angeles on the day she died. It's important to remember that intelligence documents were clear that Robert Kennedy's task was to calm Marilyn and keep her from disclosing her relationship with his brother and himself. In the end, RFK was left dealing with her numerous telephone calls to the White House and Department of Justice and all the emotional baggage the brothers created.

Noted in the diary were several entries regarding the weekend at the Cal Neva a week before she died. The Cal Neva weekend was also documented by other agencies, and a report detailing that weekend was placed in OCID's secret files.

'Frank invited me to the lodge. He said it will be fun. He said never to mention Sam at the lodge. He's Mafia.'

It appears the following entries were made after she returned home to Fifth Helena Drive. Before and after the entered items were scribbled out and not legible.

'Frank, Peter and others were there … Frank said I can't keep my fucking mouth shut … He told me to get out. I don't know why he's treating me this way … What happened to me. I was drunk. I don't remember … Did I have sex.' [sic]

Interestingly, in the diary, she noted having sexual relations with President Kennedy and alluded to significantly more sexual relationships with Robert Kennedy. The diary entries never provided detailed information as to where she and the President had sex beyond making a simple mention of 'Peter's [Lawford's] house', her house, a pool or a hotel. This would not be unusual since a person making a diary entry already knows the intimate details, and they are not authoring a romance novel for public consumption. As with all diaries, they're intended for personal use.

The diary contained several entries regarding her innermost feelings for President Kennedy. It appeared she momentarily loved him and believed the feelings were mutual. The earliest entries referred to John Kennedy as 'the President' and as their affair continued the entries related to him transitioned to 'John'. Later the entries changed to being primarily about Bobby. His last name was not noted, but it was clear she was referring to Robert Kennedy.

One notation stated: 'The President and I made love last night for the first time. He is wonderful and kind. Today he sent me two dozen red roses and chocolates!' Another entry read: 'John called he wants to see me again. He'll have me picked up and taken to the hotel.' She noted that President Kennedy suffered pain. At least once she mentioned helping him remove a back brace before they had sex.

> 'John's back is horrible … He always needs a brace and doesn't want to walk upstairs … I helped him take it off before we made love.'

She noted her apparent disappointment that he engaged in minimum physical foreplay if any, had sex, and it was over.

> 'We just kiss and have sex. I wish it was more but it's not … He always wants me to blow him … John just lies there, and I get on top of him to make love.'

Considering Kennedy's painful back injury, I assume he was physically unable to be active in bed, requiring Marilyn and his other lovers to handle the more physical aspects of sex by keeping his painful back as still as possible. This could be the reason he had a penchant for sex in the White House swimming pool, it takes the pressure off the back. Another diary entry read: 'John and I made love in the pool.'

There was one diary item indicating that the President had erectile dysfunction: 'It takes a long time for John to get hard and sometimes he can't.' This is highly likely since he was taking a daily cocktail of powerful painkilling drugs. Another, printed in all caps and underlined several times states, 'JOHN IS A SELFISH LOVER!'

There is an entry that I believe was related to the Bay of Pigs attempted invasion of Cuba:

'He was very mad because he did not stop the invasion of Cuba. He doesn't trust the CIA ... They lied to him.'

There was a short entry and, as I recall, the only passage saying the President was taking blue pills and gave her one during a tryst.

'John took a blue pill and gave me one. We made love. It made me dizzy.'

What the pill was and the reason for President Kennedy introducing them is unknown. However, while researching, I located a Kennedy White House telephone transcript in the National Archives and Record Administration. The transcript covered a brief conversation between President Kennedy and his White House physician Dr. Burkley. Calling from the Oval Office, Kennedy asked the doctor if he sent the medication to his office. Dr. Burkley informed the president that Mrs. Evelyn Lincoln [the President's longtime secretary] had the meds. The President asked if Dr. Burkley could send one of those 'blue' pills. The doctor said he would. I've consulted with medical doctors and pharmacists, and they believe that the 'blue pill' was a powerful pain medication called Demerol. At the request of the Kennedy family, public access to the President's White House medical records is highly restricted by the National Archives and Records Administration.

Another diary entry read, 'He's very worried the spacemen will die.' I assumed this referred to the first NASA Mercury Missions. Many feared astronauts Alan Shepard and John Glenn would be killed during their space flights.

The entries weren't dated, but there were notes that indicated when Robert Kennedy and Marilyn first had sex. Robert Kennedy was in Los Angeles and was staying with the Lawfords. Marilyn had dinner with Peter and Robert; then Peter left for the evening. It was then she and Robert had sex for the first time. The entry read: 'Bobby and I made love at Peter's. He wants to see me again. This is our secret.' Another entry indicated that, in the beginning, Robert Kennedy demonstrated a kinder heart than his brother and lent an ear and a shoulder to her. I noted one sentence:

> 'Bobby is gentle. He listens to me. He's nicer than John.
>
> 'Bobby said he loves me and wants to marry me. I love him.'

One OCID report stated that Robert Kennedy impregnated Marilyn and, shortly after the pregnancy was confirmed, he pressured her to travel to Mexico under an assumed identity for an abortion. As on all OCID intelligence reports, the informant's credibility ranged from 'reliable' to 'unknown'. On this report, the informant was listed as 'unknown.' A separate OCID report – not rated for reliability – said that on July 19–21, 1962, Marilyn was in Cedars of Lebanon Hospital in West Hollywood under an assumed name for a curettage or, what many presumed, an abortion.

Reading the final entries, it was apparent that Marilyn was angry with John and Robert Kennedy for using her as a sex toy and then tossing her aside. She was frustrated that they wouldn't take her calls, writing:

'They are not calling back. Bob and John used me. They used me … I told Peter they're ignoring me … I'm not going to stand for that. I'm going to tell everyone about us.'

From the diary and OCID intelligence documents, there's no question that Marilyn had threatened and planned to call a news conference to expose her relationships with the President and Robert Kennedy, and reveal national security items told to her. The final diary entries indicate that Peter Lawford had asked her to stay home because Robert Kennedy and Lawford were coming to her residence the next day, 'Peter said Robert will come tomorrow. I don't know if he will.'

Contained within the diary and OCID's secret files were one of Marilyn's last telephone calls to her part-time lover and friend, Mexican actor José Bolaños: 'I love José. He's a wonderful friend and lover.' The entry indicated that she told José of her plan to expose President and Robert Kennedy during a Press conference. He begged and warned her not to do it.

'I told José I'm going to tell the world about them. They used me. I'm not a whore ... José said don't tell anyone about this. It's dangerous.'

Some years later, Bolaños confirmed the details of this telephone conversation.

Other entries indicated she enjoyed discussing world events with the President and he disclosed what would have been considered national security secrets to her. Pillow talk transcriptions included a short passage stating: 'John does not like Fidel C and said he will be gone soon.' It has been well documented that President Kennedy and Robert Kennedy approved several plots for the CIA to conspire with the Mafia to assassinate Cuban leader Fidel Castro. According to CIA documents, at the very moment President Kennedy was shot in Dallas, Texas, a CIA agent was delivering a pen filled with poison to a Cuban assassin in Paris, France, with instructions to kill Castro.

Another diary entry indicated President Kennedy was to send more troops to Vietnam to fight Communism. The entry read: 'John is sending more men to Vietnam ... The Communists must be stopped. It will be a long war.'

On a later page of the photocopied sheets was a mention of Kennedy's nemesis, Khrushchev who, like so many before him, had been smitten when he met Marilyn at 20th Century Fox: 'Niketa [sic] is a horrible man and must be stopped. He doesn't like John and John doesn't like him. I'm scared there will be a war.'

And the most poignant of all the diary entries:

*John hasn't called. Bobby called. He's coming to California. He wants to see me.*

# XVIII: Over the Rainbow

*'No one leaves a star.*
*'That's what makes one a star.'*
— Gloria Swanson as Norma Desmond, *Sunset Boulevard,*1950.

In the Billy Wilder directed classic, *Sunset Boulevard*, the exotic and delightfully demented silent screen diva, Norma Desmond played by Gloria Swanson, one-time lover of Joe Kennedy Sr., is 'the greatest star of them all'. and wanted nothing but revenge when she was jilted by her lover, in an echo of Marilyn's own final days. In the final moments of the film – one of the great and ageless Hollywood movies – Norma flamboyantly announces she's ready for her close-up. Often scared, mostly of being alone, Marilyn's link to companionship was the telephone and it was truly subliminal that those staging her body decided that she should be clutching a phone when she was found dead. Marilyn on the phone would look *real*.

Marilyn had been using the phone to tell everyone she could talk to – and an audience of eavesdroppers that she was unaware of – that she was finally fed up of being 'used' by the Kennedy brothers and was going to spill the beans about her affairs with them. She wanted to get back at them for discarding her like soiled laundry. The opportunity for her to 'see sense'. as Peter Lawford had hoped he would be able to persuade her to do early in the day of her death, was never an option. We'll never know if Marilyn was crying wolf, bluffing to get the attention of the Kennedys who had 'ghosted' her to use today's parlance.

Up on the screen, so many, many feet tall, she was always a powerful presence. Her cherry red lipstick worn like a pirate flag, her status as a screen goddess and her innate understanding of her own sexual allure implied she was in control. She could handle a one-liner and an improper pass. She could handle herself. Goodness, she was *Marilyn Monroe*. Reality was more complex, and Marilyn was both endearing and exasperating. When she showed up for a 9 a.m. shoot at 5 p.m. while working on *The Seven Year Itch*, she claimed she'd got lost trying to find the Fox film lot. Director Billy Wilder was bemused: 'She'd been under contract to the studio for seven years.' Somehow, they worked it out. She could be eight hours late but forgiven in a second.

Her glory was hard fought for and self-willed. Her world was Hollywood where the deity is the dollar, and Marilyn was returning millions and millions of them at the box office. Hollywood wanted her to be happy, but they didn't want her to change. The eminent writer and card player, Budd Schulberg, who'd played poker at Sam Spiegel's with Marilyn on his knee, wrote about the duality of Hollywood. He called it 'double morality' and 'double vision'. Applied to Marilyn, it equates to glorifying what they couldn't stop exploiting, and exploiting the commodity they couldn't stop glorifying.

But Marilyn was not about money for the Kennedys. They didn't need her for that. Once they were finished with her romantically there was no compulsion to continue with her. Yet, like Hollywood, it was clear that they saw her as property, a chattel – somehow less than human. For a woman, still traumatised by a childhood of neglect, this must have been more painful than anything. She was – if not legally – emotionally an orphan. She was alone in her nightmares.

Marilyn never grew old on film or in the public imagination. In the 21$^{st}$ century she still retains a legendary-mythical status. She is simultaneously viewed as a victim of abuse and a courageous feminist. Her tale is a rags-to-riches-to-tragedy story. Her admirers are fervent, her detractors fevered. She was needy and giving, unable to disguise or overcome her insecurities.

The grand recorder of American life, famed for his *Letter from America* for the BBC, Alastair Cooke, reported the day after she died: 'She could never learn to acquire the lacquered shell of the prima donna or the armour of sophistication.' When her painfully short existence ended, while her body was still in the morgue, she was stonily cut up, repackaged, and presented as the creator of her own demise. Yet, her death was not by her design. She was deleted by others with selfish expediency, as neatly as a compromised hoodlum from a Raymond Chandler novel. And those who assisted both before and after the fact were much rewarded for their exemplary efforts. Most immediately and generously looked after was Captain James Hamilton, in whom Bobby Kennedy had a deep trust. Hamilton really did know all the secrets, and he was recommended by the Attorney General to Pete Rozelle the Commissioner of the National Football League [NFL] for a lucrative appointment in May 1963. Hamilton, then aged 53, became the first director of NFL security with an expansive brief and expense account to take him all across America. Pete Rozelle said: 'Jim Hamilton had come to us with the blessing of Robert Kennedy, with a massive vote of confidence and recommendation. He's here to protect the good name of our sport.' Hamilton said at the time: 'What I try to do is keep the pipelines open so as to be aware of anything affecting the good name of a team, an individual or the league itself.' Hamilton's health deteriorated, and he died in 1966 and was replaced by William Hundley, another crony of Bobby Kennedy and the Chief of his Organized Crime Division in the Justice Department.

When James Hamilton left the LAPD, he also left the most delicate of jobs, the head of the OCID. Chief Parker gave his protégé Captain Daryl Gates the post and the key to the files. Within two years, Gates became Inspector Gates [at 38 he was the youngest ever in the LAPD] and was being groomed to succeed William Parker as chief which, eventually, he did in 1978. He refined Parker's military approach to policing the City of Angels. He fine-tuned a relatively small, mobile force dependent on rapid tactical response, and created the now globally recognised SWAT (Special Weapons and Tactics) unit. But the film capital was changing with the more racially sensitive times, and Chief Gates' view of police brutality was abhorred. When he said that more black people were dying during the use of a carotid chokehold by the LAPD because their 'veins and arteries do not open up as fast as on normal people' there was widespread shock. In March 1991, a videotape of the beating of a black man, Rodney King, by four white LAPD officers, became public. Chief Gates held on to his job. In April 1992, the acquittal of the four officers was the catalyst for rioting in which more than 50 residents died. The chief stayed on at a political fundraising dinner he was attending during the first night of the rioting, while live television coverage showed a truck driver being grabbed on the street and beaten to near death. For once, the LAPD couldn't cope. The military were called in and Gates was called out. On April 16, 2010, Gates, aged 83, died in California from bladder cancer.

J. Edgar Hoover ['I have no use for this man Parker'] despised the man Bobby Kennedy called among 'America's finest' and lauded at every possibility. One of Parker's favourite photographs was a signed one of himself with President Kennedy who thanked him for organising their personal security. After Marilyn's death, Bobby Kennedy remained in contact with Parker. Together they arranged for LAPD retirees to hold positions in the private sector, and they placed LAPD officers in special Federal assignments.

Chief Parker was consumed with his work. He stayed at his desk and in command after an operation for an aortal aneurysm and resection. On July 16, 1966, after speaking at the Second Marine Division Association banquet at the Statler Hotel [later the downtown Hilton] at Wilshire and Figueroa, his heart gave out. He had just been called the 'foremost law enforcement officer in America' and given a standing ovation by his audience. He was 61 years old. His body lay in state in the City Hall rotunda where mourners – more than 3,000 of them – lined the streets to wish him a final farewell. There were so many people at 10 a.m. in the morning at St. Vibiana's Cathedral that extra police had to be called in. Mayor Yorty, despite his aggravations with Chief Parker managed to offer: 'Los Angeles and America will sadly miss our courageous and beloved Police Chief Parker…' Governor Pat Brown was there along with the Republican who wanted – and got – his job, the actor Ronald Reagan. The high requiem mass was broadcast to an overspill of about 1,600 people outside the cathedral. The hearse had an escort of 150 LAPD motorcycle cops for the seven-mile funeral procession. A military honour guard saw him buried as a police band played *Hail to the Chief*.

These three policemen – William Parker, James Hamilton and Daryl Gates –were major influences in the creation of the 20th century Los Angeles Police Department, the best known in the world through films and television. They were also pivotal in covering up the death of Marilyn Monroe. Other names are better remembered but were not as useful – essentially, they served their purpose by keeping quiet.

Pat Newcomb, aged 91 in the summer of 2021, was one of the last people to see Marilyn alive. She had worked for the Arthur P. Jacobs agency, but Jacobs fired her following scenes in August 1962, where she became hysterical with reporters and photographers covering Marilyn's death. As Marilyn's press agent, Newcomb was very much part of Hollywood but, after her client's death, she left America almost immediately She returned in February 1963, having stayed in Germany, France, Italy, Holland, Denmark and Switzerland. Then, she moved to Washington and on a $12,245 a year salary began work at the US Information Agency. She accepted an assignment with Pierre Salinger in the summer of 1964, when he ran as a Democratic candidate for the California Senate. Peter and Pat Lawford were also involved in Salinger's campaign which was orchestrated and financed by Bobby Kennedy. Salinger, who became a senator by default [he replaced the incumbent who died until the election proper], was ultimately defeated by a former vaudeville star, the song and dance man George Murphy. Pat Newcomb returned to Washington to work at the office next door to the Attorney

General, for Bobby Kennedy's Department of Justice. Later, she would return to work in Hollywood.

Eunice Murray, who died in 1994, moved from her Santa Monica apartment following Marilyn's death. Gossip from her neighbours said she 'had come into money'. She travelled to Europe and returned the following year. Others, like Marilyn's psychiatrist and physician, often supplied contradictory stories of what happened before, during, and after her death following an edited description of events.

Bobby Kennedy said nothing about Marilyn's death. Why should he? He said he wasn't there. Of course, he and his family went on to be stalked by tragedy, and the overwhelming global impact of that eclipsed the end of Marilyn. They are freeze-framed in memory, those six seconds of photographic images from Dallas on November 22, 1963, the day of JFK's assassination. Those tragic ticks of time, photographed as the Presidential motorcade glided past the Texas School Book Depository, remain the most studied and debated in US history. Jackie Kennedy in her pink suit and matching pillbox hat, JFK grinning and waving, the crowds cheering and then the gunshots that shattered the world as the victim became the ghost of charisma past.

Clearly, JFK's reputation has been tainted by hindsight, by his womanising and constant adultery, but he was not alone among America's leaders in the 1960s for being a sexual cowboy. Documents released in 2019 show behavioural links between President Kennedy and the Rev. Martin Luther King Jr. FBI files detail King's wild sexual activities with dozens of women as he crossed America campaigning against racial inequality. William Sullivan, assistant director of the FBI, wrote in a 1964 memo that King joked to his friends in his bugged Washington hotel room *he had started the International Association for the Advancement of Pussy-Eaters.* Another FBI recording claims King *looked on, laughed and offered advice* while a friend, a Baptist minister, raped one of his parishioners. The tapes said to show the assault were being held in 2019 in a vault under court seal at the US National Archives. The revelations on the tapes, in FBI summaries, were found by historian David Garrow who won a Pulitzer prize in 1987 for *Bearing the Cross* [William Morrow, 1986] his life of Rev. King. His biography also won the *Robert F. Kennedy Book Award* which is ironic for it was Attorney General Robert Kennedy who proposed and approved the wiretap on King. Garrow gave details of his finding in the British monthly magazine *Standpoint* in June 2019. He revealed the FBI planted miniature transmitters in two lamps in rooms booked by King in January 1964, at the Willard Hotel which is near the White House. FBI agents in nearby rooms listened in electronically with radio receivers, the conversations silently transferred to tape recorders. King was accompanied by a friend, Logan Kearse, the pastor of Baltimore's Cornerstone Baptist church, who had arrived in Washington with what an FBI summary describes 'as several women *parishioners* of his church'. Kearse invited King to meet the women in his room, where they 'discussed which women among the *parishioners* would be suitable for natural and unnatural sex acts'.

At one point, a senior FBI official [said to be J. Edgar Hoover] sent an incriminating tape and an anonymous letter to King calling him an 'evil, abnormal beast' and warning him that 'your adulterous acts, your sexual orgies were on the record for all time.' The letter ended with a veiled suggestion that King should commit suicide. When King learned of the tapes' contents, he is said to have told one aide over a wiretapped phone line that the FBI was 'out to get me, harass me, break my spirit'.

David Garrow said in UK interviews in June 2019, that he had spent several months digging through a King-related *document dump* on the National Archives website and found among them electronic copies of documents that were 500 pages long. In *Bearing the Cross*, Garrow discussed what he then knew of King's extramarital adventuring but admitted he had no idea of the scale or the extent of King's philandering until he saw the FBI files.

'I always thought there were ten to twelve other women, not forty to forty-five.' He said he believed that in the #MeToo era, evidence of King's indifference to rape 'poses so fundamental a challenge to his historical stature as to require the most complete and extensive historical review possible'.

J. Edgar Hoover, content to know but not show what he had on the Kennedys, was convinced that King's sexual recklessness made him vulnerable to Communists. David Garrow said that the FBI material on King includes hours of surveillance recordings that were sealed by court order for 50 years in January 1977. Yet, significant documents have been made available following judicial appeals on the disclosure of Government files; more elaborate evidence, hidden away, may finally appear in 2027. If not before.

Bobby Kennedy made his bid for Presidency in 1968, but was at the heels of Eugene McCarthy during the campaign until he beat the front runner in the California Democratic Primary on June 5. It was a time to celebrate, and the party location was the Ambassador Hotel on Wilshire Boulevard in Los Angeles. The Secret Service did not provide security for candidates, only nominees, but the LAPD, as they had always done, planned to look after Bobby Kennedy. On April 4 that year, Martin Luther King Jr., aged 39, had been assassinated in Memphis, Tennessee; Bobby Kennedy's advisers thought having uniformed police around the Ambassador Hotel for the celebration was 'too provocative'. Daryl Gates recalled the evening: 'Kennedy's people were adamant, if not abusive, in their demands that the police not even come close to the senator while he was in Los Angeles.' Normally, that wouldn't have mattered. The LAPD never wanted VIP trouble in their kingdom. If high-profile targets were in town they would, unknown to most, have an undercover cop as their driver and a plain-clothes police presence. But Bobby Kennedy and his staff were aware of this tactic and refused it.

So, officially, there were no uniformed or known plain-clothes LAPD officers protecting Bobby Kennedy that evening. After delivering his victory speech, Kennedy made his way out of the hotel through the ground floor kitchen. There he was hit by three bullets from a .22 calibre pistol. He was pronounced dead at 1.44 a.m. on June 6, 1968, at the Good Samaritan Hospital.

By then, Chief Parker and Captain Hamilton weren't around to protect Bobby Kennedy or to protect anyone at all. But their legacy of secrecy lived on that night.

OCID, as always, ignored authority and did what *they* thought was correct. Unknown until the publication of this book, is that several members of OCID *were* secretly inside the Ambassador Hotel when Bobby Kennedy was assassinated. Much of the evidence obtained by the intelligence squad detectives about that night [as the Marilyn Monroe files were for decades] remains secret, conveniently 'lost' among all the others in the history of the Los Angeles Police Department.

# PART FIVE

## The Verdict

*'Power does not corrupt. Fear corrupts ... perhaps the fear of a loss of power.'*

— **John Steinbeck,**
***The Short Reign of Pippin IV:***
***A Fabrication*, 1957.**

# XIX: Judgment

*'When rich villains have need of poor ones, poor ones*
*make what price they will,'*
— Shakespeare, *Much Ado About Nothing.*

Mike Rothmiller has spent much of his life investigating Marilyn's death and done years of extensive research into the politics of the 1960s, the CIA's activities, and OCID secret operations of the time. Through hundreds of Freedom of Information requests, he has obtained formerly classified Federal material, and, when officials refused access, he has received information from foreign sources. He dismisses the notion held by many, and fanned by novels and television and film fiction, that covering up a high-profile murder requires dozens of people to be engaged in the criminal conspiracy. Here, he offers a considered overview, recapping the findings and conclusions of *Bombshell* and offering his summing up for the prosecution to you, the reader and the jury, in the case of the death of Marilyn Monroe.

In the cover-up over the death of Marilyn Monroe, success was guaranteed because the LAPD handled the investigation under the covert supervision of Captain James Hamilton of the Organized Crime Intelligence Division. LAPD being in charge of the investigation was akin to having a Mafia Godfather oversee the investigation into a killing he ordered. The outcome was assured.

Some will find this shocking, but murder is one of the easiest crimes to commit and get away with if you follow a few simple rules – which I won't detail here for obvious reasons. Consider the past 75 years of Mafia 'hits', and the huge number of violent street killings in America – most of which remain unsolved. Why is that? It's quite simple. The fewer people involved in a crime, the less likely they are to be caught. And if you can add a fear of speaking out to the mix you can invalidate any witnesses.

The Mafia call their code of silence, *Omertà*. The code is strongly wrapped up in an idea of manhood and decrees that operatives never cooperate with the authorities. In a strange twist, many in law enforcement also obey a similar rule of silence.

For decades, the LAPD has had its code of *Omertà* which every cop knows, every cop is expected to obey, and every cop is expected to deny the existence of. This 'blue wall of silence' will always be denied by management. That is to be expected. Nevertheless, police management knows it exists and openly lies by denying it. The code must be obeyed by all cops, or they run the risk of being ostracised by their fellow officers and this can prove to be a death sentence. Cops can rely on other cops to cover their backs in dangerous situations and to race to their aid when needed. If a cop has broken the basic rule of silence, they face the real possibility of their life-saving backup just not showing up or showing up too late. Cops hate cops who snitch.

When Marilyn Monroe was killed, the LAPD ruled the city with an invisible iron fist. Illegal wiretaps, black bag jobs, beatings and pay-offs were all part of the department's currency of the day. No one dared question police authority, especially not the intelligence division or their conclusions – not the coroner, not the mayor and not the media. LAPD Chief William Parker's words weren't always believed, but they were never seriously challenged. The media understood the chief's power and especially the power of retribution – even if they had their own doubts at the time these were never given voice. And the public quite honestly would never think the LAPD would lie, especially when it came to the death of someone as famous as Marilyn Monroe. But the LAPD has a long tradition of lying.

During my years in the department, I witnessed countless lies knowingly rolled out as official truths from the lowest ranks to the chief of police. I witnessed false arrests, saw falsified reports, manufactured evidence, wilful suppression of exculpatory evidence, false testimony in court proceedings, and Chief Daryl Gates lying to the media and providing cover for his 'friends' in organised crime. This type of conduct is not new in the LAPD; it's been occurring since the founding of the department.

Marilyn Monroe's death was not a complicated conspiracy. In reality, only a handful of people were involved so it was not a complicated secret to keep. Everyone had something to gain or something to protect. And that's all the persuasion that was required to keep the secret.

The Los Angeles County Coroner is the final authority on determining official cause of death. Once the coroner has established the cause of death, it's nearly impossible to overturn without extraordinary new evidence. As a result, once the coroner declares death by an overdose/suicide, the police officially and legally close the case then quickly move on.

Just a handful of people had advance notice that Bobby Kennedy would secretly fly to Los Angeles the day that Marilyn died. The people who knew were: Robert F. Kennedy, President John F. Kennedy, Peter Lawford, Chief William Parker and Captain James Hamilton, Commander of LAPD's OCID. I believe I know the identity of the OCID detective accompanying Hamilton to Marilyn Monroe's home; however, until I'm absolutely positive he will remain nameless. Of those, not all knew of the plan to silence her, and I don't believe that the OCID detective knew about that. However, that officer became an accessory after the fact and a co-conspirator in other crimes when he and Captain Hamilton staged the scene and body. At that juncture, all those individuals were guilty of a multitude of criminal violations. They were all profoundly involved in the conspiracy and they were all required to obey the LAPD's code of *Omertà*.

I do not believe Peter Lawford had advance notice of the plot to silence Marilyn. And I'm convinced Chief William Parker did not know the ultimate plan. But Captain James Hamilton did. It wasn't necessary for Lawford or Parker to be informed of the ultimate aim. They were likely unwittingly drawn into it, and I believe that fact haunted Lawford throughout his remaining years.

After Bobby Kennedy and Peter Lawford departed her residence that night for the last time, and Captain James Hamilton and another OCID detective entered, no one knows all the steps the two cops undertook. Over the years, there has been much speculation about activities inside her home, but the fact remains that is pure guesswork. Captain Hamilton and that detective were not so foolish as to write a detailed report or discuss their actions with anyone. From the intelligence reports I reviewed and detectives I spoke with who worked OCID at the time, I believe I have the best estimate as to what Hamilton and his colleague did inside her house.

Hamilton's primary objective would have been to ensure the cause of death appeared to be an accidental overdose or suicide. Frankly, either would suffice. The two cops methodically staged the bedroom and the body to give this impression. Their second objective would be to clear the home of items related to the Kennedys – photographs, notes, letters, *diaries* – anything that might link Marilyn intimately to them. They had to work quickly and leave without being seen.

Captain Hamilton knew others would eventually arrive and discover Marilyn's dead body. He was clever. With the bedroom adeptly staged by Hamilton, the first arrivals would have noticed the pill vials and quickly assumed she had died from an overdose. Her personal physicians, when they arrived at her home, would know death when they saw it, but they could not have known they were about to become unwitting players in the cover-up. What is certain is that neither physician who prescribed her drugs wanted to accept blame for her death.

Hamilton understood the more people arriving, the more chance there was of evidence being contaminated or destroyed – either intentionally or inadvertently – making it harder to prove that her death was caused by anything other than an overdose. Items would be moved or discarded. More importantly, since the crime scene was staged, the house would not have been evaluated or searched for evidence of a crime. An overdose or suicide by drugs is a quick, simple, and straightforward investigation which does not require a skilled and highly experienced homicide detective.

When Sergeant Jack Clemmons arrived that day, he noted that there was much that did not make sense and that people in the house were behaving oddly and were not completely honest with their answers to his questions. After his initial investigation, Jack Clemmons made the required notifications. More uniformed officers arrived to secure the scene, and detectives were summoned to handle the investigation. None of the arriving uniformed officers would have known of the conspiracy. All would consider it a tragic overdose death of a famous lady and simply secure the area. What has remained a secret until now, is that Captain Hamilton dispatched a trusted member of

OCID to the residence to quietly oversee the collection of evidence, direct the uniformed officers, coordinate the photographs that were taken and then carefully watch as Marilyn's body was removed. That trusted detective was in all likelihood the individual who helped Hamilton stage the residence and was instructed to return for that purpose. In the 1960s, when a detective from OCID was at a scene, no mention of them was required to be made in any report. They were strictly off the record and worked in the shadows.

A key figure in the cover-up was Los Angeles County Coroner Dr. Theodore Curphey who had been the coroner for a few turbulent years before Marilyn's death. He was described as arrogant, nasty and rude to his employees. He also dared to reorganise the coroner's office against the wishes of the County Board of Supervisors which resulted in a Grand Jury investigation. The Grand Jury found no criminal wrongdoing, and the investigation was dropped. During his tenure, Captain Hamilton and Chief William Parker would have taken a keen interest in Dr. Curphey since he oversaw all deaths occurring within the City of Los Angeles. Having an 'understanding' with the doctor would have proved useful to the LAPD when circumstances required. OCID also would have accumulated some embarrassing and potentially criminal information on the good doctor regarding his long-standing disputes with various colleagues and during the investigation.

Some old-time detectives who worked OCID at the time said Captain Hamilton had a private conversation with Curphey, informing him the LAPD had significant evidence that Marilyn's death was a suicide by drug overdose and that is how it should be recorded. Hamilton would never have disclosed the plot to Curphey but he could make the wishes of the LAPD unambiguous. Dr. Curphey clearly understood what LAPD wanted and saw no reason to disappoint them, especially when Marilyn's toxicology test demonstrated high levels of drugs in her system. Dr. Curphey understood the power LAPD intelligence wielded in the region, and if he desired to keep his job and avoid personal problems, it was best to please them.

Captain Hamilton and Dr. Curphey both understood when the cause of death appears to be a suicide or overdose, the coroner's office handles the investigation, not the police. This simple move assured Hamilton no other LAPD detectives would become involved, and he had the knowledge that Dr. Curphey would dutifully follow his wishes. Dr. Curphey had personally conducted autopsies on celebrities and people of power from LA. However, in this case, he stepped back and ordered Noguchi, his relatively new deputy coroner, to perform the examination on Marilyn Monroe. It was an astute survival move. Noguchi, as with the vast majority of coroners, knew how to dissect a body, obtain body tissue and fluid samples for testing to determine the cause of death. However, Noguchi was inexperienced at the time and not a trained or practised criminal investigator. If needed, he could easily be manipulated by a highly skilled detective from the LAPD. Curphey could instruct Noguchi that it was an overdose death and, barring any extraordinary findings, the deputy would concur. If the deputy thought otherwise, Curphey could overrule his findings and state the cause of death. An overruling turned out to be unnecessary. Noguchi gave the verdict that Curphey and Hamilton required.

Curphey did not convene a long-established judicial procedure known as a coroner's inquest for Marilyn's death. Instead, he contacted the relatively new Los Angeles Suicide Prevention Center and spoke with its founder, the distinguished Edwin Shneidman. Curphey requested his assistance in appointing a panel of mental health experts to conduct a 'psychological autopsy' of Monroe to determine why she committed suicide. It was called a 'suicide panel', and the professionals appointed primarily worked anonymously and convened to discuss their findings and opinions. At the time, this was out of the ordinary, and its legitimacy was questioned on all fronts. A few 'psychological autopsies' had been performed earlier in various parts of the country, but it was still considered a pseudo-science and akin to reading tea leaves. Not convening an official coroner's inquest meant no witnesses would be under oath and, since the panel was a novel concept, the standard investigatory procedure would be eliminated. Without following the established protocol of an inquest, the interviews were conducted in a low-key, informal manner. Most importantly, key people were *not* called to testify; Peter Lawford was one. Lawford wasn't officially interviewed by LAPD until 1975 when OCID's Neil Spotts spoke with him as part of the re-investigation at the request of Daryl Gates. It was Spotts' clandestine mission to ensure LAPD's 1975 findings matched their original story from 1962.

On August 17, 1962, with a single sentence, Dr. Curphey fulfilled his secret agreement with Captain Hamilton. The doctor held a news conference and stated, 'It is my conclusion that the death of Marilyn Monroe was caused by a self-administered overdose of sedative drugs and that the mode of death is probable suicide.' With his official finding, LAPD quickly and conveniently closed the case and sent Marilyn to her tomb with the world wondering why she took her life.

I believe Dr. Noguchi was an unwitting participant in the ultimate cover-up. Noguchi was not brought into the 'investigation' until after the participants had staged the crime scene, and he was provided the appropriate evidence to reinforce the conclusion he reached. The good doctor believed what he was told. After the autopsy, Noguchi may have developed doubts about the story the detectives told him, but he understood he would never be able to prove them wrong. He lacked the investigative skills and knowledge to refute what the detectives concluded. He also lacked the evidence.

Noguchi would also have known that, in 1962 LA, it was not wise to go against your department chief, who could terminate your employment on the spot. He would have also understood that it would not be advantageous to create powerful enemies within the LAPD. With a simple telephone call from Captain Hamilton or Chief Parker, his career could be ruined. He chose wisely. Once the coroner officially declared her death was an overdose and a suicide, the cover-up was complete. LAPD was formally relieved from conducting a further investigation, and it could legally relegate Marilyn Monroe's death to the history books.

The cover-up remained dormant for years until the media began running stories questioning the suicide account and pressuring LAPD's chief for answers. With external pressure intensifying and since John F. Kennedy, Robert Kennedy, Chief Parker and Captain Hamilton were deceased, LAPD believed it was safe to announce they would 're-investigate' her death. The 1975 re-investigation was carried out by Spotts on the orders of Deputy Chief Daryl Gates. Spotts understood that the results must support the prior findings from 1962. Spotts took the appropriate time, spoke to some people, and dutifully determined that LAPD's previous findings were accurate and pure. Spotts, Gates, and other detectives in OCID knew the re-investigation was just for show.

In 1982, the Los Angeles County District Attorney John Van De Kamp's 'threshold inquiry' into Monroe's death and the potential LAPD cover-up was launched. Not surprisingly, a few months later he announced the District

Attorney's office had determined there was no cover-up and Marilyn had indeed died from an overdose. There was, however, a significant problem with their investigation; their primary witnesses and sources were the LAPD. Obeying the law of *Omertà*, the LA cops interviewed either had no information or had a sudden bout of amnesia. OCID detective Neil Spotts was, by then, retired from the LAPD and serving as head of West Coast security for Hugh Hefner's Playboy Enterprises. Neil repeated the story he reported in 1975 which supported LAPD's 1962 findings. The District Attorney only learned what the LAPD wanted them to know. Nothing more, nothing less. Again, the case rejoined Marilyn in the tomb.

In 1985, with Daryl Gates as Chief of Police, Marilyn returned from the grave to once again haunt the LAPD, but this time was different. Gates had alleged that years earlier the original case file had been destroyed as per regulations, but now Chief Gates proudly announced that a near duplicate of the original file had been mysteriously located in the garage of retired chief of detectives, Thad Brown. In a news conference, Gates released the record and confidently told reporters that it proved Marilyn committed suicide and the case was closed forever. The question is, if the original file was destroyed, how did Gates know the found file was a near duplicate of it? What did he compare it to?

With the publication of this book people can finally understand the conspiracies, the cover-ups and the secretive inner workings at the heart of the LAPD. The closing curtain has now fallen on the final chapter in the story of Marilyn Monroe. There will always be unanswered questions. No one will ever know what really went on in the minds of the identified players: President John Kennedy, United States Attorney General Robert Kennedy, OCID Captain James Hamilton, Chief William Parker, Dr.

Theodore Curphey, Fred Otash and, sadly, Peter Lawford. Based on the evidence and intelligence I gathered, I can only reach logical conclusions as to their motives and what was possible and probable in 1962.

I believe there was a conspiracy to take the life of Marilyn. Political motives for her killing were strong but were not justified. She didn't have to die in order to protect the Kennedys and their legacy. In 1962, there were other ways to silence an emotionally vulnerable woman. It would have been a simple matter for a bad faith psychiatrist to order her into a psychiatric hospital and declare her mentally ill. Nobody would have taken anything seriously from a mentally unstable film star. The Kennedys could have brushed off any story she told, feigning compassion and sorrow that her mental state had caused her to have such delusions. They chose otherwise.

And what did the individuals other than the Kennedys' innermost circle gain by participating in Monroe's death and the cover-up? The prime players would have understood or expected a substantial reward – either an appointment to a significant government position or the oldest form of reward, riches. After all, they were aiding the President of the United States and the most powerful law enforcement officer in the country, the Attorney General. The other players were different because they became engulfed in a conspiracy they did not consent to or even recognise was playing out before their eyes. They were pawns, manipulated into essential roles in the cover-up. Most of them were just required to stay silent. And some, like Peter Lawford, became victims along with Marilyn. As a detective, one question haunts me, and it will never be answered. After Marilyn drank the glass of liquid given her by Robert Kennedy, they left her alone as they searched her home. Out of sight of the two men, and clearly distressed, did she elect to ingest another liquid form of drug which pushed her toxicology levels into the zone of death? I can't answer that question. No one can. But, if it was a CIA designer toxin, toxicology testing at the time would not have discovered it. It was a scenario for the perfect murder.

# XX: Déjà Vu

*'How do you find your way back in the dark?'*
— Marilyn Monroe as Roslyn.
*'Just head for the big star straight on. It'll take us right home.'*
— Clark Gable as Gay.
— *The Misfits*, 1961. [The last words spoken on screen
by them both.]

At the time of Marilyn Monroe's death in the summer of 1962, LAPD and the OCID in particular could do whatever they wanted. Chief Parker and his men patrolled the streets driving Chrysler Imperials. They were in complete control and manipulated the city, using Hollywood with all its sex and glamour, lies and betrayals. It was a time when acts of criminality weren't something to be baulked at but tools to be used by the very people supposed to be protecting the public from crime.

Today, international passengers arrive at LAX, the city's main airport, through the Tom Bradley Terminal named after a former LAPD policeman who became the first African American mayor of Los Angeles in 1973. After two years of pressure from his office, he was able to wrest control of the Police Commission and, in 1975, began a purge of the dossiers held by OCID and the Public Disorder Intelligence Division [PDID]. The LAPD claimed to have destroyed two million files and with it 'highly sensitive information' on more than 100,000 individuals the LAPD suspected of being subversives. Yet, the intelligence divisions stayed in action with a combined force of more than 200 officers which, by 1978, included Mike Rothmiller. Following the 1982 attempt on his life, Rothmiller gave sworn testimony regarding the OCID's questionable and illegal practices. He recalled:

'The Los Angeles Police Commission was stunned and appalled by what I told them. For years, the various chiefs of police kept the commission in the shadows and explained that this was necessary so the division's operation could keep the Mafia out of Los Angeles. Of course, that was a lie – since early in the 1920s, Los Angeles had been home to a thriving Mafia family living and 'working' the southern California dream. Just like the East Coast mobsters, the Los Angeles Mafia had various LA mayors, chiefs of police, judges and police officers on their payroll.

'Acting quickly after my testimony, the infuriated Police Commission enacted the first attempts to reign in OCID and hopefully put an end to its illegal activities. Chief Daryl Gates and OCID Commander Stuart Finck did not object to the oversight since it was up to them to report OCID's operations to the commission. It was comical to believe Gates would report the truth to the commission. He claimed no violations, knowing the commission had no method to disprove his claims.'

Mike Rothmiller is the former OCID detective cited in the following report in the *Los Angeles Times* from January 30, 1985:

'The Los Angeles Police Commission adopted Tuesday the first formal set of guidelines designed to regulate the operations of the Police Department's Organized Crime Intelligence Division (OCID). Scheduled to go into effect immediately, the new standards restrict the division's operations solely to organized crime operations, limit intelligence-gathering on public figures and require investigators to record the dissemination of intelligence materials to outside law enforcement agencies. In addition, the guidelines call for an annual inspection of the division's files, and they will allow the Police Commission for the first time to participate in the yearly audits of the division's activities. The guidelines were mandated by the settlement last year of the American Civil Liberties Union lawsuit charging that the Police Department's since-disbanded Public Disorder Intelligence Division (PDID) had illegally spied upon law-abiding citizens. A former Organized Crime Intelligence Division detective testified in a deposition given to the ACLU that members of the organized crime unit had engaged in political spying.'

In 1992, following the Los Angeles riots, Chief Gates left the force but as the Police Commission considered his successor, Mike Rothmiller's book *LA Secret Police. Inside the Elite LAPD Spy Network* was released. It provoked an extraordinary response as he explains:

'The Police Commission, having read my book, requested a private meeting to discuss LAPD malfeasance. A secret meeting was arranged in a restaurant in Orange County, California, about 50 miles from LAPD headquarters. This was done to avoid the very real possibility the commissioners would be the target of OCID surveillance. During the meeting I provided insight regarding LAPD intelligence operations and my opinion on the desired qualities of a new chief. Fortunately, weeks later the commission chose a new chief from outside of the old LAPD hierarchy.

'The incoming chief, Willie Williams, then read my book and that was enough. He locked down the OCID offices and refused to allow its detectives in. Through an influential Los Angeles businessman, I warned Williams that OCID would retaliate and from that day forward he must exercise caution in all his law enforcement and private activities. I also offered to provide a list of the LAPD staff officers he could trust and those he could not. He didn't understand that you can't stop a rattlesnake from biting by holding its tail. You must cut off its head. Unfortunately, Williams did not heed my advice, and OCID did what it does best. As I predicted, a few weeks later under relentless pressure from OCID and the rest of the LAPD old guard, Chief Williams proved weak, crumbled and reopened OCID.

'What I knew, and Williams never even suspected, was that before he even set foot in southern California, members of OCID had already spent weeks gathering intelligence on Williams, in and around the Philadelphia area. The day he was sworn in as chief, OCID had already accumulated a quiver of embarrassing arrows they were ready to launch. Within weeks, OCID had fed rumours of his misconduct to their contacts in the media and placed him under surveillance.

'Since Williams was an outsider coming from the Philadelphia Police Department, his appointment had inflamed longtime LAPD staff officers who were overlooked for the position. Additionally, Williams was the first African American chief of police in Los Angeles. With the residual racism of the Daryl Gates era still gnawing away within some LAPD staff officers, Williams would never have an easy time as chief. There were dozens within the LAPD hierarchy actively seeking to bring him down. He was an outsider and his authority needed to be crushed.'

During his tenure as chief, Williams pressed for increased hiring of female officers and spoke out about the need to address rampant sexual harassment and discrimination within the ranks. He increased the size of the department and advocated for reforms drawn up in 1991 by the Christopher Commission, which had been formed by Mayor Bradley after the assault on Rodney King, to review LAPD training, discipline and complaint systems.

Doubts about, and resistance to, Williams' leadership soon took root. The OCID were behind most of it, they could make money grow on trees if they had to. Within a year of Williams taking over the department, Mayor Bradley had been replaced by Richard Riordan. Williams found himself alienated as police union officials and rank-and-file cops grew increasingly hostile to him. In 1995, a letter from a former high-ranking LAPD official to the Police Commission led to an investigation into claims Williams had accepted free accommodation from a Las Vegas casino. Williams denied it, saying it was part of an orchestrated smear campaign. The commission produced receipts showing that Williams and his family had accepted free rooms on several occasions. Williams said the rooms had been provided in exchange for the gambling he and his family had done. On June 4, 1995, *Newsweek* magazine ran the following piece on the investigation:

'Los Angeles Police Chief Willie Williams has been dogged for months by rumors of misconduct. Williams has called the allegations "utterly false," but in mid-May the LA police commission reprimanded him for allegedly lying about accepting free hotel rooms in Las Vegas. Williams' lawyer says the chief is the victim of a smear campaign by city hall. But *Newsweek* has learned that his real enemies may be closer to home: inside the LAPD. Police sources say detectives in the Organized Crime Intelligence Division conducted an unauthorized investigation of the chief, including surveillance of his trips to Las Vegas, then leaked their findings to discredit him. "This was a rogue operation to get rid of Williams," says a police source. The source says that OCID detectives compiled a "dossier" on Williams's Vegas activities, then passed the information to Stephen Downing, a retired LAPD deputy chief and close associate of ousted chief Daryl Gates. It was a letter from Downing to the police commission in December that launched the official investigation of Williams. Gates denies any effort to discredit his successor. "I had absolutely nothing to do with getting this information on Williams," he says. A spokesman for the LAPD had no comment.'

The commission concluded Williams had lied and reprimanded him, but he survived and tried for a second five-year term as chief in 1997 but his public approval ratings had fallen. The OCID had won. He was replaced by Bernard C. Parks, an African American and a veteran LAPD insider. [Parks was in place during a police brutality scandal and only served one term.]

Mike Rothmiller understood how the LAPD worked and, more importantly how the LAPD and the OCID protected themselves above all else. He recalls a time during his service when a major threat instigated drastic action:

In the late 1970s and early 1980s, the Los Angeles chapter of the American Civil Liberties Union (ACLU) was engaged in a heated lawsuit with the LAPD's Public Disorder Intelligence Division (PDID). The heart of the ACLU's suit was alleged illegal spying. Of course, the ACLU was correct, and a settlement was eventually reached, imposing guidelines on how the unit could conduct future intelligence operations. Chief Daryl Gates and Captain Stuart Finck became extremely nervous during the lawsuit. They were afraid that the ACLU may discover that OCID was also involved in illegal spying. With such a legal giant knocking down LAPD's secret closet door, Gates ordered an immediate purge of OCID records which chronicled illegal operations, including spying on politicians and the rich and famous, some of whom were not even suspected of any criminal activity.

Each detective team within OCID was assigned a letter of the alphabet and ordered to review every intelligence card and all records listed under that letter ASAP. It was a massive undertaking since there were decades of accumulated documents and, frankly, it was a dreary job none of the detectives relished. In theory, each report was to be read, and if it wasn't defensible in court as a legitimate organised crime investigation, it was to be removed and forwarded to a section lieutenant for approval to be *officially* removed from the filing system.

However, OCID's detectives quickly tired of this time-consuming process and initiated their own unauthorised paper shredding campaign. Without reading the reports, they'd rip a handful of documents from the file and proceed to the shredder. The line of detectives awaiting use of OCID's commercial paper shredder grew steadily. Soon, the shredder broke under the weight of the work. A new shredder quickly appeared, and the destruction of thousands of top-secret documents and photographs resumed. One afternoon while I was shredding documents, I was approached by Captain Stuart Finck. He stood quietly and watched as I fed dozens of highly sensitive documents into the shredder's grinding teeth.

'The one thing I dread is the day an ACLU attorney gets into the files,' Finck lamented. 'That would be the day the entire lid is blown off the police department.'

'I know,' was all I said as I fed another handful of documents into the shredder. Finck walked away, and I suspect he was nervously pondering his future if anyone like the ACLU ever did get into the OCID's files. He must have known that Chief Daryl Gates would quickly toss him under the bus to save his own skin.

When a reporter asked long time OCID detective Ed Lutz about the purge, he said, 'I personally took files to the incinerator and burned them.' But some records, he said, were boxed up and carted to archives 'who knows where'.

In theory, the only archives able to store OCID's records were the California State Archives and the City of Los

Angeles Archives. Both have informed me they have no OCID records. So which archives did Ed Lutz believe were housing the files for safe keeping? The primary question remains; where are the thousands of remaining OCID secret dossiers and who has access to them?

We know that, instead of destroying the highly classified material, many OCID detectives opted to 'take care' of them at their home. And, as Neil Spotts did, sell the information to the highest bidder. This is significant since OCID's secret dossiers spanned over seventy years and not all were destroyed. In 2018, I called the Discovery Unit of the LAPD to determine if the old OCID files were obtainable under the California Public Records Act (CPRA), under Government Code (GC) sections 6250-6270a, also known as the California Freedom of Information Act (FOIA). The answer I received was quite humorous but not surprising. The LAPD representative stated that all OCID files are 'considered active investigations and therefore not subject to release' and quoted the sections of the law stating that release would 'disclose investigative techniques, jeopardize ongoing investigations, related investigations and law enforcement procedures.' I informed the person that I am a former OCID detective, and I'm fully aware of OCID's past techniques, investigations and procedures. Then I quickly embarked on a fascinating exchange with the representative.

'You said all OCID files are classified as active investigations. Does that include the 70-year-old files?'

'Yes.'

'Are the investigations I opened and closed while in OCID considered active?' I asked.

'Yes.'

'Are the investigations conducted by the old 'Gangster Squad' from the 1930s still active investigations?'

There was a moment of silence and then a cautious, 'Yes.'

'Are the files on Lucky Luciano [who died in 1962], Al Capone [who died in 1947] and Paul Kelly [who died in 1936] considered active investigations?'

'Who are they?'

'Old time mobsters.'

'Then those investigations are still active.'

'Thank you for your help.'

This conversation is a prime example of LAPD doing what it does best, protecting its secrets. As with the federal government, even under FOIA requests or subpoenas, they'll decide which documents, if any, are eligible for release. In most cases, if the requested records will prove embarrassing or involved illegal activities carried out by surveillance teams, they'll reply that there are no relevant records for your request. At that point, your only option is to file suit, although LAPD are counting on you to walk away and forget the request. However, if you do file suit, they will drag it on for years, hoping to bleed your financial resources and chip away at your desire to keep fighting. The City of Los Angeles has unlimited resources, while most individuals do not have the financial capability to fight a multi-million dollar protracted legal battle. And consider this, in the rare event you won the legal battle, and the LAPD was ordered to turn over the documents you initially requested, they'll just say they were unable to locate those records, or that they have been 'accidentally' destroyed. You may win an expensive battle, but you will always lose the war.

As well as revealing the truth about how Marilyn died, this book also provides a small window into the decades of secret and, at times, illegal intelligence operations carried out by the LAPD's Organized Crime Intelligence Division and the part that Captain James Hamilton played in Monroe's death. The move to replace Hamilton upon his departure for the NFL with Daryl Gates was a shrewd one by Chief William Parker. It meant important secrets were secured, and of course it couldn't hurt his chances of a possible appointment as FBI director. It also presented the ideal opportunity for Gates to learn the finer points of utilising the power of LAPD intelligence to further his own ambitions.

Gates came to view the OCID as his personal detective agency and he never hesitated to use it to consolidate his own power and protect his friends, both within and outside the LAPD. When a detective, and longtime buddy of Gates, was the prime suspect in a murder, Gates quietly ordered that the investigation be dropped, and the detective quickly retired. The OCID was created to target and surveil gangsters and the Mob – something I always encouraged and pursued, but Gates relished learning the secrets of the rich and famous, especially celebrities and politicians. He delighted in his regular secret briefings by the captain of OCID which always included the latest scandalous information unknown to the media. In the vast majority of cases, the celebrities and politicians were never aware they were targets of OCID. As a diner savours their favourite dessert, Gates always savoured surreptitious photos as part of the briefings.

Gates also knew that knowledge meant political influence. During the 1970s, California Governor Jerry Brown was always a prime target. During Brown's 1980 presidential run, he attended a fundraiser in New York. OCID detective Norm Bonneau learned that several New York Mafia members would be in attendance. A senior member of the Colombo crime family had a friendly encounter with Brown who left the fundraiser with a nice donation from the group. Both the FBI and the OCID had photos of the event. OCID's Commander Stuart Finck, on orders from Chief Daryl Gates, told Bonneau to arrange a meeting with Brown. At the meeting, Bonneau handed Brown the photos and asked if he knew the men in the pictures with him were mobsters. Of course, Brown claimed he did not know and promised to return the donation. The meeting ended with Brown thanking Bonneau for the information and 'his newfound support from the LAPD.' I was a member of OCID at the time and understood that this meeting wasn't so much a favour to the Presidential candidate as a threat. This was OCID's favoured method of intimidating politicians, a way of letting the politician know LAPD had embarrassing or career-ending information that they could release at any time, a chilling warning to all politicians. More importantly, this tactic also plants the 'seed' in the mind of the politician, 'If OCID knows this, they probably know my other secrets.' All politicians have secrets they wish to remain locked in the closet. These tactics worked wonders and convinced many in politics and the media to become friends of Gates. Governor Jerry Brown never knew that when he was in Los Angeles, the telephone calls he made from his state vehicle were intercepted by an OCID informant and dutifully turned over. There were no secrets from the spies funded by California's taxpayers.

OCID under Daryl Gates were actively building dossiers on influential figures from both Los Angeles and further afield from Bishop John Ward of Los Angeles to J. Edgar Hoover. Chief Gates bragged to Lew Wasserman, head of the entertainment giant MCA, that he knew every time Wasserman flew to Las Vegas. It was true – I reviewed Wasserman's dossier. But his dossier contained far more sensitive information about Lew and his family than just the details of his flights to Las Vegas.

Gates' most prized dossiers were primarily maintained under lock and key in his office. These were the secret dossiers LAPD maintained on virtually all members of the news media in southern California. From the reporters to the heads of the television companies, radio stations and newspapers, Gates had it all. And developing informants within the media was an additional bonus. OCID enjoyed a cadre of cooperative reporters willing to do its bidding. I know because I traded information with a few reporters. Shelby Coffey, the former editor of the *Los Angeles Times*, was a frequent target of OCID on Gates' orders and his dossier was extensive. Pulitzer Prize winning journalist and *Times* reporter, David Cay Johnston angered Chief Gates with his reporting on the LAPD. Gates immediately retaliated, and Johnston became a target of both LAPD intelligence divisions: OCID and PDID. On April 6, 2010, just after Gates died, Johnston published a scathing essay titled 'Daryl Gates' Real Legacy'. In it, Johnston chronicled Gates' intelligence operations and how he became a personal target of LAPD intelligence and harassment.

Gates boasted that he sent an undercover LAPD intelligence cop masquerading as a Communist to Moscow and Havana for some time. That is true, it was done for the CIA. Gates authorised members of PDID to have sex with women from various political organisations to gain their confidence in order to gather intelligence. If the detective contracted a venereal disease it would be classified as 'Injured on Duty' (IOD) and the city would be required to pay all medical costs and pay for time off. If the detective later infected his wife, girlfriend or both, I'm certain a lawsuit against the city would follow. If the woman from the political organisation became pregnant, I suspect the city would be held liable for support.

When Leon Panetta, a member of Congress, visited Los Angeles, he was under surveillance by OCID. Clandestine photographs were taken of him and the people he met. Panetta later became the director of the CIA and it is ironic that the man who became America's spy chief, was spied upon by the LAPD.

Morris Shenker was an attorney and principal owner of the then Dunes Casino and Hotel in Las Vegas. In the late 1970s, when he was awaiting a flight in the Western Airlines VIP lounge at LAX and was using the club's telephone, I witnessed an OCID supervisor enter a back room and tap into his conversation. Listening in on private telephone conversations was not uncommon.

Professional sports were not immune from OCID spying and secret dossiers. Los Angeles Dodgers' longtime manager, Tommy Lasorda, who died in January 2021, was a target of OCID surveillance, all the while Chief Gates publicly proclaimed his friendship with Lasorda. When Carroll Rosenbloom, owner of the Rams football team, drowned at Golden Beach, Florida in 1979, OCID launched an investigation. They believed Mob friends of Rosenbloom's wife, Georgia, had murdered him. Of course, it was not murder. However, OCID filed away all the rumours and innuendos in his, and his widow's, already substantial dossiers. When she later married Dominic Frontiere, an Italian composer, her dossier exploded, as did her new husband's. In 1986, Frontiere was convicted of tax evasion for scalping 1980 Rams' tickets he received from Georgia. The owners, managers, and some players of the LA Lakers, LA Dodgers, and California Angels were also targets of OCID. I know. I read the reports and saw the surveillance photographs.

Gates had his favourite detectives in OCID who would secretly gather intelligence on other high-ranking members of the force. He was infuriated when he learned that a few of his deputy chiefs and assistant chiefs had their own favourites secretly gathering intelligence on *him*. However, Gates reasoned correctly, if he demoted or tried to fire them, they would release the embarrassing information they had accumulated on him, which would cause him unforeseen work and personal problems. As a result, everyone kept their mouths shut, and life went on.

The end of Gates came only after the case of Rodney King and the resulting riots. Gates knew his time was up. He could no longer muster support or twist the arms of the city council to save his job and he resigned.

Prior to Chief Daryl Gates' death at Dana Point, California, in April 2010, he was aware that more inquiries were going on into the death of Marilyn Monroe. In retirement he had remained adamant that the LAPD version of events was correct but was said to be *disquieted* by Mike Rothmiller's revelations in *Secret Police* and his note in reference to Marilyn's OCID file. If he was troubled by the truth the irony might not have escaped him, or the effectiveness of the long arm of time. It was on May 7, 1978, in the auditorium of the Los Angeles Police Department HQ, that during a promotion ceremony, he greeted Mike Rothmiller on stage, warmly shook his hand and presented him with his detective badge. There were words about truth and justice and the need to search for both. Detective Mike Rothmiller took Chief Gates at his word. Perhaps, because of that, Marilyn Monroe can now rest in peace.

# POSTSCRIPT: THE TRUTH AT LAST

*'I'm selfish, impatient and a little insecure. I make mistakes, I am out of control and at times hard to handle. But if you can't handle me at my worst, then you sure as hell don't deserve me at my best.'*
— Marilyn Monroe, 1958.

'Wild' Bill Parker and Chief Daryl Gates are now dead, but the LAPD goes on and I expect there to be a reaction to the revelations in *Bombshell*. I fully expect the LAPD to personally attack me through their media sources. That has always been the first response to officers and former officers whose words they believe further tarnish their already battered image. LAPD will undoubtedly attack the overall Monroe story since it provides a vivid insiders' account into her death, which they do not want the public to know. When I published *LA Secret Police. Inside the LAPD's Elite Spy Network,* I revealed that I had read a top-secret intelligence report into the assassination of Senator Robert Kennedy. The report clearly stated that ten bullets were recovered from the victim and the pantry area of the Ambassador Hotel. The revolver of the convicted assassin, Sirhan Sirhan, was only capable of holding eight rounds, and he never had the chance to reload before he was subdued, and the gun wrestled away from him. Do the math, and you will understand the implications. That intelligence investigation remains one of LAPD's most closely guarded secrets. It has never been released, and I doubt it ever will, but I provided written sworn testimony on August 23, 1992, for a Grand Jury regarding that secret file and the ten bullets.

I will be disappointed if the LAPD does not wheel out a few former members of OCID, probably some from my time. They will proudly wave the LAPD flag of innocence, claim the files did not exist, and openly denounce me. That is fine. This is how all government agencies respond, and I expect nothing less. Maybe those cops will see it as retribution because I testified on behalf of the ACLU regarding OCID's illegal spying. My testimony caused them a great amount of grief.

In *LA Secret Police*, I also mentioned reading Marilyn Monroe's OCID dossier, her diary and the dossiers of John F. Kennedy and Robert Kennedy. At the time and in the years since, the LAPD have never claimed the files do not exist and have never disputed my statement. Why? Because they knew it was true.

In July 1992, the *Los Angeles Times* printed a story about the OCID files. The article states: 'Unit old-timers figure there were 5,000 files at the peak, about 50 labeled "special investigations," one of those reviewing the death of Marilyn Monroe.' That article was published after my book was released but the *Times* did not receive that information from me. Yes, Monroe's file was in OCID's hands and probably is still in the hands of the LAPD.

The OCID investigations into Marilyn Monroe's death have all been to confuse and distract from the truth. The inquiry led by Daryl Gates following the 1975 *Oui* magazine article was laughable. Its only objective was to support the falsehood that LAPD was not involved in a cover-up of Marilyn's death. Every OCID detective I asked about the second investigation laughed and said: 'It was complete bullshit.'

In among those 'special investigations' I reviewed, aside from the Monroe homicide and the assassination of Senator Robert Kennedy, were the murder of mobster Bugsy Siegel and the infamous 'Black Dahlia' murder of Elizabeth Short. The 'Black Dahlia' file contained scores of troubling details. Those secret investigations will never be released because they will prove embarrassing and probably prove a criminal cover-up by the

LAPD. A brief intelligence investigation was even conducted into the November 1981 drowning of actress Natalie Wood even though her death did not occur within the LAPD's jurisdiction.

The citizens of Los Angeles must ask themselves if the LAPD has changed since Daryl Gates departed? The answer is blurred and all I can say is it has changed *somewhat*. On paper, LAPD intelligence has changed for the better. There is now an LAPD policy mandating how and when intelligence investigations are to be conducted. However, there were many such policies in place during my time and they were ignored. I find it difficult to believe the LAPD brass no longer cherishes or keeps records of the steamy tidbits uncovered by LAPD intelligence.

I hope this book has helped to explain how the culture of the LAPD in the 1960s allowed one of the most scandalous cover-ups in history to occur. After I told a friend about my investigations into Marilyn's death, he asked a really interesting, important question: 'I know you always admired President Kennedy and Robert Kennedy, how did you feel uncovering this information?' It was a difficult question to answer. It was true, I had always admired the Kennedys and was saddened when they were murdered. My wife and I purchased a portrait of President Kennedy in the 1970s and it is still on display in our home. President Kennedy and Robert Kennedy did a great amount of good for the country. Yet in this situation, I was a detective and had to follow the evidence. So, personally, it was a painful investigation, but it had to be done. I wish the facts proved otherwise, but they didn't, and it saddens me.

Mike Rothmiller, July 2021.

# BIBLIOGRAPHY

Adams, Cindy Heller: *Lee Strasberg: The Imperfect Genius of the Actors Studio* [Doubleday, 1980]

Aldrich, Richard J.: *The Hidden Hand: Britain, America and the Cold War Secret Intelligence* [The Overlook Press, 2002]

Allen, Maury: *Where Have You Gone, Joe DiMaggio?: The Story of America's Last Hero* [Dutton, 1975]

Allgood, Jill: *Bebe and Ben: Bebe Daniels and Ben Lyon* [Robert Hale, 1975]

Anderson, Janice: *Marilyn Monroe* [Hamlyn, 1983]

Arnold, Eve: *Marilyn Monroe: An Appreciation* [Knopf, 1987]

Axelrod, George: *Will Success Spoil Rock Hunter?: A New Comedy* [Samuel French, 1956]

Bacall, Lauren: *By Myself* [Knopf, 1980]

Baker, Carlos: *Ernest Hemingway: A Life Story* [Scribner, 1969]

Bartlett, Donald; Steele, James B.: *Empire: The Life, Legend and Madness of Howard Hughes* [Norton, 1979]

Beauchamp, Cari: *Joseph P. Kennedy Presents His Hollywood Years* [Faber & Faber, 2009]

Bigsby, Christopher: *Arthur Miller* [Weidenfeld & Nicolson, 2008]

Block, Alan A., *Masters of Paradise, Organised Crime and the Internal Revenue Service in The Bahamas* [Transaction, 1991]

Bosworth, Patricia: *Montgomery Clift: A Biography* [Bantam, 1980]

Breslin, Jimmy: *Damon Runyon: A Life* [Ticknor and Fields, 1991]

Brinkley, Alan [Edited by Arthur M. Schlesinger Jr. and Sean Wilentz]: *John F. Kennedy: The 35th President, 1961–1963 (American Presidents Series)* [Times Books, 2012]

Brown, Peter; Barham, Patte: *Marilyn: The Last Take* [Penguin, 1992]

Brown, Peter; Broeske, Pat: *Howard Hughes: The Untold Story* [Viking, 1996]

Buchthal, Stanley; Comment, Bernard: *Fragments: Poems, Intimate Notes, Letters by Marilyn Monroe* [Harper Collins, 2010]

Buntin, John: *L.A. Noir: The Struggle for the Soul of America's Most Seductive City* [Orion, 2014]

Caro, Robert A.: *Lyndon Johnson: The Passage of Power, Volume 4* [Bodley Head, 2014]

Capell, Frank: *The Strange Death of Marilyn Monroe* [The Herald of Freedom, 1964]

Carpozi, George, Jr.: *Marilyn Monroe: Her Own Story* [Belmont Books, 1961]

Carter, Graydon: *Vanity Fair's Tales of Hollywood* [Penguin, 2008]

Catterall, Peter: *The Macmillan Diaries (1950–1957)* [Macmillan, 2003]

Catterall, Peter: *The Macmillan Diaries Vol II: Prime Minister and After: 1957–1966* [Macmillan, 2011]

Cirules, Enrique: *The Mafia In Havana: A Caribbean Mob Story* [Ocean Press, 2004]

Cockburn, Alexander; St. Clair, Jeffrey: *Whiteout: The CIA, Drugs and the Press* [Verso, 1998]

Collier, Peter; Horowitz, David: *The Kennedys: An American Drama* [Summit Books, 1984]

Dale Scott, Peter: *Crime and Cover-Up: The CIA, the Mafia and the Dallas-Watergate Connection* [Open Archive Press, 1977]

Dale Scott, Peter: *Deep Politics and the Death of JFK* [University of California Press, 1996]

Dallek, Robert: *Nixon and Kissinger* [HarperCollins, 2007]

Davis, John H.: *The Kennedys: Dynasty and Disaster, 1848–1984* [Sidgwick & Jackson, 1995]

Deitche, Scott M.; *The Silent Don: The Criminal Underworld of Santo Trafficante Jr.* [Barricade Books, 2007]

Denker, Henry: *The Kingmaker* [Mayflower, 1974]

Dougherty, James E.: *The Secret Happiness of Marilyn Monroe* [Playboy Press, 1976]

Drosnin, Michael: *Citizen Hughes: In his own words – how Howard Hughes tried to buy America* [Holt, Rinehart, Winston, 1985]

Eisenberg, Dennis; Uri, Dan; Landau, Eli: *Meyer Lansky: Mogul of the Mob* [Paddington Press, 1979]

English, T.J.: *The Havana Mob,* [Mainstream, 2007].

Evans, Peter: *Nemesis: Aristotle Onassis, Jackie O and the Love Triangle That Brought Down the Kennedys* [Harper Collins, 2004]

Exner, Judith Campbell (with Demaris, Ovid): *My Story* [Grove, 1977]

Field, Shirley Anne: *A Time for Love* [Bantam Press, 1991]

Franklin, Lynn: *The Beverly Hills Cop Story* [Vantage Press, 1986]

Franklin, Lynn: *The Beverly Hills Murder File: The True Story of the Cop City Hall Wanted Dead* [1st Books Library, 2002]

Fraser-Cavassoni, Natasha: *Sam Spiegel: The Biography of a Hollywood Legend* [Little, Brown, 2003]

Friedrich, Otto: *City of Nets: Hollywood in the 1940s* [Harper Perennial, 2014]

Fursenko, Aleksandr; Naftali, Timothy: *'One Hell of a Gamble': Khrushchev, Castro, and Kennedy 1958–1964* [W.W. Norton, 1997]

Gabler, Neal: *Walter Winchell: Gossip, Power and the Culture of Celebrity* [Picador, 1995]

Gardner, Ava: *Ava: My Story* [Bantam Books, 1990]

Garrow, David: *Bearing the Cross: Martin Luther King Jr. and the Southern Christian Leadership Conference* [William Morrow, 1986]

Gates, Daryl F. (with Diane K. Shah): *Chief: My Life in the LAPD* [Bantam, 1992]

Gentry, Curt: *J. Edgar Hoover: The Man and his Secrets* [Penguin, 1991]

Ghaemi, Nassir: *A First-Rate Madness: Uncovering the Links Between Leadership and Mental Illness* [The Penguin Press, 2011]

Goode, James: *The Story of The Misfits* [Bobbs-Merrill, 1961]

Goodwin, Doris Kearns: *The Fitzgeralds and the Kennedys: An American Saga* [Simon and Schuster, 1987]

Graham, Sheila: *Hollywood Revisited* [St. Martin's Press, 1985]

Grandison, Lionel Jr.; Muqaddin, Samir: *Memoirs of a Deputy Coroner: The Case of Marilyn Monroe* [Bait-Cal, 2012]

Grobel, Lawrence: *The Hustons: The Life and Times of a Hollywood Dynasty* [Avon, 1989]

Guiles, Fred Lawrence: *Norma Jean: The Life of Marilyn Monroe* [McGraw-Hill, 1969]

Guiles, Fred Lawrence: *Legend: The Life and Death of Marilyn Monroe* [Stein and Day, 1984]

Harris, Maryls J.: *The Zanucks of Hollywood: The Dark Legacy of An American Dynasty* [Crown, 1989]

Haspiel, James: *Marilyn: The Ultimate Look at the Legend* [Holt, 1991]

Hersh, Seymour: *The Price of Power: Kissinger in the Nixon White House* [Summit Books, 1983]

Hersh, Seymour: *The Dark Side of Camelot* [Little, Brown, 1997]

Heymann, C. David: *RFK: A Candid Biography of Robert F. Kennedy* [Arrow, 1999]

Heymann, C. David: *Joe and Marilyn* [Emily Bestler Books, 2014]

Hilty, James W.: *Robert Kennedy: Brother Protector* [Temple University Press, 1997]

Huston, John: *John Huston: An Open Book* [Knopf, 1980]

Israel, Lee: *Dorothy Kilgallen* [Delacore Press, 1979]

Kelley Kitty: *His Way: The Unauthorised Biography of Frank Sinatra* [Bantam Books, 1986]

Kennedy, Robert F.: *The Enemy Within: The McClellan Committee's Crusade Against Jimmy Hoffa and Corrupt Labor Unions* [Harper and Row, 1960]

Lacey, Robert: *Little Man: Meyer Lansky and the Gangster Life* [Little, Brown and Co. 1991]

LaGuardia, Robert: *Monty: A Biography of Montgomery Clift* [Arbor House, 1977]

Lamb, Richard: *The Macmillan Years 1957–1963: The Emerging Truth* [John Murray, 1995]

Lawford, Patricia Seaton; Schwarz, Ted: *The Peter Lawford Story* [Carroll & Graf, 1988]

Logevall, Fredrik: *JFK: Volume One: 1917–1956* [Viking, 2020]

Maas, Peter: *The Valachi Papers* [Putnam, 1968]

Mailer, Norman: *Marilyn* [Grosset & Dunlap, 1974]

Mailer, Norman: *Oswald's Tale: An American Mystery* [Random House, 1995]

Manchester, William: *The Death of a President: November 20–25, 1963* [Pan Books, 1968]

McDougal, Dennis: *The Last Mogul: Lew Wasserman, MCA and the Hidden History of Hollywood* [Crown, 1998]

Messick, Hank: *Lansky* [Robert Hale and Company, 1971]

Meyers, Jeffrey: *The Genius and the Goddess: Arthur Miller and Marilyn Monroe* [University of Illinois Press, 2009]

Miracle, Berniece Baker: *My Sister Marilyn: A Memoir of Marilyn Monroe* [Algonquin Books, 1994]

Moldea, Dan E.: *The Hoffa Wars: Teamsters, Rebels, Politicians and the Mob* [Paddington Press, 1978]

Moldea, Dan E.: *Dark Victory: Ronald Reagan, MCA and the Mob* [Viking Penguin, 1986]

Monroe, Marilyn (with Hecht, Ben): *My Story* [Stein and Day, 1974]

Muir, Florabel; *Headline Happy* [Holt, 1950]

Murray, Eunice: *Marilyn: The Last Months* [Pyramid, 1975]

Noguchi, Thomas T. (MD): *Coroner* [Simon & Schuster, 1983]

Oglesby, Carl: *Who Killed JFK: The JFK Assassination* [Signet Books, 1992]

Otash, Fred: *Investigation Hollywood!* [Regnery, 1976]

Pepitone, Lena; Stadiem William: *Marilyn Monroe Confidential* [Sidgwick & Jackson, 1979]

Pileggi, Nicholas: *Wiseguy: Life in a Mafia Family* [Pocket Books, 1985]

Plokhy, Serhil: *Nuclear Folly: A New History of the Cuban Missile Crisis* [Allen Lane, 2021]

Powers, Thomas: *The Man Who Kept the Secrets: Richard Helms and the CIA* [Knopf, 1979]

Raab, Selwyn: *Five Families: The Rise, Decline and Resurgence of America's Most Powerful Mafia Empires* [Thomas Dunne Books, St. Martin's Press, 2005]

Ragano, Frank; Raab, Selwyn: *Mob Lawyer* [Prentice Hall, 1994]

Reid, Ed; Demaris, Ovid: *The Green Felt Jungle* [Trident Press, 1963]

Rosten, Norman: *Marilyn: An Untold Story* [Signet, 1973]

Rothmiller, Mike, and Goldman, Ivan G.: *LA Secret Police: Inside the LAPD Elite Spy Network* [Pocket Books, 1992]

Schlesinger, Arthur, Jr.: *Robert Kennedy and His Times* [Houghton Mifflin, 1978]

Schulberg, Budd: *Moving Pictures: Memories of a Hollywood Prince* [Ivan R. Dee, 2003]

Schulberg, Budd: *The Harder They Fall,* [reissued by Allison & Busby Classics, 2013]

Schulberg, Budd: *The Disenchanted,* [reissued by Allison & Busby Classics, 2013]

Sciacca, Tony: *Who Killed Marilyn Monroe?* [Manor, 1976]

Server, Lee: *Robert Mitchum: Baby, I Don't Care* [St. Martin's Press, 2001]

Server, Lee: *Handsome Johnny: The Criminal Life of Johnny Rosselli The Mob's Man in Hollywood* [Virgin Books, 2018]

Sherwin, Martin J.: *Gambling with Armageddon: Nuclear Roulette from Hiroshima to the Cuban Missile Crisis* [Knopf, 2020]

Skolsky, Sidney: *Marilyn* [Dell, 1954]

Slatzer, Robert: *The Life and Curious Death of Marilyn Monroe* [Pinnacle, 1974]

Smith, Matthew: *Victim: The Secret Tapes of Marilyn Monroe* [Century, 2003]

Spada, James (with George Zeno): *Monroe: Her Life in Pictures* [Doubleday, 1982]

Spada, James: *Peter Lawford: The Man Who Kept the Secrets* [Bantam Press, 1991]

Speriglio, Milo: *The Marilyn Conspiracy* [Pocket Books, 1986]

Spoto, Donald: *Marilyn Monroe: The Biography* [Harper Collins, 1993]

Stack, Robert; Evans, Mark: *Straight Shooting by Robert Stack* [Macmillan, 1980]

Starr, Kevin: *Golden Dreams: California in An Age of Abundance 1950–1963* [Oxford University Press, 2011]

Steinem, Gloria (with photographs by George Barris): *Marilyn* [Henry Holt, 1986]

Stern, Bert: *Marilyn Monroe: The Last Sitting* [Morrow, 1982]

Summers, Anthony: *Goddess: The Secret Lives of Marilyn Monroe* [Macmillan, 1985]

Summers, Anthony: *The Kennedy Conspiracy* [Warner Books, 1992]

Summers, Anthony: (with Swan, Robbyn) *Sinatra: The Life* [Corgi, 2006]

Swanson, Gloria: *Swanson on Swanson* [Random House, 1980]

Teresa, Vincent (with Renner, Thomas C.): *My Life In The Mafia* [Doubleday, 1973)

Thomas, Evan: *Robert Kennedy: His Life* [Simon & Schuster, 2002]

Thompson, Douglas: *Shadowland: The Untold Story of the Mafia's Global Gambling Conspiracy* [Mainstream/Random House, 2011]

Thompson, Douglas: *The Dark Heart of Hollywood: Glamour, Guns and Gambling – Inside the Mafia's Global Empire* [Mainstream/Random House, 2012

Tierney, Gene: *Self-Portrait* [Wyden, 1979]

Tosches, Nick: *Dino: Living High in the Dirty Business of Dreams* [Doubleday, 1992]

Tosches, Nick: *The Devil and Sonny Liston* [Little, Brown, 2000]

Turkus, Burton B.; Feder, Sid: *Murder Inc. The Story of the Syndicate Killing Machine* [Da Capo Press, 1992; reproduction of 1951 edition]

United States Treasury Department: *Mafia: The Government's Secret File on Organized Crime* [2007]

Tye, Larry: *Bobby Kennedy: The Making of a Liberal Icon* [Random House, Reprint Edition, 2017]

Von Tunzelmann, Alex: *Red Heat: Conspiracy, Murder and the Cold War in the Caribbean* [Simon & Schuster, 2011]

Waldron, Lamar (with Thom Hartmann): *Ultimate Sacrifice: John and Robert Kennedy, The Plan for a Coup in Cuba and the Murder of JFK* [Constable, 2005]

Waldron, Lamar (with Thom Hartmann): *Legacy and Secrecy: The Long Shadow of the JFK Assassination* [Counterpoint, 2008]

Weiner, Tim: *Legacy of Ashes: The History of the CIA* [Penguin, 2007]

Wilkerson, Tichi; Borie, Marcia: *The Hollywood Reporter: The Golden Years* [Coward-McCann, 1984]

Wilson, Earl: *Sinatra* [W.H. Allen, 1976]

Winters, Shelley: *Shelley: Also Known as Shirley* [William Morrow, 1980]

Wolfe, Donald H.: *The Assassination of Marilyn Monroe* [Little, Brown, 1998]

Yablonsky, Lewis: *George Raft* [Mercury House/W.H. Allen, 1975]

Zolotow, Maurice: *Marilyn Monroe* [Harcourt Brace, 1960]

Zolotow, Maurice: *Billy Wilder in Hollywood* [W.H. Allen, 1977]